Teaching All Children to Read
Michael A. Wallach and Lise Wallach

Despite all the recent efforts at compensatory
education, hundreds of thousands of children
still go through first grade each year without
learning to read. More often than not, these are
children of the poor.

The underlying assumption of the Wallachs'
study is that the major attempts at educational
compensation for disadvantaged children have
failed because of fundamental misconceptions
about what is needed to help these children learn.
After evaluating these attempts, the authors
elaborate an alternative viewpoint and describe
a tutorial program that enables children to learn
to read by the end of the first grade. They also
present the highly favorable results of their previously unpublished field research. Low income,
minority group first graders otherwise headed
for reading failure learned to read competently
with this program when tutored by community
adults.

According to the authors, many children—
especially, but not only poor children—have
trouble learning to read because they do not know
how to recognize, manipulate, and blend the
kinds of sounds that letters stand for—phonemes. The authors argue that previous attempts
to teach reading presuppose, rather than supply,
these subskills, which middle-class children
usually learn from their home environment.

An exciting aspect of this program is that it
can be taught in either a school or nonschool
setting by nonprofessional tutors. Under the
guidance of a tutor, the children systematically
master the recognition and manipulation of
sounds, the alphabetic code and its utilization,
and then the actual reading of printed materials.
Each task is mastered before the next is
introduced. The Tutor's Manual is included in
this volume.

Teaching Al

The University of Chicago Press   Chicago and London

Children to Read

Michael A. Wallach
Lise Wallach

MICHAEL A. WALLACH is professor of psychology
at Duke University. He is the author of *The
Intelligence/Creativity Distinction* and coauthor
of *Risk Taking: A Study in Cognition and Personality,
The Talented Student,* and *College Admissions and
the Psychology of Talent.* He was the editor of the
Journal of Personality from 1963 to 1972.
LISE WALLACH is a lecturer in the department of
psychology at Duke University.

The University of Chicago Press, Chicago 60637
The University of Chicago Press, Ltd., London

Library of Congress Cataloging in Publication Data

Wallach, Michael A
   Teaching all children to read.

   Bibliography: p.
   Includes index.
   1. Reading (Elementary)   I. Wallach, Lise,
joint author. II. Title.
LB1573.W315   372.4'1   75–19503
ISBN 0–226–87166–5

Contents

Preface   vii

1. Introduction   1

2. The Bursting of the Educational Reform Balloon:
   Where Do We Go from Here?   8

3. Developing Basic Skills   45

4. A Cumulative Mastery Reading Program   77

5. Applying the Program: Community Tutors
   in the Schools   108

6. Results of the Field Research   146

7. Implications for Theory and Practice   177

Appendix A: Tutor's Manual   223
Appendix B: Alpha-Picture Chart   303
Appendix C: Key Data by Child   307
References   313
Index   327

Preface

After millions upon millions of dollars and all kinds of attempts at compensatory education, educational reform, and research on cognitive development, this is still a nation in which hundreds of thousands of children go through first grade each year without learning to read. These children are not randomly distributed across the population; such failure to learn is found much more often among the children of the poor than among the children of the middle class. Wherever the faults may lie, it is hard to deny the feeling that promises have been made to these children and the society has not delivered. When children do not learn to read at the time this is expected of them, they suffer not only from that failure itself but from difficulties with all the other work in school that depends on reading competence.

But why are there large numbers of children who don't learn to read in the course of the first grade? Why do so many children seem unable to profit from the classroom instruction they receive? Reading, after all, is a rather straightforward skill, not an esoteric one. The mystery puzzled us, as it has puzzled others. Our interest in trying to solve it was made all the stronger by the failure of so much of what has been undertaken in the name of educational reform to produce demonstrable benefits for disadvantaged children—the children who need help the most. Our suspicion was that the major attempts to provide help for these children were based on some fundamental misconceptions about what was needed, misconceptions centering around such ideas as that these children's interests and motives were insufficiently engaged or that their intellects needed to be improved. We suspected, rather, that at the root of the mystery would be found something so mundane as to be easy to overlook: a simple failure to teach these children key ingredient subskills that have typically already been supplied in large degree by the home environment of middle-class children but not of disadvantaged children. These subskills are crucial if a child is to make progress in learning to read. The problem, then, would not be one of insufficient motivation or intelligence on the part of the child but of school instruction taking for granted the possession of needed subskills that had not in fact been acquired.

We believe that we have located such subskills. Of particular importance is the ability to recognize and manipulate the kinds of sounds that letters stand for—namely, phonemes. While middle-class children at the start of school typically possess accessible and manipulable concepts of these sounds, poor children very frequently do not. The belief is widespread, furthermore, that recognition and manipulation of phonemes cannot be effectively taught. We found the grounds for believing this to evaporate upon close inspection, however, and so we set about trying to do what the customary belief said was not possible. Developing ways to train these children to perceive phonemes and to blend them into words proved possible indeed; and with such training, learning to read no longer seemed a problem for the children. The training procedures that did this job, moreover, were sufficiently straightforward that they could be worked out in forms amenable for application by adults without any particular educational credentials or certification, who could use the procedures as tutors.

The way seemed open, then, for a technically feasible, fully realistic solution to the problem of teaching children to read in first grade who presently do not learn to read there. This book tells the story of the work we have been doing toward achieving that solution. The book evaluates recent attempts to come to grips with the educational difficulties of poor children; it elaborates a new point of view, one emphasizing highly systematic instruction that insures acquisition of whatever pre-requisite subskills are needed for competence at school tasks; it applies this approach to the area of basic reading instruction through the development of a tutorial program for use by appropriately supervised nonprofessionals; and it presents extensive, previously unpublished field research demonstrating that low-income, minority-group first graders otherwise headed for reading failure learn to read competently if tutored by community adults with our program. We expect the book to be of relevance to professionals of various kinds who share an interest in the cognitive competence of young children: academic psychologists and educators concerned with child development, children's learning, school curricula, and school-community relations; reading specialists; school psychologists; and school administrators—along with students of these professionals.

The book chronicles the development and use of a tool to solve a problem; but it also offers theory and interpretation as to where the problem comes from, why it has been hard to solve, and how other problems like it can be solved as well. It constitutes an instance of the fruits derivable from taking the existence of a real-world problem—here, the failure of large numbers of children to learn to read in first grade—as one's starting point and bringing to bear on that problem whatever knowledge can be found that is relevant to it, from whatever research traditions that may be germane to it. The attempt to do this brings home just how accidental and arbitrary the separations between many of those research traditions seem to be—among, for example, such professionally distinct specialty areas as cognitive development, educational psychology, reading research, psycholinguistics, and learning. It also brings home the artificiality of the distinction between pure and applied research, making evident how the cause of advancing theoretical understanding often may better be served by trying to answer questions that have their point of origin in phenomena people are grappling with in the world itself rather than by questions emerging from academically derived paradigms or models. Answering questions stimulated by such paradigms or models frequently seems to take on a life of its own, finding sufficient justification in the sheer existence of the model even though the answers fail to enhance understanding of the real-world events that gave the model its raison d'être in the first place. In a time of increasing concern as to the meaningfulness of much of the research activity going on in the social sciences, work that is aimed at solving real-world problems not only provides direct meaningfulness in its own right but can assure that theory has to do with reality and not merely with the constructions of academicians' minds.

The completion of this volume marks the end of one task but the start of another. With a tool in hand that should go a long way toward solving a pressing social problem, the next step is to see that the tool gets utilized. Toward this end, a companion publication (Wallach and Wallach 1976) presents our tutorial program in the form of an instructional kit that includes all materials needed for carrying out the program with children. We intend this kit to be used by appropriately supervised nonprofessionals of various kinds—paraprofessionals and teachers' aides in schools, community adults in other settings, and even parents with their own children. It is a self-contained instructional package that fits in with whatever reading materials may be in use in the classroom; hence it supports rather than competes with the classroom teacher's activities. We hope that what follows in the present volume will persuade professionals of the desirability of fostering and undertaking the kinds of arrangements that will make widespread use of the instructional kit a reality.

Many people have helped us in various ways at one or another stage of our research. We are grateful to the Department of Psychology, Duke University, the Department and Graduate School of Education, the University of Chicago, and the Benton Educational Research Fund for support; to the administrators and teachers of the Durham schools where we carried out pretesting and pilot work, and to the Duke undergraduates who participated with us in this work; to the administrators and teachers of the Chicago schools where we conducted our field research; to Barbara Fernandez, June

Patton, and Kaffie Weaver for administering tests; to Inez Higgins Costanzo for invaluable research assistance; to Barbara Harp, Dolores Ford, Dolores Walker, and especially Verble Roberts, who typed the final manuscript with superb care, for secretarial assistance; to the tutors applying the program in the field study, who worked conscientiously and with much devotion to the children; to our daughter Rachel for helpful suggestions and much cooperation; and, of course, to the children with whom we have been working, whose trust we hope we have fulfilled.

> *Michael A. Wallach*
> *Lise Wallach*

Durham, North Carolina
April 1975

1
Introduction

Dating approximately from the time of Jensen's statement in 1969 that "compensatory education has been tried and it apparently has failed" (1969, p. 2), more than a decade's optimism concerning what education can do to improve the life chances of poor children has turned sour. As the evidence from the intervention attempts of the sixties has accumulated and been assessed in such documents as the Westinghouse/Ohio University (1969) evaluation of Head Start programs, the Coleman Report (1966), the volume of commentaries on the Coleman Report edited by Mosteller and Moynihan (1972a), and the book by Jencks (1972a), it is hard not to conclude that the message is a negative one. Jencks sums up the situation this way: "The evidence suggests . . . that educational compensation is usually of marginal value to the recipients. Neither the overall level of educational resources nor any specific, easily identifiable school policy has much effect on the test scores or educational attainment of students who start out at a disadvantage" (1972a, p. 255). And again, "We can see no evidence that either school administrators or educational experts know how to raise test scores, even when they have vast resources at their disposal. Certainly we do not know how to do so" (Jencks 1972a, p. 95).

Jensen's response to this state of affairs, along with that of Herrnstein (1971, 1973) and others, is to wonder if the poor children not helped by this wide spectrum of educational reforms—often black in skin color—may not be genetically inferior as to intelligence. Jencks's response, on the other hand, is to argue that, whether genetically inferior or not, poor children deserve help, and since this help is beyond the competence of education to provide it should take such direct forms as redistributing income by governmental fiat. Still another response to the negative evidence is the desire to intrude more and more deeply into the family settings of poor children. The claim in this case is that the problem, while environmental rather than genetic, is so massive and deep-seated as to call for social science professionals to change the very culture of minority groups so that their children will be reared "scientifically." This is the view represented, for example, by Hunt (1969, 1973).

None of these responses seems, as we see it, to be constructive, and all end up strengthening the hand of conservatives. The Jensen position says there is little to be done. The Jencks position says the only thing worth doing is to change the economic and political structure of the society in such a manner as to redistribute its wealth. We can be rather sure, of course, that this is not about to happen. And the Hunt position says the only thing worth doing is to have experts raise poor people's children differently, which is easy to object to on ethical grounds and in any case would involve huge expenditures that are not about to be made. The upshot of such responses is support for conservative social policymakers who argue that public education cannot be expected to help the poor and that no one has anything to suggest short of state socialism and drastic governmental interference.

Not to consider these responses useful or constructive is one thing; to have something better to offer is another. The judgment that what has been tried thus far in the name of compensatory education has failed seems to be accurate. Our response to this evidence of failure differs, however, from those just enumerated. In our view there were certain fundamental errors in the way compensatory education was conceived that led to the negative results chronicled in such sources as the Coleman Report and the Westinghouse/Ohio University assessment of Head Start. These errors continue to characterize most of what gets done in the name of helping poor children better their station in life through the agency of schooling. Were these errors to be corrected, we believe that public education could be made much more effective for poor children than it has been.

What, then, are these errors? One is the belief that there is something wrong with poor children's minds. If this is the hypothesis, then the pedagogical task is to improve their minds, to make the children more intelligent. But what intelligence really is, and how by instructional activities you can make a child more intelligent in a way that will have consequences for academic achievement, seem murky issues at best. It is also an error, as we see it, to believe that, if nothing is wrong with poor children's minds, then the problem must lie in their motivations or interests. On this view, what needs doing is to engage their interests, to instill aspirations, to communicate expectations of accomplishment, to build confidence. How this is supposed to be sufficient for bringing about school competences that do not exist otherwise is, again, far from clear. Common to both errors is a conception of the child's functioning that envisions no more than two categories of determinants for school success—intelligence and motivation. We would maintain that there is a third category, quite distinct from the others, and that it is precisely this third category which is crucial for solving the problem of poor children's education. This third category is the specific skills or competences needed for coping with the demands of school. Given sufficient intelligence and appropriate motivation, it is *by no means the case* that academic skills follow automatically and easily. Yet that tends to be the typical assumption. Rather, skills need specific pedagogical development; they need to be elaborated through training.

There is nothing wrong with the intelligence of poor children, and their motivation, as we see it, takes care of itself when they do something competently and know this. What poor children *do* need more of, in our view, is specific training in the systematic development of skills or competences that are required for coping with academic work. We maintain that there has been little effort spent on figuring out what poor children need to learn in order to master such skills and on how to bring about this learning within the practical constraints of the public school setting. The one most crucial skill for academic work is reading. Because of cultural differences, component subskills involved in a skill like reading have already largely been mastered at home by middle-class children but in many instances have not been part of poor children's background. These subskills, therefore, ought to be systematically and cumulatively built up within the school context for the children who need them. Otherwise, these children will not learn to read on schedule, and thus they will begin the cycle of failure that leaves them further and further behind as ever more of their schooling comes to presuppose the use of reading as a tool. But this kind of cumulative mastery of the building blocks needed for a skill like reading is just what often fails to take place for poor children at school.

There did not seem to us to be any reason why such skill development *could not* take place for poor children at school. Rather, the situation appeared simply to be one where this task had received little attention because the problem of what is needed for school success had been wrongly defined. Because of its obvious significance as an academic tool, we decided to focus on the skill of reading and try to determine the component subskills it entails psychologically. With this done, we could attempt to design a means of delivering mastery of these subskills to a child who did not possess them, a means that would be practical as well as effective. Our hunch was that the task would be one of establishing rather simple competences that are already strong in most school-age children from middle-class backgrounds. It is all too easy to assume that these competences must be within any child's repertoire, whereas many poor children just have not had the experiences that lead them to develop. But if what was required were such straightforward competences, it should be possible to design a program of activities that would assure their cumulative mastery. What each child would be asked to do at each point in time would be a function of what he or she was already capable of and of what he or she still needed to learn. The activities could be monitored by "nonteachers"—tutors—who would be trained to follow explicit rules concerning what to do, with practice being provided for the child at each step until the child had mastered it sufficiently to proceed to the next. Following such a program's rules is not difficult for a tutor—there is nothing esoteric about it—but it does take personnel. The children must themselves perform activities, and these activities need monitoring; hence such a program is not something that could simply be presented to children audiovisually, as has been tried in the case of "Sesame Street" or "The Electric Company" on television. And the nature of the activities, involving as they do categories of sounds and meanings that are psychologically simple but physically highly complex, are beyond the scope of any computers and hence of "computer-assisted instruction."

A kind of unwritten assumption often seems to be made to the effect that the ratio of children to teaching personnel in schools should stay more or less constant as the child proceeds from grade to grade. What the preceding considerations suggest, by contrast, is that this ratio should be very low at the beginning of formal instruction to insure that needed basic academic skills get built up for children who lack them; the ratio can be much higher subsequently, when the children have learned these skills. Also suggested by what we have said is that the qualifications needed for an adult to be able to build a skill like reading competence in a low-performing child are met by large numbers of people from the same backgrounds as these children. No professional certification is needed, nor any educational credentials. The important attributes for a potential tutor—besides literacy—seem to be no more than that the person likes to work with children, is responsible, and is patient. Happily enough, these attributes characterize plenty of adults from the low-income minority group communities that also contain the children who are failing at school. Employed as "paraprofessionals" or "teachers' aides" and given training and supervision in tutoring routines that would establish mastery for a child of the subskills that make for reading competence, such community adults should be able to teach children to read who would not otherwise learn.

This book describes what happened when we applied these ideas. We found them to work well—sufficiently well, in fact, to suggest that most poor children can learn to read on schedule by the end of the first-grade year in public school, however low their "reading readiness" prognosis at the start of the year. Our results indicate that poor first graders otherwise headed for academic failure can be effectively taught to become competent readers within the first-grade year by community tutors who are trained to build systematically the children's mastery of the requisite subskills that reading entails. The nature of these subskills proved upon examination to be clear enough to permit us to design a program of sequential steps that build toward mastery of the skill of reading and that can be effectively carried out by community adults without professional or educational credentials. In this book we present the program, the considerations that led us to devise it and that determined its form, and evidence of its effectiveness in the hands of noncredentialed community tutors. The book mounts an argument for defining the problem of children's school competence in terms of the achievement of directly meaningful cognitive skills, such as competence at reading, rather than in terms of raising scores on presumptive indicators of cognitive constructs, such as intelligence; it shows how this distinction helps explain why past attempts to make education more effective for poor children have come to so little; it presents an analysis of the skill of reading that implies a clear directive as to what must be done to teach it to children who don't learn it in the customary classroom situation; it gives in full detail the program for establishing reading competence that we developed on the basis of this analysis for use by noncredentialed adults from these children's communities; and it reports field research demonstrating the effectiveness of the program under conditions of actual application.

What we aim at here, quite simply, is a solution to the pressing social problem of making public education functional and significant for poor children. Application of the program that we have developed for utilizing community adults trained to function as tutors in the public schools brings about basic reading competence for a large proportion of the kinds of first graders who otherwise fail to learn. Such application is practical and economically feasible. There already are large numbers of such adults on public school payrolls as "teachers' aides," often relegated to the performance of no more than custodial or disciplinary functions, such as keeping lines orderly in the lunchroom. Even if one did no more than train these already available personnel to tutor children with our program of materials, a sizable dent in the problem would be achieved. But there is reason, of course, to go further and to budget additional jobs for such tutors, since their use could go a long way toward eliminating the need for remedial attempts carried out several years later in the poor child's school career, attempts that often are fruitless because by then the child is far behind and has built up negative transfer and motivational hindrances from a history of prior failures. The kind of community tutor approach that we advocate could well end up saving school systems money rather than adding to costs—and could be considerably more effective for the children to boot. Who, in turn, are to train and supervise these tutors? The possibilities are extensive, running from clinical psychologists, school psychologists, and reading specialists, to teachers themselves. And what could be done for reading competence could, we expect, be carried out for competence in mathematics as well.

Next we will take a brief look at the educational reform landscape of the last decade and a half or so, to see if we can discern why so much time and effort by so many people has produced so little return. The pattern that we detect in these failures then will lead us to some questions about the theories that have guided these attempts.

2
The Bursting of the Educational Reform Balloon: Where Do We Go From Here?

Poor Children Still Fail at School

The failure of what gets done in the name of education to have much effect on the academic chances of children—in contrast to the effect exerted by family background differences—is a disagreeable fact made all the more unpalatable by the considerable effort that has recently been devoted to intervention attempts on behalf of children from low-income backgrounds. Schooling or education-relevant compensatory activities have seemed able to do little to impinge upon the overriding consequences of social class in determining the outcome of the school experience. A front-page article by education reporter Gene Maeroff in the *New York Times* of May 27, 1973, carrying as its headline, "A Solution to Falling Reading Scores Continues to Elude Big-City Schools," gives as good an example as any of the reality of this situation. Maeroff writes, "The reading scores of inner-city schoolchildren sink to new lows each year, and educators and others here and in most big cities have been unable to find ways to reverse the trend."

Viewing whatever survey evidence he could find that evaluated what has been tried out by way of varying techniques of education in recent years, Jencks sums it all up in these terms: "Our research suggests . . . that the character of a school's output depends largely on a single input, namely the characteristics of the entering children. Everything else—the school

8

budget, its policies, the characteristics of the teachers—is either
secondary or completely irrelevant" (1972*a*, p. 256). And as
Stodolsky and Lesser (1971) put it in summarizing their review of studies bearing on these matters, "Taken together,
the data on general intelligence, mental abilities, and school
achievement all give indications that general learning, first in
the home and community and later within the school as well,
is clearly associated with socio-economic status: the level of
such learning is generally lower for children of most minority
groups and children in low socio-economic status" (p. 28).
The consequence of this state of affairs is "an abysmal prognosis for most children who enter the school system from disadvantaged backgrounds" (p. 27). In the Coleman Report
(1966), we find that already by sixth grade blacks, Mexican-
Americans, Puerto Ricans, American Indians, and Oriental
Americans—all of whom have lower incomes as groups than
whites—lag considerably behind whites from the metropolitan
Northeast on customary test performances. For example, on a
reading comprehension test taken in sixth grade, the members
of such lower-income groups lag two or three grade-level years
behind the whites. And the amount of lag keeps rising as
further years of schooling pass by.

The implications of this kind of lag, furthermore, go well
beyond the absolute amounts as given in grade-level years.
These pupils can never catch up. Also, the very machinery
constituted by the basic academic skills remains so ponderous
and creaky that its potential facilitative function for a wide
range of school tasks can never take hold. The lag has generalized consequences. Thus, for example, Crano, Kenny, and
Campbell (1972), examining performance data from middle-
class suburban versus low-income inner-city ("core") elementary schoolchildren, found kinds of contrasts which they were
led to interpret in the following terms: "The assimilation of
specific concrete skills may proceed within the core schools
at a pace so retarded that the integration necessary for the
generation of abstract schema simply cannot take place" (p.
273). However one views the particular terminology here, the
point is that below a certain minimum rate of basic-skills

acquisition, the possible transfer or "ripple" effects from these skills may be severely restricted.

What such a picture means from the children's point of view, when they become old enough to understand what has been going on, is captured in the following remarks by a student attending a conference of high school pupils reading more than two years below grade level. The conference was covered by *New York Times* reporter Maeroff in the article mentioned above:

> Lux Munoz, a student at Clara Barton Vocational High School in Brooklyn, said that for many of the pupils who were at the conference the problem was one of "not having been taught to read well enough in the first grade."
> "Why did they keep passing me when they saw I wasn't keeping up in reading?" she asked. "Did they want to get rid of me instead of helping me? Now a lot of kids get to high school not being able to read and they say if they can't get jobs they will just have to go on the streets and mug and steal" (Maeroff 1973, p. 35).

When in turn Maeroff grapples with the question of how to solve this problem, his answer, like that of many others, is to recommend more of the same kinds of professionalized services and viewpoints that have failed so badly already. Thus, he feels that the taking of academic courses in the teaching of reading should be required of persons who want state certification as elementary schoolteachers, that more reading specialists doing more of the same kinds of things that they do already should be hired by school systems, and that there should be tighter state control over what persons are permitted to call themselves reading specialists. These are just the very sorts of changes, however, that past experience indicates will not make a meaningful difference. They assume the appropriateness of the customary definitions of what it means to be a reading specialist, and they assume the utility of a few additional hours of education courses on reading for prospective teachers. School-resource indices of the kinds looked at in, for instance, the Coleman Report (see Jencks [1972b]) already tell us quite clearly that little can be hoped for in such directions.

And so we can rather confidently expect that Maeroff's recommendations, if followed, would lead to still more evidence
of educational failure for low-income students despite well-
meaning efforts to help. From this outcome it is but a small
step to the position, increasingly popular among liberals these
days, of celebrating such social-class differences as virtues.
Winschel (1970), for instance, looking over a decade of negative evidence on attempts at compensatory education, finds it
possible to say: "We do not castigate compensatory education
for its failure to improve in any dramatic way the education of
the disadvantaged. Rather we question its implied promise to
eliminate those differences in ability and achievement which
are a part of the richness of a people" (p. 8). And Dyer
(1972), in the light of such negative evidence, recommends
that there be a "shift away from the usual fixation on academic
achievement as the only educational outcome of prime concern" (p. 403). In the same vein, Ginsburg (1972) advises
that schools should aim at encouraging "the unique capabilities
of the poor" (p. 57) rather than helping them meet middle-
class competence standards, and Ornstein (1972) wants school
to help the poor by being an "institution which encourages
diversity" (p. 288). This is, of course, hardly a position that
is in the interests of poor children as long as they are failing
in sizable numbers to learn basic academic skills on schedule
in school. To set up different goals for them, for whatever
excuse, amounts to a form of tracking that will keep them out
of competition with the children of the middle class.

If poor children still fail at school despite the recent wave
of attempts at improving what education has to offer, what
then have these attempts been like? We turn first to work at
the preschool level.

Preschool Intervention Attempts Fail to Compensate

The Head Start programs of a few years back have been subjected to rather extensive evaluation. This evaluation has taken
the form of assessing the impact of those programs on the

scores from various tests that fall largely within the psycho-metric intelligence testing tradition, such as the Illinois Test of Psycholinguistic Ability or the Metropolitan Readiness Tests. The hope, essentially, was that the experiences taking place during the course of twelve months of a Head Start program before regular schooling began would bring poor children's performances on intelligence-type tests up to average as defined by national norms. If this could be achieved, it was assumed that a corresponding rise in school success would be the result. As Daniels (1972) put it, "raising the IQ of preschool chil-dren" was seen as the way "to assure scholastic success in regular elementary school" (p. 184).

When the results of such psychometric test evaluations ap-peared (see Hawkridge, Chalupsky, and Roberts 1968; West-inghouse Learning Corporation/Ohio University 1969; Smith and Bissell 1970), there ensued considerable debate as to their interpretation, but it was hard not to conclude that they were very disappointing. As Cicirelli (1970) has noted, reference to national test performance norms indicates that, viewed against such an absolute yardstick, Head Start clearly failed to remedy in anything like the necessary degree the effects of the children's poverty background—if it was helpful to any degree. This point remains clear even if one feels, as do Camp-bell and Erlebacher (1970a, 1970b), that the essentially nega-tive evidence as to relative gains for experimental compared with control groups is difficult to evaluate. This difficulty exists, as they see it, because the controls tended to come from more privileged family backgrounds than the experimentals; while this bias was adjusted for statistically in the analysis of results, they question whether one can view such statistical matching as sufficient to really equate the groups. It seems hard to dis-agree in any case with White's (1970) conclusion that, evalu-ated by the kinds of test measures mentioned before, the effect of the nationwide Head Start effort was small in magnitude at best and therefore of questionable practical utility in the form in which it was carried out.

The major response to the disappointing results of Head Start has been the argument that the psychometric intelligence testing tradition—central to the evaluational work that was done—led investigators astray on what sort of assessments to conduct in order to measure intelligence and what sort of interventions to prescribe in order to enhance it. Whatever really took place in Head Start classes—and White (1970) points out that social adjustment goals may well have predominated over cognitive goals in much of what actually happened —the prescriptive rhetoric as to program objectives emphasized teaching that would overcome the kinds of deficits measured by inferior performances on the traditional panoply of psychometric yardsticks such as IQ test scores. What has been viewed as misleading about reliance on the intelligence testing tradition is the kind of analysis of the intelligence concept which that tradition provides. This analysis, it is believed, does not do justice to what intelligence is really about and therefore cannot offer useful guidelines for assessment or enhancement of intelligence. Instead of what is considered to be an arbitrary dissection of intelligence into such components as verbal ability, reasoning ability, spatial ability, and numerical ability— or verbal test scores and performance test scores—and an equally arbitrary assembling of component scores into overall composites such as the IQ, it has been proposed that the perspective on children's intelligence developed by Piaget offers a theoretically more cogent basis for deciding what to evaluate and teach.

A shift from more conventional IQ-type measures of intelligence to Piaget-derived measures of intelligence has in fact been viewed by many as the basis for a revolutionary advance in compensatory education at the preschool level. As Zimiles (1970) points out, "The area of conceptual functioning—how children order events and govern their inferential thinking, how they utilize thought to recreate and understand reality— which has only begun to receive systematic study since the recent rebirth of interest in Piaget's work, is minimally represented in most assessment studies. Yet, many observers tend to regard this sphere of functioning as lying at the core of the intellectual disability observed in disadvantaged children" (p. 239). Zimiles correctly notes that just because traditional psychometric intelligence tests correlate modestly with school-defined competence does not imply that raising a child's scores on those tests will correspondingly increase the child's success in school (the basic rationale for what was done in programs such as Head Start). Since the correlation between conventional intelligence test scores and academic competence is imperfect, to say the least, scores of the former kind could go up for reasons that have nothing to do with improved academic skills. What Zimiles does not seem to realize, however, is that this point constitutes an equally telling argument against trying to raise a child's status on any other presumptive index of intelligence such as measures of Piagetian notions of "conceptual functioning." Zimiles, like the advocates of evaluation by psychometric intelligence-type tests whom he criticizes, continues to believe that the intelligence of poor children is deficient and that the task therefore is to improve it, with the expectation that this will then automatically transfer to increased academic competence.

Without questioning this assumption that poor children are characterized by fundamental deficiencies of intellect that need correction if the children are to succeed in school, various researchers have done as Zimiles advocates. The results of such work, however, do not look particularly more promising than what came from the psychometric intelligence-testing tradition that the work aimed to replace. Thus, for example, Sigel and Olmsted (1970) were led by Piagetian considerations to concentrate on "classification training" as what poor children needed for their intellects. This training gave the child "the opportunity to identify various attributes of objects and subsequently to use this information as bases for classification. He is encouraged to build and rebuild classes and to combine and recombine classes of objects" (pp. 309–11). The effects of the training could not even be shown to generalize to tasks calling for what Piaget would consider cognate intellective operations such as multiple classification and multiple seriation. The possibility that any of this should meaningfully help poor children in school seems remote indeed, yet Sigel and Olmsted feel it appropriate to conclude, "In sum, we believe that the training programs do have educational heuristic value" (1970, p. 330). In a related vein, Stendler-Lavatelli (1968) argues that Piagetian tasks offer the pedagogical key for repairing the intelligence deficits she ascribes to poor children. For example, part of the machinery of intellect that she considers deficient in this way is logical thinking. She believes that "culturally disadvantaged children are retarded in logical thinking," and for that kind of reason "these children will be severely retarded in school learning" (p. 372). Thus she used Piaget-based instructional procedures aimed at undoing this presumptive deficiency in logical thinking with disadvantaged four-year-olds. Little seemed to come of this attempt, but she nevertheless feels that the answer is to proceed with more work of the same kind. Weikart (1972) puts the article of faith behind this approach quite clearly when he says of Piaget-based curriculum programs that "They omit training in specific areas, such as reading or arithmetic, treating these skills as inevitable outcomes of basic cognitive ability" (p. 34). He too utilizes Piagetian tasks to make up for presumed intellective deficits in poor preschoolers, with positive effects that, at best, seem small in magnitude.

Further disappointments of this kind seem to have brought as their major consequence the conclusion that the deficits of intelligence assumed to cause poor children's school failures simply are more massive and pervasive than was first envisioned and therefore are in need of still earlier and more thoroughgoing repair. In other words, more of the same gets prescribed even though it has been of little help thus far; only this time around the recommendations get more expensive, the invasions of privacy deeper, and the degree of professional expertise presumably needed to cope with the problem greater. Instead of just trying, for example, to induce poor children to think abstractly, one now provides training "designed to foster the precursors of abstract thinking," as Blank (1972, p. 114) puts it. Similarly, Sigel and his collaborators (Sigel, Sechrist, and Forman 1973) now work with two-year-olds instead of five- and six-year-olds and try to foster what they view as the very essence of representational thought through such means as seeking to teach the child to "consider things that are not present" (p. 32), although later oral language does not suggest that poor children have any particular difficulty in doing this. One gets ever deeper embroiled in trying to elucidate and measure what intelligence "really" is, and ever further from the reality of the school achievements these children need and do not exhibit.

What made the Piagetian reconstruction of the intelligence concept seem like such a revolutionary advance over the psychometricians' use of the concept was that it offered investigators like Hunt (1961, 1968, 1969, 1973) a basis for moving away from what they saw as the conservative belief that intelligence is fixed. Instead, they believed that in Piaget they had found potent prescriptions for forms of early experience that should increase a child's intelligence and thus had found a solution to the educational problems faced by disadvantaged children. That Piaget should have been read this way in any case seems ironic because the forms of early experience that he sees as feeding intellectual development are so basic as to be the property of all children, not just those who are economically privileged. His writings led Hunt and others, however, in the direction of imagining that serious early experience-deprivations characterized the children of the poor. These deprivations would be made up for by preschool instructional programs that provided "an opportunity to encounter a wide variety of objects and circumstances" as well as "an opportunity to imitate a wide variety of models of action and of motor language" (Hunt 1968, p. 327). In general, there seems no reason to think that poor children have less opportunities along these lines than middle-class children. Yet it is experiences of these kinds, characteristic as they seem to be for the early development of all children, that Hunt and those in his tradition now specifically undertook to reinforce in disadvantaged children. And the failure to show the strong positive effects desired leads only to a recommendation (Hunt 1973) that the same strategy be intensified.

What we find in the more intensive pursuit of this strategy is, for example, the following. Weikart and Lambie (1968;

Lambie and Weikart 1970) have undertaken to teach low-income mothers to carry out routines with their infants aimed at facilitating such matters as "visual pursuit and permanence of objects," "construction of the object in space," and "development of causality." Thus, the mother is supposed to learn to stimulate "development of the notion of recognizable object" for her infant through such activities as these: "Present two different colored objects to baby lying in supine position to stimulate baby to look from one object to another. . . . Shake a noise maker on either side and above head to stimulate baby to locate object. . . . Present two stationary objects to baby in sitting position to stimulate baby to look from one to another." (Lambie and Weikart 1970, p. 390). There is no reason, however, to imagine that infants in low-income families lack experiences with these kinds of effects. Indeed, Piaget considers such intellectual achievements as the object concept and causality to be highly invariant acquisitions. The same holds for the child's use of speech for purposes of communication—something, again, which is universally present and yet forms the basis for what Lambie and Weikart want low-income mothers specifically to stimulate. And in describing a comparable kind of Piaget-influenced "infant curriculum," Meier, Segner, and Grueter (1970) make clear that they view its justification as depending on whether it faithfully represents elements in the Piagetian theory of intellectual development, even though if Piaget is correct that development ought not to be very malleable and the forms of early experience on which it depends should be widely available. Seemingly lost from focus is the problem at issue—the failure of school-age children to learn school skills.

How these elaborate and expensive infant-curriculum plans are rationalized is quite revealing. The terms used to justify them treat as nonproblematical the link between enhanced intelligence and the goal of improving school achievement when the child reaches school age; what is viewed as the problem is how to bring about that enhancement of intelligence, and here the Piagetians see the Piagetian formulation as giving them the tools they need along with the recommendation that intervention very early in the poor child's life is what is called for. The grounds for believing the poor child's intelligence to be deficient in the first place and therefore in need of improvement are never really questioned. After all, these children *do* fail at school when they arrive there, don't they? With many other reasons besides real differences in intellect always available to account for whatever differences are found on intelligence assessors, and with the stark facts of poor children's academic failure constituting the social problem that stands in need of solution, a strategy which seeks to help poor children do better in school through early experiences that are hypothesized to make them more intelligent seems strikingly indirect. Why not help them directly with school skills?

Higher-Quality School Resources Fail to Compensate

What about attempts to improve educational quality during the years of schooling? During the 1960s data came in from work trying to boost school resources, with evaluations that led to the Coleman Report (1966) and related materials (Flanagan and Cooley 1966; Mosteller and Moynihan 1972a; Jencks 1972a). The drift of the evidence reinforced pessimism once again; differences in quality of school resources as defined in various ways seemed to show little or no effect on the school-related achievements of students. In particular, higher quality school resources were not found to compensate for the effects of a disadvantaged family background. Such evidence should perhaps have come as no surprise, in that it had been present in various forms for a while (see Central Advisory Council for Education 1967; National Education Association, Research Division 1967; Stephens 1967). The difference, however, was that it came now in the wake of concerted attempts to better the situation.

Consider this example of the negative evidence. A New York bank (Landes 1969), studying 150 schools in New York City with student enrollments that were 90 percent or more black and Puerto Rican, looked at the per pupil expenditures at these schools during the 1967–68 academic year. The average per capita expenditure was $839, which was well above the 1968 national average of $623, and the variability of expenditures in that group of 150 schools was extensive, ranging from $529 per pupil at the low end to $1,560 per pupil at the high. No relationship was found between the amount of money spent per pupil and reading-score improvement from one year to another, even though some schools were spending about three times as much as other schools on each student. And in general, of course, the reading-competence levels of the pupils were low. Evidence of this kind, multiplied manyfold as to, for example, the ways in which school quality was assessed, added up to the picture presented in the Coleman Report (1966), which Mosteller and Moynihan (1972b) summarize in these terms: "The pathbreaking quality of the [Coleman Report] had to do with its analysis of the relation of variation in school facilities to variation in levels of academic achievement. It reported so little relation as to make it almost possible to say there was none" (p. 15).

With family background relating substantially to variation in academic achievement, it became natural for Coleman and others seeking environmental changes that could improve educational outcomes for poor children to take, essentially, the same course as Hunt and those in his tradition. Thus, the call now is for earlier and more massive interventions than were first envisioned, reaching into the very structure of the family. As Coleman (1972) puts it, in referring to the Coleman Report findings, "I have used evidence from the study to draw strong policy conclusions from the absolute level [of school effects], arguing that the low absolute level of effect means that a more radical modification of a child's environment than that provided by schools is necessary to induce achievement in children whose family environments do not insure learning" (p. 163). This is just what conservative politicians want to hear, of course, since it gives them a rationale for not spending money on education; and the "more radical" modifications of environment called for are easily criticized as being too costly to be practical and involving tampering by the state with the personal affairs of some of its citizens. On this last point, furthermore, conservatives will be joined by many on the left.

Since the Coleman Report's negative evidence plays such a major role in documenting the current view that improving school resources does little for academic achievement, our first question must be to consider whether this evidence is in fact appropriately interpreted as negative. If that interpretation seems correct, we can then consider further why it turned out that way. The major line of criticism directed at Coleman's interpretation has come from Bowles and Levin (1968) and Hanushek and Kain (1972). The way the Coleman Report developed its evidence can be seen from this excerpt from the report: "The first finding is that schools are remarkably similar in the way they relate to the achievement of their pupils when socioeconomic background of the students is taken into account. It is known that socioeconomic factors bear a strong relation to academic achievement. When these factors are statistically controlled, however, it appears that differences between schools account for only a small fraction of differences in pupil achievement"(1966, 1: 21). In the Bowles–Levin and Hanushek–Kain critiques it is argued that the Coleman procedure, as just described, underestimates the effects of school-quality differences on student achievement by giving family background the credit for whatever tendency there is for families of higher socioeconomic status to send their children to better schools. As Bowles and Levin (1968) put it, "The survey made the arbitrary choice of first 'controlling' for student background and then introducing school resources into the analysis. Because the student background variables . . . served to some extent as statistical proxies for school resources, the later introduction of the school resource variables themselves had a small explanatory effect. The explanatory power shared jointly by school resources and social background was thus associated entirely with social background" (p. 15).

Coleman (1966, 1:330) has an answer to this kind of criticism; it is that the student's background obviously came first in his actual history, and hence it is only appropriate to hold constant the effects of that background on pupil achievement

when determining the extent to which differences in school
resources themselves have effects on such achievement. This
answer does not seem satisfactory, however; Coleman's method
of analysis, assuming as it does that effects which might be
attributable either to background or to school resources are
always caused by the former, puts just that much more inference between the evidence and its interpretation. It seems only
fair to ask, therefore, whether the case against school effects in
these data requires Coleman's causal assumption. The answer
from extensive reanalyses of Coleman Report data by Smith
(1972) and Armor (1972) seems to be that without this causal
assumption one still comes out with the same interpretation. In
other words, Coleman's grounds for believing that pupil
achievement differences have little connection with school
quality differences are in fact even stronger than was first
thought.

Armor (1972) in his reanalysis used the national sample of
elementary schools that had provided the Coleman Report data,
eliminating some schools for such reasons as having elementary
and secondary units combined (the final total was more than
1,500 schools). The academic achievement of sixth graders in
these schools was the object of study, with such achievement
assessed by a verbal test yardstick that correlated in the 90s
on a school-to-school basis with other kinds of academic
achievement indices, suggesting therefore that something like
overall academic competence as reflected on objective tests
was being evaluated. How, in turn, were family background
and school quality assessed? It will be desirable to consider
these assessments in some detail in order to indicate what the
type of information collected by Coleman was like.

The family background of the sixth graders in each school,
aggregated by school, was defined by intactness of family
structure (whether both parents were living at home), occupational status of the father (whether he was in a white-collar
occupation or not), a household items inventory (whether such
items as a daily newspaper, dictionary, encyclopedia, car, telephone, and record player were in the student's household or
not), and a measure of the educational level achieved by the

child's parents. School quality was defined by how many of twenty-six possible items about personnel and equipment believed to be implicated in producing better academic achievement characterized each school—such as, for example, whether the school had speech therapist services, mental health services, one or more remedial teachers, special classes of various kinds, a librarian, one or more guidance counselors, a principal with an M.A. degree or higher, a principal's salary of $9000 or more, twenty-six or fewer students per teacher, less than 5 percent annual teacher turnover, free textbooks, 1,500 or more volumes in its library, no split sessions, textbooks with an average age of four or less years, no improvised rooms, and 180 or more days in the yearly session. Also used to define school quality were three further measures: a professional background index for a school's teachers, reflecting the quality and extensiveness of the teacher's formal education and such additional matters as whether the teacher regularly reads two or more national educational journals; an objective test measure of the verbal sophistication level displayed by a school's teachers; and each school's annual per student expenditure for teacher salaries.

To evaluate the relative importance of information about family background of the students, versus information about the quality of the schools they attended, for predicting the sixth-graders' academic achievement, Armor's approach was to construct for each predictor being considered in a particular analysis its appropriate "beta weight," or standardized regression coefficient. A beta weight represents the amount of predicted change, calibrated in standard deviations, of the criterion—in this case sixth-graders' academic achievement—when a given predictor is increased by one standard deviation, all other predictors in the set under consideration remaining the same. The beta weight suggests how powerful the predictor is, therefore, in affecting status on the criterion. The size of a beta weight depends on the extent of a given predictor's unique influence in predicting the criterion, plus an apportioned amount of the influence it shares with whatever other predictors are also being considered. Beta weights thus are responsive to relationships that may exist among the predictors. Influence that these predictors jointly possess in predicting the criterion is apportioned accordingly among them. In the Coleman Report all such influence was assigned by fiat to one particular class of predictors: that is, all influence in predicting academic achievement shared between family background and school quality indices was assigned to family background alone by controlling for it first. What is gained in Armor's kind of analysis, then, is that no particular causal assumption is made.

What happens in Armor's analysis? It leads essentially to the same conclusions that Coleman reached. Thus, for example, in a regression analysis for all elementary schools in the sample (Armor 1972, p. 216), raising the household-items index one standard deviation lifts academic achievement .34 of a standard deviation; and raising the parent-education index one standard deviation lifts academic achievement .18 of a standard deviation. On the other hand, raising the teachers'-professional-background index one standard deviation actually reduces academic achievement .02 of a standard deviation; and raising the teachers'-salaries index one standard deviation lifts academic achievement only .07 of a standard deviation. If in turn we draw a contrast between the four family-background measures as a group and the four school-quality measures as a group in their power to predict academic achievement—perhaps the most meaningful comparison of all—the following picture emerges. Raising the index of intactness of family structure, occupational status of father, the household-items inventory, and educational level of parents all one standard deviation, lifts academic achievement .67 of a standard deviation; while raising the index of twenty-six school-personnel-and-equipment items, professional background of teachers, verbal sophistication level of teachers, and per-student expenditure for teacher salaries all one standard deviation lifts academic achievement only .05 of a standard deviation. The minimal effect of the school resources here, as against that of the family backgrounds of the students, is striking indeed.

The reanalysis by Smith (1972) was similar to Armor's but was limited to schools in the North. As with Armor, Smith's results showed that the Coleman conclusion does not depend on controlling for family background first, when looking at the relationship between school quality and academic achievement. Consider, for example, the following zero-order correlation coefficients (Smith 1972, pp. 331–32) between various predictors and academic achievement for sixth-grade Northern black and white students, respectively (zero-order correlations meaning, of course, that nothing is controlled in regard to them): with reading material items from the household-items inventory (presence in the home of a daily newspaper, dictionary, and encyclopedia), .21 and .23; with the appliance items from the household-items inventory (presence in the household of such items as a refrigerator, telephone, and car), .23 and .22; but, on the other hand, with teacher level of verbal sophistication, .08 and .05; and with the number of dollars spent per pupil for instructional purposes, .07 and .04. Smith furthermore has shown that from the magnitudes of the means and standard deviations for the various school-quality measures, their lack of clear relationships with academic achievement cannot be accounted for in terms of restriction of range. In other words, plenty of variation is found in such school-quality indices, but this variation simply has little to do with the children's academic achievement.

What the Armor and Smith reanalyses show, therefore, is that without controlling for family background when studying the potential role of school-quality differences in students' academic achievement, it nevertheless remains the case that such differences in school quality matter little if at all—while family background matters a great deal. As Smith (1972) puts it in summarizing his reanalysis, "The overall results should be clear to policy-makers and researchers alike. With regard to the differences among schools in resources that we conventionally measure and consider in making policy, there are few that give us any leverage over students' achievement" (p. 315). We can be quite confident, therefore, about what the Coleman data tell us; their negative message about school-quality effects is not an artifact of a mode of analysis which throws to family background whatever degree of explanatory power family-background and school-quality differences may share.

This negative evidence finds ample further corroboration in other recent surveys as well. Take, for instance, the results from the study conducted in fifteen countries by the International Association for the Evaluation of Educational Achievement (see Thorndike 1973). With major conclusions echoing what emerged from the Coleman materials, this extensive investigation found school-resource predictors—type of school and variations in practices within schools—to have little influence over students' level-of-reading competence. Family-background predictors, on the other hand—parents' level of education, socioeconomic status of parents, the presence of printed materials at home—were found to possess considerable influence over the students' reading levels. What such results boil down to in terms of specific attempts to improve educational quality for low-performing students, can be seen, for instance, from Wessman's report (1972) on the results of "Project ABC"—a very expensive program designed to give disadvantaged minority-group boys "a better chance" through special compensatory programs in connection with their secondary school education. After two years of the special programs, reading comprehension was no better than for matched controls not in such programs. Joining the growing chorus of those who have carried out careful evaluative research on school-quality manipulations and are pessimistic about the results, Wessman concludes: "The unimpressive scholastic results confirm the need for realistic appraisal of the contributions and limitations of such endeavors" (p. 371).

Parallel to the bad news that has been arriving from assessments of current attempts to make education more effective is a reevaluation by certain educational historians of the role traditionally ascribed to public schooling for immigrant groups in the nation's past. The official view, still widespread, has been that the public schools played a pivotal role in giving the immigrant poor the skills they needed to gain advancement opportunities. For example, the black psychologist Kenneth Clark (1973) simply assumes the validity of this view and invokes it as a basis for refuting Coleman-type evidence about the insignificance of the public schools for combating the effects of poverty. Such evidence, Clark says, flies in the face of "our national history—a history in which previously deprived groups of European immigrants, themselves handicapped by the burdens of language and cultural differences, came to America and used public schools as the chief instrument for their own economic and social mobility" (p. 118). What the revisionist historians of education suggest, however, is that the public schools never served this purpose in the past; that their ineffectuality in the face of socioeconomic background differences did not begin in recent times but has been more or less of a constant (see Lazerson 1973; Greer 1972; Katz 1971). Despite certain excesses of interpretive zeal to which Lazerson calls attention, it seems fair to conclude that this new look at the history of public schooling indicates that school failure for the children of the poor has always been with us. It has been with us in sufficient degree, furthermore, to suggest that there is nothing unique about the current problem of poor blacks not succeeding in school; this simply is part of the general problem that public schooling never did much for the poor, whatever their race or ethnic background.

Higher quality school resources, as these have been defined now and in the past, thus do not have much of a success record in helping poor children with their academic problems. What are the implications of this record? The answer from those who take the evidence seriously is that at best, these problems will not really yield to anything short of remedies that change family background itself. The academic problems of poor children are seen to be so intractable as to require the deepest environmental manipulation—a manipulation far deeper than schools have it within their power to provide and one that is thus either very costly, very obtrusive, or both. Mosteller and Moynihan (1972b) state the matter this way: "The most promising alternative would be to alter the way in which parents deal with their children at home. Unfortunately, it is not obvious how this could be done. Income maintenance, family allowances, etc., seem a logical beginning" (p. 43). At worst, of course, the family-background effects have been viewed as essentially referring to hereditary matters about which there is nothing to be done anyway.

There is another kind of answer that can be offered, however, and it is this. While many kinds of extensive differences in school resources have been documented and found ineffectual, perhaps little that is genuinely appropriate to the academic needs of poor children has really been tried. When school "quality" has varied, perhaps it has done so in ways that have little bearing on the learning tasks that children from low-income backgrounds really must grapple with if they are to have a chance to cope successfully with the demands of school. The programs of school resource enrichment that have led to the negative evidence have, by and large, not involved real changes in what goes on pedagogically for a child. More teachers, more reading specialists, more books in the library, higher salaries to attract more qualified personnel, fewer students in the classes, newer textbooks, more special classes, more days in the school year—none of these imply anything concrete about how something is taught. Neither do team teaching, the open classroom, ungraded classrooms, or higher standards of teacher certification. The actual pedagogical procedures under any of these conditions of "enhanced school quality" tend to be unaffected. And these pedagogical procedures have been developed for middle-class children, not poor children.

It may be the case, therefore, that we as yet know next to nothing about how effective public education might be for the poor children who currently experience academic failure in such large numbers. If we do not have this knowledge, it is because most of what has been done in the name of improving the quality of education has not proceeded from a consideration of what these children need pedagogically by virtue of the differences in family background that characterize them. What the home situation of middle-class children usually provides by way of already achieved school-relevant masteries has not been taken seriously. Rather, how such masteries were acquired gets left in the background, and the implication is accepted that they were learned at school when in fact they were learned at home. This leaves the schools thinking that they teach what is needed for the acquisition of basic academic skills while the reality is that much of what is needed never takes place for poor children. They don't learn it at home the way most middle-class children do, and what is done at school never recognizes the enormity of the prior masteries presupposed by the school's instructional approaches. If this interpretation of the negative evidence about school-resource effects is correct, it suggests that the starting point for knowing what school should involve for poor children must be an understanding of how a given form of wanted academic competence gets achieved—such as, for example, skill at reading. There must be an adequate psychology of the skill to be learned. Then one can consider how the steps revealed by that analysis of the skill can be systematically taught in school for children whose homes have not already done the job.

Soon we will consider this possibility further and explore its implications. First, however, let us briefly comment on two additional kinds of compensatory education attempts which once again seem based on inappropriate views of what is needed. These further attempts seem headed toward the same dashed hopes that we have looked at thus far. Both attempts start essentially with the idea (one we indeed share) that the problem for poor children is not one of inadequate intelligence. The assumption is made, however, that if their intelligence is adequate then the only remaining possibility for what can be wrong must be, by and large, in the sphere of motivation. Attention therefore is directed toward trying to improve how the child feels about his or her competence in relation to the task demands of school.

Enhanced Teacher-Expectancies Fail to Compensate

Most of the effort at improving the child's motivation in school has taken the teacher's beliefs about the child's competence to be the culprit. According to this view, the cause of poor children's academic problems stems from teacher expectations that these children will fail. The difficulty, of course, is that teacher prophecies to the effect that poor children will have academic trouble may simply be truthful assessments of what actually happens under the usual school circumstances; such prophecies need not be causing what occurs. In order to evaluate whether teacher expectancies actually are playing a causative role, therefore, researchers have tried to manipulate teacher expectancies experimentally and to determine whether differences in the academic performance of the students taught by these teachers follow suit. While there has been much eagerness in recent years to blame the teacher's attitude for poor children's academic failure in this way, the charge does not really seem to stick as soon as one looks at the experimental evidence.

The tendency to scapegoat the teacher for poor children's learning failures is an understandable reaction to the frustration of finding the problem as bad as ever, or getting worse, despite the help that school authorities have tried to provide. If teachers and their administrative supervisors say they are trying everything they can and that these children still don't learn, then—granted a belief that poor children are not inadequate in their intelligence—a natural next step is to infer that the schools must be prejudiced against the poor. This presumption of a powerful cause-effect relationship between teacher attitudes and poor children's academic failure is apparent, for example, in the following reaction by several black social scientists to the bad news from evidence of the Coleman Report type as reviewed in Jencks's book: "Many among those of us who have worked in schools know that schools share the larger society's distaste for the poor. By grade 9, the average poor child has not acquired the basic school skills that are prerequisite to successful matriculation" (Edmonds et al. 1973, p. 80). The implication is that if only teachers did for the poor what they do for middle-class children, then poor children would learn. Instead, however, the teachers have it in for the poor and in various ways therefore fail to provide the motivational supports—rewards, encouragement, praise, expectations of success—that will lead a child of normal intelligence to achieve in school.

A modicum of "radical chic" can attend this way of viewing the matter, of course. The role of elementary-school teacher does not enjoy high prestige in the American occupational structure, and the role can often be aspired to by persons who themselves come from relatively humble socioeconomic origins or are members of the sex that traditionally has been expected to keep its occupational aspirations modest. Intellectuals may find it relatively easy and self-satisfying to accuse such persons of attitudinal shortcomings that produce the very problem the teachers say they are trying to solve. And it is possible, of course, for a Herbert Kohl (1968) to point to instances where a teacher's narrow-mindedness can have pernicious effects. To jump from such observations to the belief that teacher expectancies are the seat of poor children's academic difficulties, however, as many have recently done, is something else again. We will turn first to examples of the rather sweeping claims that have been made in this regard, and then look at some experimental evidence.

Rist (1971) made observations in a ghetto school that no doubt have considerable generality. What these observations of black kindergartners and second graders demonstrated is that teachers treat the children in a somewhat differential manner depending on clues as to which children, in the customary public-school setting, are likely to show greater academic success. The clues are not random, however, or the choice of a malicious mind; rather, although Rist does not seem to understand this, the clues have a record of high veridicality as a basis for inference. And while the title of his article refers to "the self-fulfilling prophecy in ghetto education," Rist has no evidence for that claim, only for the point that, if you look at what the teacher is doing, you find that she tries to give more support and encouragement to the students who she infers are more likely to profit from what she knows how to do pedagogically. The teacher bases her inferences on whatever information she has about prior academic achievement, and in the absence of information of that kind she relies upon social class indications such as the extent to which the child's language behavior approximates middle-class norms, what she knows about the education level of the parents, what she knows about their income level, and so on.

It is hardly unreasonable for the teacher to make inferences upon the basis of clues which, as we have seen from studies like the Coleman Report, do tend to be highly correlated with academic success. Moreover, that there are differences in the ways teachers tend to treat children, depending on these clues, in no way demonstrates that these differences are responsible for poor children's learning failures. Yet this is exactly what Rist takes his observations as implying. If the teacher treated the poor children in her class the same way she treated the middle-class children, according to Rist, the poor children would learn as well. The teacher simply needs to be even-handed in her bestowal of support.

Rist argues for this belief on the basis that such even-handedness is all that *could* be missing if poor children are as intelligent as the others. The possibility escapes him that what poor children may need in order to develop academically, despite adequate intelligence, is very different from what suffices for middle-class children, because of differences in how much school-relevant prior learning has gone on at home—and that what poor children need is something the usual teacher has neither the time nor the training to provide. What Rist seems to be trying to do is to write off all evidence of the Coleman-Report type for the pervasive role played by family background in children's academic achievement as a fiction that the teacher makes true by believing.

When you apply this theory of the pernicious teacher as an explanation for the ills of an entire public school system, you find, for example, the kind of broadside that Stein (1971) has directed at the New York public schools. The logic that leads her in this direction is the same as in the case of Rist. Stein argues—appropriately, we should add—for the adequacy of poor children's intellects, pointing to such evidence as the subtlety and complexity of their verbal communication and the visual and auditory discrimination powers they exhibit in learning the ins and outs of their neighborhood environments. But if poor children are intelligent, her argument continues, then the only reason why they fail in such large numbers to learn to read in the New York public schools must be that their teachers have it in for them. If the teachers simply did for them what they do for the middle-class children, the poor children would learn. Instead, the teachers are withholding support and encouragement, are expecting the worst for these children academically instead of the best, and that is what causes the problem. The psychological account behind Stein's position is quite blind to the possibility that a normal intellect on the child's part and the support that teachers know how to provide may be far from sufficient to give a poor child a skill like reading competence, even though these things do the job for the middle-class child. Left out of this picture is the idea that what may have to occur in addition is an elaborate process of skill development that largely goes on at home for the middle-class child but which redounds to the teacher's benefit in the classroom. When that process does not go on at home, the teacher is not in a position, either logistically or in terms of her training, to provide it.

In a book which takes the notion that poor children are "deprived" to be a "myth," Ginsburg (1972) follows the same path as Stein and Rist. Interestingly enough, he treats the Rist paper as supporting the proposition that, "If the child is poor, the teacher may not think him capable of academic success and her belief may in fact help to fulfill this prophecy" (Ginsburg 1972, p. 55). As we have seen, however, all that Rist's observations document is the first part of that proposition—that clues about a child's socioeconomic status influence some aspects of how the teacher treats the child, not that such treatment differences cause the school successes and failures that subsequently take place. It seems hardly surprising, in fact, that teacher beliefs about a child should have some effect on her behavior toward the child. Rubovits and Maehr (1971, 1973) have essentially provided experimental support for Rist's observations along this line by randomly identifying some children as gifted and others as average for student teachers who were to interact with the children in a teaching-like situation. The student teachers tended to give somewhat more support and encouragement to the children who had been assigned the gifted label; for example, they gave these children more praise for what they said than they did for those called nongifted. Rothbart, Dalfen, and Barrett (1971) found approximately the same sort of thing. These are the kinds of teacher treatment differences, then, that are invoked in explaining how the teacher's attitude is supposed to generate a self-fulfilling prophecy. But is there evidence for the claim that when a teacher expects more from a child this does in fact cause the kinds of academic gains that would account for the difference in school success between middle-class and poor children?

Rist, Stein, and Ginsburg all seem to agree that there is such evidence. They also agree, furthermore, in citing an experiment by Rosenthal and Jacobson (1968a, 1968b) as having demonstrated just this. According to Rist, Rosenthal and Jacobson's work supports the point that "the teacher's expectations of a pupil's academic performance may, in fact, have a strong influence on the actual performance of that pupil" (1971, p. 72). As Stein puts it, Rosenthal and Jacobson have "confirmed experimentally" the " 'self-fulfilling prophecy' effect of the teacher's low opinion of the child" (1971, p. 154). And Ginsburg summarizes the Rosenthal-Jacobson experiment in the following terms: "These investigators conducted an experiment in which teachers were told that certain disadvantaged students would show 'dramatic intellectual growth.' These predictions were allegedly made on the basis of a test of 'academic blooming'; in fact the experimenters selected the children randomly and lied to the teachers. Subsequent tests revealed that the potential bloomers bloomed. For example, their IQ scores were higher than those of other children whom the teachers did not expect to show dramatic intellectual growth. It would appear, then, that teachers' expectancies can influence children's academic performance" (1972, p. 55).

Whether the experiment by Rosenthal and Jacobson shows anything like this, however, seems highly questionable. It has been extensively criticized as methodologically inadequate in a variety of respects (see Snow 1969; Thorndike 1968, 1969; Elashoff and Snow 1971), and, as would be expected from such inadequacies, has not been replicated with any kind of clarity. Yet, as the citations by Rist, Stein, and Ginsburg serve to illustrate, it has been very influential. Although we don't want to belabor the points of criticism that already have been made by others, the ease with which the study's claims have been accepted requires us to give it some further attention.

For the Rosenthal-Jacobson experiment, random samples of children in fast-, medium-, and slow-track classrooms in grades one through six were described to their teachers as likely on the basis of a presumptively valid intelligence test to show an academic spurt in the course of the year. These were the "experimentals"; their classmates were the "controls." We would like to have objective tests that evaluated gains in academic subject-matter areas for the experimentals and controls from one year to the next—obviously, teachers' report cards would not do because the differential expectations instilled in the teachers could influence their report-card grading regardless of how the pupils really performed. Objective, nationally normed tests of subject-matter competence in reading, language, and arithmetic were available, but only for some of the classes in the study. None of the comparisons made by Rosenthal and Jacobson showed the experimentals doing better than the controls on these objective achievement tests at the conventional .05 statistical-significance level by a one-tail test (1968*a*, pp. 196–97). Rosenthal and Jacobson concentrated their attention, however, not on academic competence measures that would have at least a relatively clear intrinsic meaning but on what was supposed to be an intelligence test yielding an IQ index. It was this IQ measure that carried the major empirical burden as to what has been claimed for the study.

As critics have pointed out, the IQ measure used—a relatively unfamiliar one, Flanagan's Tests of General Ability (TOGA), involving "verbal" and "reasoning" items—did not have adequate IQ norms for the youngest children. Yet it is *only* in the case of the youngest children—those in grades one and two but not in grades three through six—that significant expectancy effects were found. Snow (1969), for example, notes that "pretest reasoning IQ means for Grade 1 (tested in K) are 47.19 and 30.79 for 16 middle and 19 low track control Ss, and 54.00 and 53.50 for 4 and 2 experimental Ss, respectively. The average for all first grade children is 58. Were these children actually functioning at imbecile and low moron levels? More likely, the test was not functioning at this age level. TOGA does not have norms below an IQ of 60. To obtain IQ scores as low as these, given reasonably distributed ages, raw scores would have to represent random or systematically incorrect responding. Presumably the published conversion tables were extrapolated, even into the chance score range" (p. 198). Snow's comment is that "Readers should wonder why other mental ability information, already available from the school or obtainable without undue additional effort, was not used along with TOGA" (1969, p. 198). And as he also indicates, "The authors rely on simple gain tests (i.e. tests of the difference between difference scores), even though many mean pretest differences between treatment groups equal or exceed obtained posttest differences" (1969, p. 198). When many mean pretest score differences between experimentals and controls equal or exceed posttest score differences, it is hard to see any warrant for comparing gain scores—and, indeed, difficult to make anything of the results.

These are examples, then, of some of the problems with the TOGA IQ evidence to which critics have called attention. Even if those IQ scores meant anything, furthermore, the differences in gains between experimentals and controls were not found to be greatest for the children in the slow-track classrooms but rather for those in the medium-track classrooms—an embarrassing result, since the whole point of the Rosenthal-Jacobson argument is to do something that will help the lowest-performing children. These are, after all, the ones who most need help, the ones that Rist, Stein, and Ginsburg are talking about in the first place. As Rosenthal and Jacobson themselves note, "That was a surprising finding, for it had seemed most likely that the slowest-track children would have shown the greatest advantage attributable to a change in their teachers' expectations. It was they who had the furthest to go, and, in general, it is the children thought to be 'slowest' academically who have been most often discussed by educational theorists as most affected by the teachers' expectations" (1968b, p. 238). It is more than a surprising finding, however. It renders any evidence from the study even less relevant to the problem it purports to address.

We can understand from the foregoing why such difficulty should be encountered in trying to replicate what Rosenthal and Jacobson demonstrated, since it is not clear that they demonstrated anything. The failure to find meaningful effects on pupil performance as a function of experimentally induced teacher expectations in elementary-school settings comparable to the setting of the Rosenthal-Jacobson study includes replication attempts by Claiborn (1969), Fleming and Anttonen (1971), José and Cody (1971), Pellegrini and Hicks (1972), Dusek and O'Connell (1973), and Mendels and Flanders (1973). As an example, the Mendels and Flanders' experiment found that inducing teacher expectations to the effect that disadvantaged first graders had hidden academic potential and might spurt academically in the course of the school year had no effect on the children's reading level, reading achievement grade, or arithmetic achievement grade—even though these assessments were mediated by teacher subjectivity—and had only a marginal and unstable effect, which the authors characterized as "negligible *for all practical purposes*," on an IQ measure (Mendels and Flanders 1973, p. 209, italics theirs). To give another example, Pellegrini and Hicks summed up their replication attempt in these terms: "the results of the study failed to support the general utility of attempted manipulations of expectations as a means of enhancing intellectual growth in children. More importantly, the results suggest that prophecy effects in studies of this kind may be an artifact of a methodology which confounds attempts to induce different levels of expectation with teacher familiarity with the criterion instruments" (1972, p. 418). The only circumstance under which Pellegrini and Hicks found any teacher-expectation effect on pupil performance at all was when induction of a positive expectation was coupled with making the teacher familiar with the type of intelligence-test items used on pretest and posttest, and when in addition the items in question were of a nature that would permit easy coaching for the test. The authors point out that the conditions of the Rosenthal and Jacobson study were such that the same kind of specific coaching for the test could account for whatever apparent expectancy effect was found there.

More generally, if teacher expectancies really were causing the problem of poor children's school failures, we could well have expected a much more positive picture to emerge from the intervention research that we reviewed earlier in the chapter. Both the work covering the preschool years and that concerned with higher quality resources during the years of regular schooling has included countless instances of experimental designs where enhanced teacher expectancies were confounded with whatever else was being manipulated. In other words, the teachers thought the programs instituted would benefit the children. If such expectancies themselves had the power to do much, they should have produced something quite different from the largely negative evidence that has emerged from this work. Even the attention, support, and encouragement that result from a one-to-one tutoring relationship with an adult over an extensive period of time are not sufficient per se to do much for the academic achievement of the tutored child; what matters is the nature of the pedagogy delivered through such a means, as we will see later when exploring the implications of tutoring research by Ellson and his collaborators (Ellson, Barber, Engle, and Kampwerth 1965; Ellson, Harris, and Barber 1968).

It seems, then, that—despite its attractiveness to many— experimental support cannot in fact be mustered for a teacher-expectancy interpretation of poor children's failures in school. The following statement by Stodolsky and Lesser seems to come closer to the mark in describing the teacher's situation than the accusations of teacher prejudice that we noted before: "Most, if not all, teachers want to teach effectively and to see their students learn. We do not believe the cumulative deficit in achievement of disadvantaged students reflects any willful or determined attempts on the part of teachers to 'keep these students down.' Nor do we think it reflects laziness. The most parsimonious assumption would seem to be that teachers are not effective and students are not learning at an adequate rate

because techniques have not been devised which produce desired learning outcomes in many children whom we label
disadvantaged" (1971, p. 35). Or as Jencks puts it, "Most
educators just don't know how to teach these children much.
Nor do I" (1973, p. 152).

Improve the Learner's Self-Concept Directly?

When provision of adequate motivational supports has been
viewed as the answer to poor children's school problems, enhancement of teacher expectancies has most often been seen
as the way to provide those supports. Sometimes, however,
the approach taken looks directly to the child's self-concept in
relation to school, recommending that one try through some
kind of training to shore up or refurbish that concept. There
is little evidence that anyone really knows how teachers could
build up children's self-concepts as such, however, and still less
evidence that their doing so would lead to increased academic
achievement. Trying to improve the learner's self-concept in
any direct way, thus does not seem any more promising an
approach than enhancement of teacher expectancies turned out
to be. Like the latter, however, it seems increasingly popular
these days and therefore requires some further comment.

Presumably, the rationale for improving learning by enhancing the learner's self-concept comes from observations of a
relationship between adequacy of self-concepts and adequacy
of learning. While the evidence is far from clear, instances
certainly can be cited where—as indeed would seem plausible
—"self-confidence" or "self-esteem" or "sense of control over
the environment" is positively related to academic achievement. Thus, for example, Trowbridge (1972) did find that,
within each social-class grouping (although not when lower
and middle socioeconomic status groups were combined),
elementary-school children showed a positive relationship between self-esteem and academic achievement, the latter assessed
in terms of reading-level scores and scores on objective achievement tests. So, too, the Coleman Report (1966) contains
evidence of substantial relationships between educational

achievement and a student's sense of being able to control
what effects the environment has. And Stephens and Delys
(1973), comparing poor children in Head Start classes with
middle-class children in preschool settings, found the middle-
class children to possess a stronger sense of control over environmental events than the poor children.

Suppose, then, that one assumes—despite some evidence that
doesn't really fit the foregoing pattern (see Trowbridge 1972)
—the presence of the kind of relationship suggested by the examples just given. Does this mean that a lower self-concept is
the cause of lower academic achievement? This seems again
and again to be the interpretation made. Dyer (1972) seems to
take it for granted that the direction of causation must run
from "pupil's self-perception" to "pupil's achievement" when
he discusses the Coleman Report data mentioned above. Making this same kind of point from the Coleman Report data,
Beshers (1972) argues that the first task of the school is "the
inculcation of attitudes of self-confidence and self-respect"
(p. 529), although how this is supposed to create for the
student academic proficiencies that don't otherwise exist is left
unanswered. Indeed, the stance adopted by Beshers seems to
be one of simply *assuming* that improving the self-concept will
improve academic performance, as when he says, "We assume
that increased feelings of self-control will lead to other improvements in the educational achievement of the students"
(1972, p. 536). And Stephens and Delys (1973) make the
recommendation that compensatory programs for poor children
"be expressly aimed at enhancing the development of internal
control expectancies" (p. 670). Elkind (1972) even argues
that, if a child is not learning how to read, what is important
is not to help him learn but rather to buttress his self-concept:
"If, for whatever reason, a child in our society is not reading
by the end of first grade, he already begins to feel that he is a
'flop' in life. . . . In helping such children, the major task is
not to teach them to read but to refurbish their self-concept"
(p. 19).

But why assume that the causal direction runs from self-
concept to academic achievement? Stephens and Delys (1973)

give as their reason for making this assumption their finding that poor children already have a weaker sense of internal control in preschool than do middle-class children. But the fact that this already occurs in preschool by no means implies that it is responsible for the later school failure of the poor children. Not only may there well be factors in these children's poverty backgrounds that lead both to the weaker sense of internal control and to the poorer academic achievement, but already at preschool age the children, enrolled as they are in Head Start classes, are encountering demands set by Head Start teachers that could engender feelings of somewhat less control—and we are talking in any case about small self-concept differences.

What causal relation there is between adequacy of self-concepts and adequacy of learning seems much more likely to run from adequacy of learning to adequacy of self-concept than the other way around. To view the problem of poor children as one of a need for a stronger sense of confidence or control over the environment ignores the question of to what extent such a feeling will be realistic. If one teaches children competences with which they can successfully cope with environmental demands, on the other hand, then their own experience will tell them they possess greater control over what happens to them; an enhanced sense of internal control will be a natural consequence of what they can do. Yet, ironically, Stephens and Delys even go so far as to caution against teaching competences on the ground that this may make the poverty-background child excessively reliant on the teacher and thereby weaken the child's sense of internal control even more!

While the Coleman Report evidence of a correlation between the student's sense of control and academic achievement has, as we noted, been used to argue that the prime need is to make students feel greater self-confidence or a greater sense of internal control, the fact is that a look at the absolute levels of felt control expressed by the students in the Coleman Report data immediately calls this recommendation into question. As Mosteller and Moynihan (1972b) point out, more impressive than the correlational evidence is the Coleman Report's finding

"that such a large number of students, black and white, report
that they *do* have a sense of control of their destiny, *do* have
a healthy, even exaggerated, sense of their ability" (p. 26).
Since large proportions of all students already possess rather
high levels of self-esteem and sense of internal control, and
since academic achievement for groups such as blacks or students from low-income backgrounds still is poor, it seems
doubtful indeed that the answer to the academic achievement
problem will be to try to make students feel more confident
about themselves.

The notion of repairing presumably deficient self-images thus
does not seem headed for any greater success in improving
poor children's academic achievement than the other approaches
that have been tried. An adequate sense of self-esteem or of
self-origined control over environmental events no doubt is
important for a child to possess, but, insofar as it is lacking,
it seems more appropriately viewed as a likely consequence of
increased academic competence rather than vice versa. At the
least, we seem relatively clear about why making a person
more competent academically could well result in *feelings* of
greater competence too; but it remains somewhat of a mystery
how making a person feel more competent, assuming it could
in fact be done, could generate academic skills that were absent otherwise. That one should attempt in this manner to
sneak up on academic achievement by undertaking to do something about the learner's self-concept can only suggest a belief
that nothing of a more learning-centered nature remains to be
tried. Our belief, by contrast, is that nothing really close to the
process of academic skill-acquisition itself has yet been given
half a chance.

Taking the Task of Instruction Seriously

Before trying to change the home, or writing off what the
public schools can do, or blaming the teacher for insufficient
supportiveness, or trying to strengthen the child's self-confidence—or giving up because huge expenditures get made but
don't seem to accomplish much—we would suggest that the

task of instruction for poor children needs to be taken much more seriously than has been the case thus far. Implicated in one way or another in the strands of work on compensatory education that we have examined in this chapter is the attitude that the cognitive aspects of pedagogy are relatively non-problematical and that nothing remains to be done to improve them. Where academic instruction has been the focus, what has been done tends to boil down to quantitative increases in the kinds of tools and remedies used already; the implication is that actual pedagogical procedures, developed though they were for middle-class children, leave nothing to be desired for helping poor children.

Perhaps the most disturbing aspect of this situation is that, if anything, current views seem to be moving ever further from what is needed. As evidence arises from psycholinguistic research (see Labov, Cohen, Robins, and Lewis 1968; McNeill 1970; Burling 1973) that poor children in no sense suffer the "language deprivation" that once was ascribed to them, the inference is appropriately made that the complexity and sophistication of their language means that they can't be suffering from serious inadequacies of intellect. This in turn is taken to mean—again appropriately, as we see it—that attempts to make poor children "more intelligent" are misguided. But then the conclusion is drawn that what poor children need in order to succeed in school has to do with motivating them, engaging their natural interests, encouraging them, since it is assumed that adequacy of intellect means that instruction will take care of itself if appropriate motivation is present. In a presentation typical of this viewpoint, Ginsburg (1972) concludes, "It is a mistake to think that the poor child must be taught" (p. 179). Granting that there is a social-class difference in the extent to which reading-relevant activities have been going on at home during the years before formal schooling begins, Ginsburg nevertheless argues that, since the poor child's intellect is adequate, all the child needs at school in order to overcome this background handicap with respect to reading is "a literate environment" (p. 188)—an encouraging, supportive classroom atmosphere with literary materials to feed an interest in reading when it naturally arises in the child.

Ironically enough, the position Ginsburg advocates is similar to that espoused by someone whom Ginsburg would recognize as an archconservative—Stanley—who not only believes that poor children suffer from intellectual inferiorities but that compensatory education can do little to make them more intelligent (1973). He too believes that it is futile to push the child, that one must wait until the child is "ready" to learn, though he advises this because he believes the poor child to be less bright, while Ginsburg advises it from believing the need is to depend on the poor child's self-directed activity. Ginsburg and Stanley also are led to agree that it is a mistake for school to emphasize reading so much for poor children anyway.

But what if it is *not* true that, for an intellectively intact mind, learning will take care of itself as long as the motivational conditions are propitious for it? What if family-background differences mean that many poor children have not built up the subskills at home during the preschool years that are presupposed by the way in which formal instruction proceeds in basic academic subjects such as reading? Then these subskills would have to be specifically and systematically elaborated by suitable training if the child from a low-income background is to have a chance to profit from schooling; far from not needing to be taught, the poor child rather would need teaching of a much more explicit nature than is customarily provided. The cognitive aspects of pedagogy, in short, rather than more or less being taken for granted, would have to become the very focus of our concern.

What, then, is involved psychologically in teaching a child to learn a skill? And what bearing does this have on a poor child's mastery of a skill like reading? We turn to these questions next. Our choice of reading as the particular skill on which to concentrate derived from the clearly pivotal role that it plays in school success, as documented, for example, by Fitzsimmons, Cheever, Leonard, and Macunovich (1969). Bereiter and Engelmann (1966) expressed the matter as well as anybody when they wrote, "If a child fails in reading during the primary grades, his chances for success in any other academic area are greatly reduced" (p. 274). The best period to focus on seemed to be the beginning; once a child falls behind it becomes harder and harder to catch up. Further, it seems reasonable to expect that acquisition of reading skill does not simply proceed in a linear fashion but rather passes through an early "crystallization" phase such that, once a certain degree of facility is achieved, a barrier has been crossed and further skill development becomes far easier than it was before.

3
Developing Basic Skills

Prerequisite Skills in Learning

Suppose a boy of school age is unable to sing—to carry a tune. He doesn't like singing, and when the children are learning songs in school he pays little attention. His hearing has been tested and it is normal. One teacher may feel he has not had enough positive experience with music. She arranges for him to play musical games as a means of changing his negative attitude. He comes to like music better as a result, but he still can't sing. Another teacher may feel he needs more training than the other children, and therefore arranges for him to have additional individual practice on the songs the children are learning. He tries to respond to the training, but he still can't carry a tune. What is to be concluded? That the child is genetically tone-deaf? Too often, indeed, in such cases, and analogous ones, that is precisely the conclusion drawn. But another, quite different, sort of possibility exists—that there are foundational skills the child does not yet possess which are prerequisites for making use of the training he was receiving, and that he simply needs to be taught these preliminary skills.

Leontiev (1957) reports on just such a teaching program with a group of children who were not learning to sing despite prolonged attempts at instruction. They were unable, at the beginning, to match with their voices the pitch of a continuously sounding tone. Training in such vocal matching was the first step. When this was accomplished and the child now could readily match a given pitch, the sounds were turned off after being matched and the child learned to continue singing the tones independently. Then the child learned to match tones "from memory," starting to sing only after the sounds were turned off. When the child finally became proficient at matching a tone after an interval of a number of seconds had elapsed, training in reproducing simple melodies was begun. It is reported that, using this series of steps, progress was rapid, and there was success for all the children.

We believe that, far more often than is realized, children at school are essentially in the situation of the children Leontiev described who needed special training in order to be able to sing. Teaching at school, we submit, continually assumes foundational skills that some children have not yet acquired, and if such children do not receive training in these preliminary skills they cannot be expected to benefit from what goes on in their classrooms. This point is perhaps easiest to see in the higher grades. If a child has not learned basic arithmetic, he or she clearly will not be prepared to undertake studies in the more advanced parts of mathematics. If a child has not learned how to read, he or she will not be able to benefit from training that depends on the use of reading—as almost all of a child's schooling after the first few grades does. A child who has not learned adequately in the primary grades is, rather obviously, at an enormous disadvantage in the grades that come later. It is, however, also true, and not so obvious, that complex foundational skills *already* are required for success *at the very beginning of formal schooling*; that classroom instruction from the very start assumes the presence of skills which some children, most often the children of the poor, simply have not yet acquired.

Teachers try, of course, to avoid this state of affairs; they try to teach the children what is needed. Not only, however, is it sometimes difficult to tell just what *is* needed, but teachers have a large number of children in their charge and often simply find themselves without sufficient time to do what they would like for each one. The upshot, frequently, is that some children do not yet know such things as how to count when their class is working on arithmetic, or how to recognize letters when their class is working on spelling; in short, they do not have the skills they need in order to make sense of what is being told to them in class and of what they are supposed to be doing. And when this is the situation for a child at the start of school and it is not remedied, the child inevitably falls further and further behind as time goes on.

There can be little doubt that it is poor children, especially, who often have not yet acquired the prerequisite skills for undertaking schoolwork at the time when they enter first grade. Although as we discussed in chapter 2, there seems to be no reason to think that poor children lack such broad kinds of experiences as those involved in, say, the representation of absent objects or the recognition of causality, middle-class families (as well as the preschools to which they often send their children) do seem much more likely to indulge in and encourage specific activities that foster school-related achievements. Word games take place, there are nursery rhymes, there is play with letters and numbers. The frequent stress in current popular writing and in commercial toys and games on school readiness and ways to improve it can only act to exacerbate such differences between the middle class and the poor, since, by and large, it is middle-class families that come upon such material and are in a position to take advantage of it. In a study by Milner (1951), for instance, substantial relationships were found between indicators of social class and of reading readiness.

A concrete example of what this adds up to in practice is the following rather striking social-class discrepancy that became evident in our observations and will be further discussed later. In order to be able to make use of the relations between letters and sounds in learning to read, a child must, of course, be able to recognize the sounds when they occur in spoken words. But large numbers of the low-income first graders with whom we have worked had great trouble "hearing" the sounds in words when we tried to have them do so. Savin, in a recent paper (1972) and in the discussion following it in Kavanagh and Mattingly (1972), also reports such problems among poor children, as does Venezky (in press). Middle-class children, on the other hand, frequently seem to find sound recognition to be a very easy task even well before the start of school. In one middle-class preschool we visited, in fact, the *four-year-olds* were already quite competent not only at recognizing a word's starting sound but also at producing that sound for almost any word that we could give them!

The effect on a child in school of continually lacking the skills needed to make sense of what he or she is supposed to be doing must inevitably be a drastic one. It seems to us likely, indeed, that the "low motivation" and the "inattentiveness" so often attributed to poor children who aren't doing well academically simply arise as a direct consequence of the situation in which they find themselves. How can a child be expected to keep paying attention when that child cannot understand what he or she is supposed to attend to? How can a child be expected to keep trying when that child keeps failing even to comprehend what he or she is supposed to try? On the other hand, the change that can be brought about by making it *possible* for the child to do what is asked of him or her in such cases is profound. Slavina (1957), for instance, describes work with children of seven and eight who were having very serious trouble with arithmetic. The children were regarded as "intellectually passive" and at first were given experiences with games involving numbers in order to change their negative attitudes. Although their attitudes toward numbers improved, their difficulties with classroom arithmetic problems persisted. It was then realized that the basic problem was not one of attitude but rather that the children lacked the actual knowledge essential for carrying out the arithmetic they were to do. While they knew the names of the numbers in order from one to ten and their written symbols, they did not understand number sequences and did not realize that one of two successive numbers is always greater or less than the other by one unit. The children were given a graduated sequence of training, starting with actual manipulations of external objects, then imagining such manipulations without being able to look at the objects and, only after that, going through the operations without reference to anything concrete. At the end of this training, it is reported that they were able to proceed in new arithmetic learning with ordinary classroom methods quite as well as the other children.

In our own observations of first graders at the schools where we have worked, we would again and again see poverty-background children who did not seem to care, would not try, would not pay attention to what was going on. But when what was asked of them came reasonably within their reach, these same children frequently appeared to be utterly transformed; now they were eager, intense workers, with a devoted concentration hard to match. Indeed, we occasionally had the opportunity to observe a very direct relation between a child's attitude and the possibility of the child's doing what was asked of him or her. In the development and pretesting of our tutoring program, it would sometimes happen that children were still asked to perform tasks for which they were insufficiently prepared. The child would then become negative, would not work, would try in one way or another to get out of the situation. When, subsequently, the task was made easier, the child would immediately shift behavior, again becoming involved, hardworking, and eager.

Estes (1970) puts the general points at issue here well: "When standard methods fail to produce learning in an individual of apparently normal ability, the usual initial response of the trainer or teacher consists in increasing the incentives for successful performance or in instigating larger amounts of practice. However, no increase in motivation and no amount of practice can be expected to produce learning if essential constituent habits or skills are missing from the individual's repertory owing to some defect of previous experience" (p. 88). Clearly it is of crucial importance to provide such essential constituent habits or skills when they are missing, if children not learning adequately in school are to be helped to learn better.

The most critical tool needed for all the rest of school learning would seem to be reading; almost everything else to be learned in school depends heavily, after the first few years, on being able to read. But hundreds of thousands of poor children do not learn to read adequately in these first years of school. The reason most of these children fail, we submit, is that, they simply lack the prerequisite skills that would enable them to make use of the training that is available in their classrooms. The development of these prerequisite skills can, we believe, be excellently provided for if community adults carry out appropriate forms of tutoring. The rest of this chapter will spell out the grounds for these assertions. We shall give our reasons for urging tutoring for the children who are expected to have difficulties learning to read, and we shall discuss in detail what seems needed psychologically for establishing basic competence in reading. Finally, we will consider what general alternatives there are to providing prerequisite skills to the children who lack them, and we shall argue that anything other than providing the prerequisite skills inevitably leads to these children falling further and further behind in school.

Tutoring in Reading

The magnitude of the reading problem among children from low-income backgrounds, especially those from minority groups, is sufficiently great to have received widespread recognition. When the children of the poor do badly in school at reading, furthermore, it dooms them in a way that is not the case for middle-class children. The latter are subject to home influences which will seek to compensate for what has not been learned at school, whereas the former children are much more dependent on whatever the school does for them—or fails to do. This general point, which is suggested by some of the findings in the Coleman Report (1966; see also Harvard Educational Review 1969), constitutes an additional argument for the importance of using increased school resources specifically for disadvantaged children—that is, those children for whom the added resources will make the most difference. Because reading is a key to all academic progress, it is crucially important for the school to provide that skill to children from low-income backgrounds. The start of school, in turn, seems clearly to be the optimum time to provide extra help in the fundamentals of reading for children who need such help. To wait longer means there will already be cumulative failure and frustration; furthermore, later remedial efforts inevitably have to counter unproductive if not simply erroneous approaches that the child has developed toward written material in the meantime.

How, then, may one assure the appropriate and timely development of reading skills in the children who presently fail to learn? Note first that it is not a matter of all or almost all the children in a particular set of schools needing help, and hardly any other children needing it. Rather, it is a matter of some children in just about every school needing such help, although the proportions of course will vary. Jencks (1972*b*) has described as the Coleman Report's "most important and most neglected single finding" (p. 86) that at a given grade level the range of academic achievement variation encountered *within* any single school is not much less than the range of variation overall.

To help the particular children who need assistance in virtually every school, individual tutoring suggests itself as a particularly suitable method. For one thing, it is a method feasible to implement on a wide scale, one that does not require pervasive changes in existing institutions or in the procedures currently followed by schools and educators. It also seems potentially to be an ideal way of providing exactly what we believe the children need: instruction which induces their active involvement and which systematically builds up to more complex skills from simpler ones, always assuring that the simpler skills are mastered before moving on to others that presuppose them.

Consider what is going on in school for those children who do not learn to read. Despite all the differences that exist in classroom situations, one problem seems almost omnipresent: these children are not involved, they are not "paying attention." Typically—when they are still only six or seven—they will make an effort if individually called upon. But as soon as the teacher's attention is no longer specifically focussed on such a child, the child tends to "leave the field" again. Most of the time that instruction is going on in a group situation—as, in classrooms, it almost always is—these children are simply "not there." To induce them to make a beginning at learning to read, individual tutoring should be able to capture and maintain their active involvement in a way that the classroom cannot. Even more critical than its role for active involvement, however, individual tutoring offers the possibility of maximizing the learning process by tailoring what is asked of the child to what that child in particular knows already and what he or she in particular needs to learn. It can be adapted specifically to what the given child can and cannot do at each point in time, asking of the child the performance only of such tasks as he or she can undertake with success. Individual tutoring does not have to presume prerequisite skills; it can, instead, be oriented toward cumulative mastery, providing for the development of each skill as it is needed.

We believe the children of the poor, rather than lacking sufficient intelligence or confidence or motivation, tend to lack certain quite specific reading-relevant skills, simply because they have not yet had the experiences required for their development. The required experiences, moreover, can be effectively provided by individual tutoring at the start of school for those children who need them. In later chapters we will provide evidence for this belief. At this point let us consider who is to do the tutoring. In our estimation, responsible adults with minimal formal qualifications who come from the same communities as the children themselves and get along well with children, can be excellent tutors if appropriate materials and supervision are provided. Indeed, their cultural similarities to the children make such adults especially well suited for the tutor role. Not only is there a shared background of knowledge, customary behavior, and expectations, but the forms of spoken language—a significant factor in relation to beginning reading (see Baratz and Shuy 1969; Williams 1970; Burling 1973)—are the same as well.

Our approach to helping disadvantaged children who are presently failing in school thus moves toward meeting another need, that of adults who are themselves from disadvantaged backgrounds for employment. Large numbers of such adults are searching for job opportunities in this society. Some already have appointments as teachers' aides or paraprofessionals but with activities that seem minimally productive of academic gains for the children. The tutoring plan that we hope to put into effect would open up a significant role for these adults, involving a type of position as beginning reading tutor for which many of them should be able to qualify and for which on-the-job training would be given. In providing this role, the plan would also represent a constructive response to the call for increased participation by the community in school affairs. Competence in reading is a goal that school and community can readily agree on as desirable for first-grade children to achieve. Involvement of community adults as tutors for this purpose in the schools will, on the one hand, show the community that the school is genuinely committed to helping their children and, on the other, show the school that community adults can help the teacher reach a significant academic objective.

Previous Work on Tutoring

In recent years, as the tremendous needs in this area have become more and more apparent, fairly widespread efforts have been made to provide individual tutoring in one form or another for children experiencing difficulties with reading. Books have been written encouraging such efforts and offering advice and general guidelines for lay tutors (see Pope 1967; Cohen 1969; Kohl 1973). Under a variety of institutional arrangements, tutoring programs have been instituted in many schools and communities. Although a number of these programs have reported successes (Schoeller and Pearson 1970; Shaver and Nuhn 1971; Vellutino and Connolly 1971), tutoring has often been found ineffective. When older children tutor younger ones, for example, it is a frequent finding that the children being tutored gain very little, although the children doing the tutoring may gain appreciably (see Cloward 1967;

Gartner, Kohler, and Riessman 1971). Indeed, tutoring procedures that might be expected to be very beneficial can turn out to be no help at all. In a study by Ellson, Harris, and Barber (1968) that was designed with great care, a group of children (who were to serve as controls for a special kind of tutoring to be discussed further below) were given daily tutoring for a full school year by carefully trained tutors using extensive materials and methods provided by reading specialists. There was no noticeable gain from the tutoring.

Just what, concretely, takes place in the course of tutoring clearly is of critical importance for whether it will be effective or not. And it is of particular significance if a tutoring program not only is successful but is described with sufficient specificity so that it can be followed successfully by others. Two tutoring plans that have been extensively worked out and described in this way, and that have given evidence of success in a number of research studies, are the programs of Staats and of Ellson and their collaborators (Staats and Butterfield 1965; Staats, Minke, Goodwin, and Landeen 1967; Staats 1968; Staats, Minke, and Butts 1970; Ellson, Barber, Engle, and Kampwerth 1965; Ellson, Harris, and Barber 1968). The Ellson group's work has, in fact, resulted in the publication of tutorial programs that are being put to wide use in conjunction with some popular basal readers. Let us consider the Staats and Ellson programs in more detail.

The Staats group has worked mostly with junior high school students as tutees rather than with children starting school. Stories obtained from standard reading-instruction sources have been used, with material reinforcers (tokens, to be exchanged for money or other objects of the student's choice) for correct responses. New words appearing in each story would be taught first, then the student would read paragraphs of the story, and finally the student would read the whole story and answer comprehension questions. The tactic followed with any given story was essentially that the tutor would prompt the student when he or she could not read a particular word or answer a particular question correctly (or would allow the student to make a self-correction), would give the student the opportunity to try again as often as necessary, and would reinforce error-less units of performance.

The Ellson group's "programed tutoring," carried out with first-grade children, is somewhat closer to what we are pro-posing. "Programed tutoring" refers to a set of detailed and rigidly prescribed instructional procedures followed by the tutor that have evolved over a number of years with a con-tinuous attempt at improvement. The content of these proce-dures is closely tied from the start to the reading instruction in the children's classrooms. The programs aim essentially at the teaching of sight reading, comprehension, and word-analysis skills. They specify precisely where correct responses are to be followed by reinforcement—in the case of the Ellson group, social rather than material reinforcement—and exactly what the tutors should do when errors occur. These routines attempt to assure appropriate attention on the child's part, provide hints or prompts whenever feasible rather than simply tell the child the correct response, and ultimately give the child the opportunity to do again correctly whatever was done incor-rectly.

Both the Ellson and Staats groups—as well as others follow-ing their procedures (Camp and van Doorninck 1971; Cramer 1971; McCleary 1971)—have found highly encouraging evi-dence of real success, and have found such evidence with tutors few of whom had any education beyond high school and some of whom had less. In the two major studies by the Staats group (Staats et al. 1967, Staats et al. 1970), differences between tutored students and controls on the ability to read a sample of the words in the tutoring material were significant at the .01 and the .001 levels, respectively. In the Ellson group's most extensively reported study (Ellson et al. 1968), children given programed tutoring for two fifteen-minute peri-ods a day during the first-grade year were significantly different at the .01 level from their controls on all of the tests involving the preprimer, primer, and reader used in the tutoring. On the other hand, again both for the Staats and the Ellson programs, it has been difficult to demonstrate positive effects of a *general* kind on reading competence—effects on tests not specifically pertaining to the content of the tutoring.

Neither program, in fact, goes much further than ordinary classroom procedures in an attempt at systematic skill development. Both programs place their emphasis from the very beginning on the reading, with comprehension, of whole words in continuous prose, without attempting to build up to such reading from work on constituent subskills. If one could do as well as these programs have without providing for systematic skill development, it seemed likely to us that one could obtain really striking results if one *did* arrange for such development. As will be seen below, this turns out, in fact, to be the case. How, then, may the systematic development of prerequisite skills in reading be provided for?

Systematic Development of Prerequisite Skills in Reading

It is almost a truism to say that just about any skill or subject-matter to be learned—reading, mathematics, or other school subjects, as well as, for example, the playing of a musical instrument or learning to draw in perspective or learning to ski —can be broken down into component parts; that these parts can be arranged in a cumulative, hierarchical manner such that the learning of the later parts builds systematically upon what has been learned already; and that learning will be efficient to the degree that it proceeds along the lines of such a hierarchy. That is, skills of a more preliminary kind ought to be mastered before more difficult ones are attempted, and maximal use ought to be made at each step of what the learner knows already in the development of what he or she is yet to learn. While the application of this general principle to educational practice has been urged from some quarters (see particularly Ausubel 1966; Bloom, Hastings, and Madaus 1971; and Gagné and Briggs 1974), its impact on American education, especially in the teaching of reading, has been limited. One crucial component skill in reading—a skill that is virtually always present by the time a child grapples with the task of learning to read—is understanding of the spoken language. Another clear component skill is knowledge of letter-sound relationships, the "alphabetic code." What our principle of systematic cumulation suggests is that the child must be thoroughly trained to "break" that code, to transform the visual forms of letters into the sounds they represent, so that printed words can be recognized by turning them into the words of the spoken language that the child already knows. However, as several centuries of controversy on how to teach reading attest (see Mathews 1966), this suggestion entails certain problems.

For one thing, the relation between individual letters and sounds in our system of writing is complex and quite imperfect, as is clearly described by Smith (1973). Further, it is widely observed that even when a word is spelled in a straightforward, regular manner and a child knows the sounds corresponding to the letters in it, the child still may not be able to blend these sounds together and recognize the word (see Chall, Roswell, and Blumenthal 1963; Vernon 1971; Savin 1972). And even when a child does manage to "decode" a printed word and pronounce it correctly, the child may simply be "word-calling" and not thinking of its meaning—a practice which is frequently believed to be encouraged by teaching that stresses letter-sound relationships (see Anderson and Dearborn 1952; Goodman 1968). Given these problems—as well as what is often regarded as the tediousness of teaching reading with a focus on the alphabetic code—there have been strong pressures against such an approach for a long time. Around the beginning of the century, in close connection with the rise of progressive education, training in letter-sound relationships was widely abandoned as an educational practice in this country. Teaching of words as wholes became prevalent, with emphasis on their overall configuration instead of on the specific letters in them and the sounds to which these letters corresponded. This pedagogical development drew support from psychological research showing that fluent readers do not process printed material on a letter-by-letter basis. Perhaps especially influential was the finding that such readers can identify words almost as quickly as single letters (see Cattell 1885). The sponsors of the whole-word approach also frequently viewed themselves as following the prescription of Gestalt psychologists (for example, Wertheimer 1945; Köhler 1947) to the effect that one should recognize and deal with wholes as such.

The complete rejection of letter-sound training did not last long, and some teaching of the alphabetic code is again widespread. But the approach taken to beginning reading instruction in this country is still far from systematic. Some reading programs teach a sound for each of the letters at the start; others do not. Some begin with whole words and then try to teach ways of analyzing them. But, no matter what the approach, systematic consideration of constituent subskills and provision to assure their acquisition is generally lacking. Even the reading programs that do teach a sound for each of the letters fail to make any provision for the children who do not learn these correspondences readily, not to speak of the children who fail to understand what such a task is all about. Further, even the reading programs that start by teaching letter sounds still tend, in the beginning, to teach most words as wholes, with the connection to the letter-sound training being mostly left to the child to figure out by himself or herself. The approach adopted by most reading programs in the United States can perhaps best be described as a kind of genial eclecticism. The assumption seems to be—and indeed this is sometimes even asserted—that if the child doesn't learn to read one way then the child will learn to read another way, and therefore there is no need to make sure that the child learns anything in particular. Perhaps it is not surprising, then, that each year hundreds of thousands of first-grade children fail to learn anything at all.

In what follows, we shall consider in more detail the practice of teaching words as wholes. We shall argue that the developments in psychology which are often cited as supporting this practice do not, in fact, favor it. We shall contend in addition that to learn words as wholes is an enormously inefficient procedure and, indeed, for more than a very few words, perhaps an impossible one. Then we shall return to a further examination of what can be expected from systematic teaching that

builds on letter-sound relationships. We will argue that it has
been a mistake to regard the irregularities of these relationships
or possible problems with blending or with comprehension as
militating against a focus on letter-sound correspondences; that
these issues imply, rather, an *all the greater* need for teaching
to proceed in a systematic manner.

To view Gestalt psychology as supporting the teaching of
words as wholes is based, we believe, on a rather serious mis-
understanding of the Gestalt argument. The Gestaltists never
intended to discourage analysis of wholes or concern with
parts. Rather, they were urging the consideration of parts that
are structurally significant instead of arbitrary subdivisions and
of the roles of these structurally significant parts in wholes.
This misapplication of Gestalt psychology is especially ironic
in view of the Gestaltists' overriding concern with maximizing
the possibility of meaningful learning and understanding—by
means, indeed, of considering the structural roles of parts in
wholes—to which the rote learning of whole words as such
stands in direct opposition. As for the processes by which
fluent readers accomplish their reading, while it is true that
such readers do not proceed letter by letter and are seldom
concerned with sounding out words, this hardly means that
letter-sound relationships have played no role for them. Children who are fluent readers do, after all, rather consistently
seem to know these relationships, although they may have had
to pick up this knowledge on their own. Indeed, the ability of
fluent readers to process printed material smoothly and rapidly
in large chunks probably depends in an essential way upon the
building up of these chunks from smaller units—just as it is
necessary for a pianist to spend long hours slowly practicing
simple phrases before the pianist is able to render perfectly a
rapid and complex piece of music on sight.

What seems most questionable, however, about the idea that
words should be learned as wholes is the huge amount of learning required in order to do so. In this approach each word,
essentially, must be learned afresh, as if it were a completely
new and different symbol, except that the confusion and interference from the constant repetition of letter elements in dif-

ferent sequences make matters even worse. An enormous amount of memorization is called for, and the fact that the same letters keep recurring serves, not as a source of positive transfer, but only to make that memorization even harder. The learning of whole words by rote becomes increasingly difficult, furthermore, as the size of the learner's word repertoire increases. When the learner is dealing only with a few words that look quite different from one another, the difficulty may not be insurmountable. In the case of the words "boy" and "airplane," for example, it may not be too hard for a child to learn which is which. As the number of words increases, however, the differences among them must inevitably become smaller, and the difficulty of making discriminations correspondingly greater. It is much more difficult to learn to distinguish the letter configurations "boy" and "dog," for instance, than "boy" and "airplane." It seems highly doubtful, as a matter of fact, whether a child ever does learn to read many English words by proceeding only on a whole-word basis. As we mentioned before, whether they are explicitly taught this or figure it out for themselves, children who can read a sizable number of words also seem to possess a goodly amount of knowledge concerning letter-sound relationships. This knowledge may well be essential if they are to get very far in learning to read—and they certainly seem to need it if they are to learn to read efficiently.

But if we are correct about the significance of knowing letter-sound relationships, then it is essential to create arrangements that will bring about such knowledge in all children and to do so sufficiently early in the game that they can make use of it in learning to read. Recall what has been said about the development of specific school-related skills among poor children at the start of school. These children are far less likely than their middle-class peers to have been taught the letters of the alphabet and are very frequently unable to pick up the sounds in words when an attempt is made to have them "hear" these sounds. Most middle-class children, when beginning school, seem to have little trouble with such "hearing"; indeed, they can often themselves produce the sound that a word starts with and also the letter that represents that sound. It should hardly be a surprise, therefore, when, in reading programs that do little to make sure that children can recognize sounds in words and know letter-sound relationships, low-income children often fail to learn.

Let us now return to a consideration of the way in which teaching a child to read should, as we see it, best proceed—namely, through systematic skill development which focusses directly on the relations between letters and sounds. We shall try to show that it has been a mistake to view the irregularities of these relations, or the problems with comprehension and with blending, as militating against this approach. That there are numerous variations in the sounds corresponding to given letters is clear, although a large majority of letters are relatively constant and only a much smaller number are highly variable; also, there is much less variation when one considers common letter *sequences* than when one only considers letters individually. Some of the sound variations that occur can be subsumed under rules of various sorts, but to subsume most of them would seem to require a huge number of rules indeed —and would always leave a sizable number of exceptions anyway. Further, some of the rules required could not be stated in terms of letters and sounds alone, as, for example, the kind of rule needed, at the level of whole words, for "ph" in "haphazard" or "shepherd" as against "ph" in "telephone" or "prophecy." Since it even is the case that two different words with different pronunciations can be spelled identically (for instance, "*lead* pencil" and "the horse in the *lead*"), sounds clearly cannot be fully determined by letters.

The point that keeps being forgotten when such irregularities are cited—as in the extensive arguments advanced by Smith (1973)—is that there is no need for letters to be *completely* determinative of sounds in order for the knowledge of typical letter-sound relationships to be enormously useful to the child. Again, without any such knowledge, each word essentially must be learned afresh, as if it were a completely new and different symbol (except for the confusion resulting from recurring letters). Armed with some knowledge of letter-sound relationships, on the other hand, one can very often figure out printed words that one would not recognize otherwise even if they do not quite follow the rules one knows. A spoken word, after all, may be mispronounced quite seriously and still be recognized, even in the absence of any other clues. And there almost always are other clues, of course, when in reading one comes across a word one cannot immediately recognize. A great deal of information is provided by context, information that, while usually insufficient to determine an unrecognized word completely, very often is sufficient to determine it when used in combination with knowledge about its letters and their usual sounds. Also, a child often knows that a word he or she is trying to read is one of a small number of alternatives on which the child remembers working. If the child knows the fundamental letter-sound relations and how to use them, it is then often easy to tell from the letters which alternative it could be. It should, thus, be a great deal easier to learn words if one knows something of the connections between letters and sounds than if one receives no clues as to sounds from the letters.

Sometimes the objection is raised that, even when printed words have been transformed into oral language, one still must make the transition from oral language to the meaning of the words, while it is perfectly possible, instead, to go directly from printed words to meaning (see Goodman 1968, 1973; Smith 1973). Why, therefore, bother with teaching letter-sound relations, when the child could proceed directly from print to meaning at the outset? But going directly in this way takes, of course, an enormous amount of learning, since here again each word must be mastered as a separate entity. The step from oral language to meaning, on the other hand, is extremely easy and in fact usually is quite automatic for anyone who knows the given language.

That there are variations in the sounds corresponding to the letters, then, or that these correspondences could in principle be bypassed, does not by any means gainsay the utility of a child's knowing the letter-sound correspondences that are typical. Consider next the concern that emphasis on letter-sound relationships encourages "word-calling" and thereby hampers the development of comprehension. It certainly is true that a child who is struggling to decipher a word may be much too involved in that task to pay a great deal of, or even any, attention to the word's meaning. And when that child reads a phrase or sentence containing a number of words that have to be struggled over laboriously, comprehension is likely to suffer. But surely when the mechanics of deciphering have taken too much attention and time, one can have the child go back over what has just been read until these mechanics become smoother; and as the child comes to recognize the words without too much difficulty, so it will become possible, in the case of most beginning reading material, for the child to comprehend what those words are saying. Chall's (1967) review of clinical studies in her carefully done book, *Learning to Read: The Great Debate*, supports the view that when beginning readers experience difficulties with comprehension this is generally a consequence not of too much emphasis on decoding but rather of trouble with decoding and, as a result, with word recognition. The comprehension difficulties seem to disappear when the child becomes competent at decoding and then at recognizing individual words. Furthermore, as Chall makes clear, experimental and correlational studies tend to show a positive relationship between a teaching emphasis on letter-sound relations and reading skill as assessed by various measures that include tests of comprehension. And the evidence for this positive relationship seems, if anything, most appropriately regarded as a fortiori, since it emerges despite the considerable slippage that occurs regarding assessment of what teachers actually do in their teaching—slippage that probably plays a large role in the frequent finding that "methods" make much less difference than "teachers" in the results obtained. Of particular significance for our purposes, the advantages of a letter-sound emphasis seem especially pronounced for slow learners and for children from poorer socioeconomic backgrounds, who are of course just the children least in a position to pick up knowledge of the alphabetic code apart from specific tuition at school.

The evidence, then, does not support the view that focussing on letter-sound relationships in beginning reading is disadvantageous for comprehension—quite the contrary. When a beginning reader has trouble with comprehension, this seems to be the result, mainly, of lack of skill in decoding. Of course, if an *advanced* reader exhibits comprehension difficulties, this will be the result of causes of a different order (perhaps, in many cases, because the decoding facility was developed too late for the child to have had sufficient practice in reading easier material), and such a reader will need a different type of help. But, again, one cannot argue from the needs of the advanced reader to the needs of the beginner. Thus, despite frequent assumptions to the contrary, neither the irregularities in letter-sound correspondences nor the importance of comprehension appear to militate against centering on the alphabetic code in teaching beginning reading. But what about the crucial point that some children—most often poor children, but sometimes middle-class children as well—seem quite unable to *profit* from such training? As we have already noted, poor children are frequently found to be incapable of recognizing letter sounds when they occur in words. To children who have not developed this ability, talk about sounds and about relating sounds to letters just does not make much sense—and doing something like blending sounds into words seems quite incomprehensible.

That many children have these kinds of problems about sounds is a fact that has been frequently noted in the literature and is very familiar to teachers. This fact is widely regarded as a powerful argument against systematic instruction that focusses on letter-sound relationships, at least for the children in question. If a child cannot even recognize sounds, let alone put them together, what point could there be in trying to instruct that child in letter-sound relationships? The belief is widespread that such children, in any case, must be taught to read by other methods, at least until they mature to the point of being able to benefit from letter-sound training. But—provided it is possible—should not one rather *teach* the children to recognize and to combine sounds, if they have difficulty doing these things? After all, the children who have such problems are going to be the very ones least likely to develop a grasp of the alphabetic code on their own. Instead of putting off anything about sounds in the training of these children—or by-passing sounds altogether—should not one rather *give them the prerequisite skills they need* in order to be able to make use of training in letter-sound relationships?

It seems to have become part of the conventional wisdom that one cannot do this, that there is in fact no way effectively to help large numbers of children who experience difficulty with sound recognition and blending and that all one can do is wait for their readiness to mature (see, for example, Roswell and Chall 1956–59; Kavanagh and Mattingly, 1972, p. 328). When one inquires into why this belief is held, strikingly little basis can be found for it. The major reason for the belief probably is just the fact that what efforts have been made to teach these children about sounds often fail. But those efforts turn out upon inspection to *presuppose* in large degree the very skills they seek to impart! The kinds of rhyming and sound-matching tasks included in many reading readiness programs, for example, most likely can be performed only by children who *already* are fairly well along in their development of competence at recognizing and manipulating sounds. In our estimation, hardly a beginning has been made at trying intensive, systematic modes of instruction which genuinely train the children in the prerequisite subskills in question rather than take them for granted. Nothing has been done, for example, which approaches the systematic, step-by-step training discussed at the beginning of this chapter for children who had trouble learning to sing.

The belief that children cannot be taught recognition of sounds and blending also is sometimes based on what is understood to be the cause of the children's difficulties. Large numbers of first-grade children—especially from disadvantaged backgrounds—have been found to obtain low scores on standard auditory discrimination tests, and deficiency in auditory discrimination has widely been regarded as a major source of their reading problems (see Wepman 1960; Deutsch 1964; Plumer 1970) It may be noted that even if this were the case, perceptual discrimination is by no means unamenable to training (see Fellows 1968; Gibson 1969). Even more to the point, however, it has now been shown that low scores on the standard tests of auditory discrimination are not due, typically, to problems in discrimination at all. With modifications in test procedures that remove irrelevant sources of difficulty, Berlin and Dill (1967) and Blank (1968) have found that children otherwise scoring low perform comparably to other children.

Rather than having a deficiency in auditory discrimination, the children who have difficulty understanding talk about sounds and about relations between sounds and letters seem to lack readily accessible, manipulable concepts of the kinds of sounds at issue, the sounds to which letters are related, or "phonemes." While these children seem able to distinguish between words that differ in single, closely related phonemes— for example, they can distinguish "bad" from "dad," "bed," and "bat" (the work of Shvachkin 1948, and Garnica 1973, indicates that such distinctions are generally feasible even for much younger children than we are talking about)—they are unable to deal with phonemes in abstraction from their contexts (see Mattingly 1972; Savin 1972; Gleitman and Rozin 1973; Venezky, in press). For example, they cannot say whether "bad" and "borrow" start with the same sound, or whether "so" consists of the sounds "ss" and "oh." Such problems are hardly surprising in view of what the concept of a phoneme is like. For one thing, it is a classificatory kind of concept, and the dividing lines are by no means obvious until one learns them. They are not the same in all languages; for example, there is nothing in some Oriental languages that corresponds to our division between the sounds for "l" and "r." Another clear source of difficulty is the fact that a great many phonemes cannot exist in isolation. They can neither be pronounced by themselves nor be produced alone by artificial means. And to make matters still more complicated, the same phoneme in the context of different syllables is frequently quite different acoustically, which has led a number of workers to the view that articulatory as well as auditory mechanisms are strongly involved in phoneme recognition (see Liberman, Cooper, Shankweiler, and Studdert-Kennedy 1967; but see also Gibson 1969; Norman 1969, for critical considerations).

That phonemes are not simple concepts, however, hardly means that their recognition and manipulation cannot be taught. Clearly, lots of people acquire considerable skill in dealing with them. There is no basis, then, for simply assuming at the outset that effective instruction along these lines cannot be provided. What seems called for are ways of making the phonemes and their distinguishing features—the attributes that differentiate one phoneme from another—salient. Although phonemes cannot, of course, be literally pointed at, there would seem to be various means of drawing attention to them. For example, awareness of given sounds can be heightened by "tongue twisters." "Peter Piper picked a peck of pickled peppers" can serve admirably to concentrate a child's mind on the sound for "p." As another example, saying a word that includes a given sound and then saying it again with that sound segregated off by pauses from the rest of the word—"sun . . . s - un"—should be of help; especially if this is done repeatedly with a variety of words that include the same sound. While most consonant sounds cannot be segregated in this way from *all* other sounds and will have to be accompanied by some vowel sound, abstraction of the consonant sound should not be too difficult if the same vowel sound—for example, "uh" or "eh"—is always used with the different consonant sounds. And since articulatory mechanisms seem to be highly significant in the definition of phonemes, it should be especially helpful if the learner himself or herself could be brought to pronounce series of words that include given sounds, and to say such words both in the normal way and in the way that isolates by pauses the sounds at issue. One also can make extended use of typical "concept formation" or "concept attainment" procedures for the purpose at hand—giving children exemplars and nonexemplars of words containing particular sounds, having them indicate whether or not a particular sound was used in each instance, and letting them know if they were correct or not. One can devise procedures such as asking whether a given sound occurs at the start of each of a series of words, and when the child wrongly says that it does, one can let the child hear what the word would sound like if indeed it *did* start with that sound. And so on. It would be necessary, of course, to work on the recognition of sounds with each child until that child had learned to distinguish most of the significant sounds from one another. This is difficult to do in a classroom situation but is readily feasible in tutoring.

Once children have learned to recognize sounds in words—to analyze words *into* sounds—it should be much easier for them to learn to blend sounds—to synthesize words *from* sounds. Here too there would certainly seem to be useful ways to help children instructionally. Thus, to induce an understanding of what is wanted, one can make the task very easy at first—telling the child a few quite different short words, saying that one of these words will be pronounced sound-by-sound, doing this, and having the child guess which word it is. If the child still has trouble identifying the word, one can blend some of its sounds together oneself, and see if the child gets the word, and as a last resort blend all its sounds, providing the answer. Then one tells the child the alternative words in the set once more and tries again. As before, it would be essential to continue practice on such tasks until a child had thoroughly mastered them, and only at that point move on to more difficult blending tasks, using letters instead of sounds and providing less information about alternative possible words. And as before, such tailoring of instruction to the individual child's needs is easy to arrange with tutoring but is hard to do in the classroom.

Such methods of helping children with the analysis and synthesis of phonemes are not unknown. Related suggestions can, for example, be found in Durrell and Murphy (1964), Zaporozhets (1969), Elkonin (1971), and Venezky (in press). They are especially well elaborated in the *Structural Reading Series* (Stern and Gould 1963; Stern, Gould, Stern, and Gartler 1968), a program explicitly designed to foster learning by developing structural understanding as urged by Gestalt psychology. But such suggestions have had little impact and have been only sketchily utilized at best. Most to the point, they have been surprisingly neglected by those who argue that skill in dealing with sounds must be allowed to mature and that there is no way in which instruction can help children who are not otherwise "ready."

The fact that many children—especially children from low-income backgrounds—have trouble with sound recognition and blending once more, then, does not mean that the teaching of beginning reading should not focus on the alphabetic code. On the contrary, a grasp of the code seems crucial, and the children who have difficulties dealing with sounds will be all the less likely to develop this grasp on their own. What their difficulties *do* mean is that, quite simply, these children need to be taught how to deal with sounds before they are taught anything that depends on this knowledge. The problem we have identified is that *the attempts made to teach these children presuppose, in effect, that the child already possesses in large degree the very skills that have to be acquired.* Since, more often than not, these skills *are* in fact already possessed by middle-class children, due to the learning going on in a literate home environment, this situation works to their detriment much less often than it works to the detriment of minority group children from poverty backgrounds. If a child has not learned certain skills, in other words, there should be no mystery as to why teaching attempts that presuppose those skills fail.

In this section we have been following two closely related lines of argument. The first has been concerned with establishing that reading is a complex skill which, like other complex skills, is best learned by systematically cumulating the mastery of its component subskills. This implies a sequence which starts with establishing competence in the recognition and manipulation of sounds and mastery of the alphabetic code and then proceeds to the utilization of that code in reading printed material with comprehension. The second line of argument has been concerned with the fate of the many low-income children who begin school lacking the wherewithal to cope with sounds and letters. We have pointed out that the reading instruction to which these children typically are exposed at school fails to develop the prerequisite skills they need in order to profit from classroom activities, and as a consequence such children experience considerable difficulty at learning to read.

Our tutorial program is designed to remedy this situation by providing the children with systematic training that establishes what is called for.

Alternatives to Teaching Prerequisite Skills

Before presenting our tutorial program in more detail, we will consider what ways there might be, other than giving training in the skills they need, to help children who lack prerequisite skills. What most often happens, of course, is that these children are just processed along anyway even though they are not learning adequately, with the result that they fall further and further behind. Two alternative ways to try to help them, other than by training them in prerequisite skills, have recently been encouraged, but as we see it each of these still results in the children's falling progressively further behind. One of these alternatives is to wait for the needed skills to develop by maturation; the other is to attempt to bypass these skills and to teach by rote. Each alternative offers some temptation to a busy teacher who is responsible for a classroom of children with widely disparate levels of achievement. Each alternative, moreover, has been lent some support from certain developments within the field of psychology in recent years. Yet we believe that these alternative policies fail completely to remedy the plight of the children who enter our schools lacking needed skills, and furthermore that the philosophies underlying these alternatives in fact encourage some of our worst practices.

Consider the maturation alternative first. That a policy of waiting for maturation has the consequence of leaving the children in question at an increasing disadvantage can be readily seen. Those who possess the prerequisite skills are in a position to profit from the classroom instruction and thus go on to learn more; meanwhile, the children without these skills receive little or nothing. Such "waiting until readiness develops," sometimes regarded as a necessity forced upon teachers by the impossibility of effectively doing anything else, has recently received positive encouragement as an educationally desirable approach from advocates of "open classrooms" and others impressed by the evidence for relatively immutable stages of cognitive development (see Ginsburg 1972). There is no point, these writers say, in trying to teach anything until the child is ready for it, and there will be no problem once the child is ready. Thus Ginsburg (1972), in advocating open education as the appropriate pedagogical strategy for helping poor children with school tasks, considers it an error to believe "that knowledge is most effectively acquired through systematic instruction" (p. 17). Rather, he wants to wait until the child's self-defined developmental schedule—given a generally supportive environment—makes the child ready to absorb what is to be learned. He notes, for instance, that "If for some reason [the child] has no interest in reading, even for a few years, many teachers in open schools will let him be" (p. 229) —and he agrees with that practice.

Such an approach hardly seems in the interest of poor children, however, unless competition among age-mates—for indications of merit and capability, for access to particular classes or particular schools, for all the forms that preferential treatment can take—were miraculously to disappear from the American educational scene. Waiting for readiness to mature is obviously going to place children whose skills are less developed at a tremendous disadvantage. It seems the height of unrealistic optimism to expect that competition of the kinds mentioned could simply be abolished. There *are*, after all, scarcities in the resources and opportunities that can be made available to children, and it is difficult to imagine their allocation being determined without recourse to criteria of achievement. When debates on these matters take place—see, for example, Wing and Wallach (1971)—they concern not whether achievement criteria should be used but which achievement criteria are meaningful. Waiting for maturation to occur simply decides these matters by fiat in favor of middle-class children.

The grounds, furthermore, for believing that the kinds of cognitive skills at issue develop by "maturation" are in fact quite tenuous. It is true, of course, that children may eventually acquire a variety of school-relevant competences without receiving explicit tuition in them, as in the case of their sooner or later becoming capable of recognizing sounds in words without being specifically taught to do this. Such an outcome does not at all imply, however, that these skills develop simply as a result of growth quite apart from anything the environment provides along the way. Still less does it say that the environment could not be constructed in such a way as to facilitate the development of these skills, as by using pedagogical methods of the kind we discussed earlier to help children in dealing with sounds. Waiting for readiness to mature is hard to justify, then, if there is something one can do to facilitate acquisition of the skill in question. The social consequences of waiting are to hold down those who are disadvantaged already.

What of the other alternative—trying to bypass prerequisite skills and to teach by rote instead? Rote teaching is, as we have already seen, widely practiced in American education. It takes place when words are taught as wholes without the drawing of any connections between the letters and sounds in the words. Another frequently encountered kind of rote teaching occurs when children are asked to memorize the results of addition and subtraction involving small numbers—"number facts"—without any consideration of the relation of these results to the number sequence. Such educational practices are widespread with children from all types of backgrounds. It is our conviction, however, that most of the children who learn adequately under these conditions in fact do so because they already possess enough of the fundamental skills at issue to be able themselves to discover relevant relationships or connections, even though these are not pointed out to them in the classroom. This possibility is not available for children who still know little about letters and sounds or about numbers—the situation frequently of children with a poverty background.

The still greater use of rote methods when children are not learning adequately, especially the increased use of rote methods with disadvantaged children, has received considerable encouragement recently from Jensen (see Jensen 1969, 1973, 1974). Jensen believes that there are two types of learning-relevant abilities, what he calls "Level I" and "Level II." As he puts it, "Level I ability consists of rote learning and primary memory; it is the capacity to register and retrieve information with fidelity and is characterized essentially by a relative lack of transformation, conceptual coding, or other mental manipulation intervening between information input and output. Level II ability, in contrast, is characterized by mental manipulation of inputs, conceptualization, reasoning, and problem-solving; it is essentially the general intelligence (g) factor common to most complex tests of mental ability and standard tests of intelligence" (Jensen 1974, p. 99). According to Jensen, many disadvantaged children, while quite comparable to other children in Level I ability, are so deficient in Level II ability that they are best taught by rote. The empirical basis for Jensen's view is the finding in various studies (for instance, Jensen 1974) that children at different socioeconomic levels differ relatively little in performance on simple memory tasks with familiar items ("Level I ability"), while children's socioeconomic status is more strongly correlated with their scores on intelligence tests ("Level II ability"). Given the well-known problems of interpreting scores on intelligence tests obtained from groups of different backgrounds, however, this finding can hardly be taken to support a real difference in cognitive ability. Familiarity with the kinds of test items involved, and—even on the so-called "culture-fair" tests—facilitation of development of the particular cognitive skills called for, vary widely among different groups. And quite apart from all this, children from lower socioeconomic levels are likely to have much less rapport with the tester and to be much less motivated in the test situation than middle-class children— factors that have been shown to impinge rather strongly on test scores (see Ginsburg 1972).

But even if disadvantaged children *did* possess less of what Jensen calls Level II ability—which we do not believe is the case—could they possess so little of it as to justify rote teaching as the method of choice? Jensen's own way of describing Level II cognitive functioning makes it hard to see how this could be the case. Level II abilities, he says, "involve self-initiated elaboration and transformation of the stimulus input before it eventuates in an overt response. Concept learning and problem solving are good examples. The subject must actively manipulate the input to arrive at the output" (Jensen 1969, p. 111). And, "The capacity for transfer of training is one of the essential aspects of what we mean by intelligence" (Jensen 1969, p. 104). Note, however, that the very concept of a permanent object, manifest among almost all one-year-olds, requires self-initiated elaboration and transformation of stimulus input (see Piaget 1954; Wallach 1963). The earliest use of language, similarly, would be quite impossible without such processes (see Brown 1973). And transfer of learning— the application of learning to new situations—occurs whenever learning manifests itself, since no situation is ever exactly the same as a previous one. Almost all children, then, possess in substantial degree what Jensen describes as Level II abilities. Only the very youngest or the most severely retarded might perhaps be described as incapable of actively manipulating stimulus input or of transfer. Jensen's recommendation that large groups of disadvantaged children would be better off if they were taught by rote can hardly be supported by arguing that they possess too little by way of Level II abilities to benefit from other instructional methods.

Besides the points made thus far, there are in addition some strong direct arguments against extensive teaching by rote. One of them has been clearly stated by Jensen himself in a different context: "Material that is learned by rote association and repetition may appear as gains on an achievement test, but it does not necessarily become consolidated or integrated into the usable, transferable knowledge that we associate with intelligence. Unless it is constantly rehearsed, such knowledge acquired by rote quickly fades and is unretrievable" (Jensen 1973, p. 89). Material learned by rote, in other words, is difficult to retain. Not only is retention difficult but, for most material, rote learning is extraordinarily inefficient. We discussed earlier how learning words as wholes means essentially that every word has to be learned afresh without any help from prior learning. Such continual learning from scratch is the nature of the case for all rote learning. Since no account is taken of possible relationships among the items that are to be learned, each must be learned as a separate entity. When there *are* interrelationships that could be utilized, however, to require that each item be learned anew creates the burden of a great deal more to be learned than is necessary. Finally, a third argument that bears remembering is the simple fact that much of the knowledge one would like children to acquire cannot be handled on a rote basis. While the point seems obvious, to forget it is to drastically lower one's sights as to what will be expected of a child. As Cronbach (1969) puts it, "the cut and dried answers that can be learned by rote are not the answers that one needs if he is to cope with a changing world and to live an appreciative and expressive life" (p. 193). And even on the level of the most mundane of skills, pure rote learning just will not take one very far. The learner always must face the task of applying appropriately what has been learned, and this can hardly ever—if at all—be provided for without going beyond rote memorization. With retention more difficult, with learning considerably less efficient, and with much of what children should know not even capable of acquisition by rote, it is hard to see how greater use of rote methods in teaching will help children who have learning difficulties. As with waiting for readiness to mature, more teaching with rote methods would seem rather to insure that the children who are already behind will simply become more so.

In this chapter we have argued that classroom instruction generally turns out in fact to presuppose prior mastery by the child of crucial subskills that are necessary achievements along the route to reading competence. This situation is no problem when the needed prerequisite skills are mastered at home, as will often be the case for middle-class children, but it becomes a crucial problem when the home does not supply what is needed, as will often happen with children from low-income, minority group backgrounds. Under these circumstances, apparent mysteries arise when some children—usually children of the poor—seem unable to learn to read despite the school's best efforts. The mysteries disappear when it is understood that the very nature of the instruction taking place at school presupposes, rather than supplies, skills which the child must acquire. We have examined what these skills seem to be, the kinds of training procedures that should be conducive to their development, and how noncredentialed personnel functioning as tutors should be admirably suited to provide them. What has been shown here in regard to reading has implications, we feel, for other areas of academic competence as well, and indeed—as our consideration, at the start of the chapter, of learning how to sing suggests—for the learning of any skill.

The tutoring program that we have developed represents an attempt to devise a fully practical method of delivering to non-learning children the skills they lack in the basic area of reading. The intent was to arrive at an approach that would be feasible for implementation on a broad scale. We turn next to a discussion of what the program is like.

4
A Cumulative Mastery Reading Program

General Principles Underlying the Program

Our tutorial program was designed with several objectives in mind. First and foremost, of course, its aim was to make children competent at reading. Moreover, it was to do this for any and all children who might be encountered in a first-grade classroom. Furthermore, the program was to be so designed as to maximize the feasibility of its use, wherever it was needed, by people without any particular educational credentials. No particular assumptions were to be made, or requirements imposed, concerning what went on in the children's classrooms— and the program was to be effective in the hands of any adult who was literate, responsible, patient, and worked well with children.

We argued in the last chapter that learning to read, like learning other complex skills, is best accomplished by systematically cumulating the mastery of its component subskills; and we tried to show that this implies, first, establishing competence in the recognition and manipulation of sounds, in use of the alphabetic code, and in blending, and then the effective application of these competencies in reading printed materials. The tutorial program consists of a series of tasks for the child to undertake which are designed to deliver these skills. Each task is to be mastered before the child goes on to the next, with the first tasks being extremely simple and the later tasks gradually building on the mastery of the earlier ones in small enough steps to assure the feasibility of continual progress. The child works under the ongoing guidance of the tutor, who, following explicitly detailed procedures, gives the child what help is needed to perform each task correctly and tells the child when correct performance has been attained. The program specifies just how the tutor is to begin each task, exactly what to do in response to whatever the child might do, and the precise criteria of performance the child must meet in order to go on to the next task.

The aim throughout is to make possible the child's doing correctly what he or she is supposed to do, to let the child know when he or she does it correctly, and to give the child some practice at doing it correctly. We are thus following a principle familiar to operant psychologists; namely, when you want to teach someone to do something, it generally is more effective to focus on what the person *is* to do rather than on what the person is *not* to do, and it generally is more effective to get the person to *do* it rather than to talk a lot with the person about it. At the same time, we are applying this principle in the context of the kind of careful analysis of cognitive processes associated with cognitive psychologists. We have here a blend, then, of ideas from the cognitive camp about what to learn and ideas from the operant camp about how to learn.

The program has three parts. In Part I the child learns to recognize sounds at the start of words, learns to recognize the shapes of letters, and learns to connect these letter shapes with the sounds. In Part II the child gains skill at recognizing and manipulating the sounds in any position in a word, including their blending, by work with the sounds and letters in short, regularly spelled words. Part III utilizes the child's regular classroom reading materials, adapting itself to whatever reading fare the teacher may be using. The child learns to read whatever words are not known already by a process that carefully builds upon the child's knowledge of letter-sound relationships but also supplements it where necessary. When the child can recognize the words used in a given segment of text well enough, the child reads the text and briefly discusses it to assure comprehension. Depending on the child's performance, further work on the same material then ensues or the child proceeds to the words in the next segment of text. The specific procedures will be described more fully below, and the entire tutor's manual is presented in Appendix A.

While we attempted to design the program in such a manner as to provide for the systematic cumulation of component sub-skills, it by no means represents the only possible way to do this. We would not claim it is essential to follow such aspects as having the child learn one phoneme for each letter before starting to blend phonemes. One could, for example, first work with a restricted group of phonemes—having the child learn to recognize them, to associate them with the appropriate letters, and to blend them into words—and only then start working with other phonemes. Such variations probably make little difference in the child's learning, but some seem more practical to set up for tutors than others.

As mentioned before, our aim was that use of the program should bring about reading competence for any and all children found in first-grade classrooms. Lack of prerequisite skills— the problem to which we have called attention as a pivotal cause of learning failure—was to be minimized by the overall sequence of tasks and the requirement that each task be mastered before proceeding to the next. Further, we did all that we possibly could to set up the tasks themselves and the procedures to be followed with them in such ways as to insure that every child would be able to progress at every step, that no child would "get stuck," finding a particular task impossible and being unable to go on. One of the means employed toward this end was a careful attempt to provide quite specifically for the child's utilization of what had been learned earlier, when that could be of help in work on a new task. For example, when the child is confronted with words he or she does not know how to read, the routines of the program require the child to say the sounds for the letters out loud and blend them together. The child is concretely shown just how to make use for purposes of solving the problem at hand of the skills the child has acquired in transforming letters into sounds and in manipulating sounds. Wherever it was relevant, transfer was not left up to the child but was deliberately built into the program.

We also made continual strong efforts, as we developed the program, to discover whatever troubles could derail a child from making progress and to find ways of avoiding them. There is, of course, no automatic means of guaranteeing, for any given task, that every child will understand what he or she is supposed to do and be able to do it; but it is all too easy to assume this is going to be the case when in fact it is not. In order to develop a program which makes it possible for every child to succeed in mastering what is asked for, a crucial requirement is to try to anticipate whatever difficulties children might encounter and to try to find further ones empirically. Then—and only then—can the problems be removed or ways of dealing with them built into the program. Just attempting to anticipate possible problems in this way made it immediately evident that we had to make sure about such matters as the following: that a child would not be able consistently to give correct responses on the basis of irrelevant cues like spatial position or other inadvertently provided indicators; that a child would not be asked to distinguish between sounds which, in the child's dialect as opposed to our own, were too similar or were identical; that a child would not be able merely to learn specific responses to particular stimuli without making the intended abstractions—for example, a child would not be able to learn to connect particular sounds and particular pictures without noticing any relationship between these sounds and the *names* of the pictures.

Trying the program out on a pilot basis, in turn, was an important means of discovering sources of difficulty that hadn't occurred to us through an armchair approach. Much of the program was pretested by the authors and a group of undergraduates working with us. In order to try to discover as many unanticipated problems as we could, we carried out some of this pretesting with disadvantaged children who not only were selected by their teachers as particularly lacking in readiness skills but were still in kindergarten rather than first grade. How very difficult it can be for some children to recognize sounds in words became evident to us at this point, and we then tried out and incorporated a number of special additional techniques to facilitate such recognition, along with various smaller modifications which had to do mostly with assuring that the child understood what the task was and getting the child to carry it out. Such changes will be discussed further when we describe the program below.

After completion of this pilot work and of the changes in the program that resulted from it, the program was then applied in a field experiment set up to approximate as closely as possible for one school year the normal conditions of the program's use. In this field research, forty children from two inner-city public schools received a daily half-hour of tutoring by community adult nonprofessionals who were trained in the program's procedures. Some further modifications were made at that point. These children—along with control children to be described later—had been selected on the basis of scoring sufficiently low on readiness tests administered in the fall that the prognosis was poor for their learning to read during that academic year. Of the forty tutored children, thirty-seven were beginning first graders and three were in "slow-learner" second-grade sections. More extensive description of the various aspects of this field research is provided in chapters 5 and 6.

In sum, the tutorial program consists of an easily administered series of tasks which the child is to master in sequence, so designed that this cumulative mastery should lead to the child's learning to read. A great deal of effort was devoted to making sure that the procedures given for each task would be such that every child would be able to master it. Let us now look at the program in more detail.

Part I: Learning to Recognize Shapes of Letters and the Sounds They Are Usually For

The aim of Part I is to teach the child to recognize sounds at the beginning of words, to recognize the shapes of letters, and to connect the letters with the sounds. One sound is taught for each letter, and the sounds and letters are taught in alphabetical sequence. While there may be advantages in teaching more than one sound for some letters right at the start (Levin 1963) and in using a sequence other than alphabetical (Gibson 1969, p. 433), these seem to us minor in comparison with the simplicity gained by the procedure we follow. For most letters, it is clear which sound is the most typical one; for vowels, we arbitrarily chose what is generally referred to as "the short vowel sound"—the vowel sounds in "back," "leg," "pin," "cot," and "run." Only lowercase letters are used at this point, since most of the letters in normal text are lowercase, and it seemed likely—and turned out to be true—that capital letters could readily be picked up as needed in Part III.

There are ten steps to be followed with each letter (except for "a," where only the first five steps are used, as the later steps require that the child has been taught more than one sound and one letter). These steps are to be followed in the order given, with precise specifications provided as to when to leave one step for the next. After all the steps have been completed for one letter, they are followed for the next letter, and so on, until all the steps have been gone through for all twenty-six letters. At that point Part I has been completed and the child moves on to Part II. A description of the steps —which are given fully in Appendix A—comes next.

Step 1: Introduction to the Sound
The tutor introduces the sound to be worked on and illustrates it by a tongue-twister sentence containing a large number of words starting with that sound. For example, for the letter "h," the tutor says, "A lot of words start with the sound *h*. Like in this sentence: *H*arry *h*ad a *h*orrible *h*eadache and *h*ated to *h*ear *H*enry *h*owl." (Our notation convention is to italicize a letter when referring to its sound.) The critical sound is emphasized each time it occurs at the start of a word. After the sentence is given, each of the words in it that starts with the sound at issue is repeated several times. First the tutor says the word and has the child say it after the tutor. Then the tutor says the word again, this time separating the starting sound from the rest of the word with a pause in between, and now

the child repeats the word this way also. This sequence is followed for each of the relevant words in order. Thus, the following dialogue takes place after the tutor gives the sentence for *h*:

Tutor: Harry
Child: Harry
Tutor: H-arry
Child: H-arry
Tutor: had
Child: had
Tutor: h-ad
Child: h-ad
Tutor: horrible
Child: horrible
Tutor: h-orrible
Child: h-orrible
Tutor: headache
Child: headache
Tutor: h-eadache
Child: h-eadache
Tutor: hated
Child: hated
Tutor: h-ated
Child: h-ated
Tutor: hear
Child: hear
Tutor: h-ear
Child: h-ear
Tutor: Henry
Child: Henry
Tutor: H-enry
Child: H-enry
Tutor: howl
Child: howl
Tutor: h-owl
Child: h-owl

The primary purpose of Step 1 is, of course, to draw the child's attention to the critical sounds and to provide some initial instigation towards developing concepts of them. It also should aid the child, at the beginning, in coming to understand what is meant by "the sound at the start of a word," a notion which to many first graders originally has little or no meaning. The procedure also is one that most children find enjoyable. Having the child not only repeat the words that start with the critical sound but also repeat them again with the starting sound separated off by a pause from the rest of the word provides the child with a strategy the child can use for telling when a word starts with that sound. Some of the children in our pretesting group did not learn to recognize any sounds until we introduced such repetition of words with the initial sound separated off by a pause.

Step 2: The Two-Picture Game
Step 2 makes use of "game-pictures"—simple line drawings showing objects whose names begin with the various sounds for the different letters. The child is shown two pictures at a time, one whose name begins with the sound being worked on and one whose name begins with any of a variety of different sounds. The child is to name the pictures and to say which one starts with the critical sound. Work on Step 2 is continued with different pairs of pictures until the child meets the rigorous criterion of seven correct choices in a row.

The tutor assures that the child knows the names of the pictures before having the child choose the one whose name starts with the sound at issue. Sounds which in some dialects are identical or very similar—for example, the vowels at the start of "astronaut" and "Eskimo"—are never contrasted with one another. The pictures to be used get shuffled, and the correct one in a pair is sometimes shown on the right and sometimes on the left, so that the correct picture will not be given away by irrelevant cues. The child is required to make a commitment to one picture or the other, rather than, for example, being allowed to point between them or at both of them.

If the child chooses the wrong picture, a specific correction procedure is followed. To illustrate this, suppose the names of the pictures are "window" and "violin," and the child chooses the violin as starting with *w*. The tutor then says, "No. It's violin, not wiolin." The tutor then points to the window picture and says, "Window starts with *w*. Say 'w-indow.' " The child then repeats "w-indow."

The object of Step 2 is, of course, to provide further help in forming the concepts of the sounds. When the child makes an error, the reason for the tutor's contrasting the name as it really is with the name as it would be if it started with the sound chosen by the child, is that such a correction procedure should aid in differentiating the sound at issue. (The procedure suggested itself to us when we happened to come across a reference to "the two *th* sounds, as in 'this' and in 'thunder' " —and were momentarily puzzled. The puzzlement immediately disappeared when we tried saying one of the words with the starting sound belonging to the other.)

Even with the aid that has been described, some children in the pretesting had trouble reaching criterion. We therefore included another procedure, to be added if the child has a hard time without it. In this case, after the child names each of the two pictures, the tutor points to them in turn, saying their names with a pause after the starting sound, and has the child repeat the names this way. Only after that is the child to choose which picture starts with the given sound. All children were then able to reach criterion, and on later letters the special help became unnecessary.

Step 3: The Yes-No Game
Step 3 also makes use of the game-pictures. Now, however, they are shown one at a time. Half of the pictures used have names that start with the sound at issue, while the remaining half have names that start with various other sounds—different sounds from those used for contrast in Step 2. The child is asked to name the picture and to say whether the name starts with the sound at issue or not. Again, work is continued until the child answers correctly seven times in a row. And again, the tutor assures that the child knows the name before the child says whether or not it starts with the critical sound, no pictures are used that require discriminations between sounds that may

be too much alike, and efforts are made to avoid giving away the answer by irrelevant cues.

There now are two correction procedures carried out for wrong answers, depending on whether the name of the picture on which an error was made does or does not start with the critical sound. To illustrate, suppose the game-picture depicting a hat is shown for the sound *a*, and the child says "hat" does start with *a*. The tutor then says, "No. It's hat, not at. Hat doesn't start with *a*." Or, suppose the game-picture depicting an ambulance is shown for *a* and the child says "ambulance" doesn't start with *a*. Then the tutor says, "A-mbulance. That does start with *a*."

The function of Step 3, like that of Step 2, is to provide further help in developing concepts of the sounds or phonemes at issue. Unlike Step 2, Step 3 forces consideration of the phoneme boundaries; the child must decide whether each exemplar offered falls within the boundaries for a given phoneme or not, rather than, as in Step 2, choosing which of two instances is a better fit. Consistently correct responding in Step 3 thus calls for greater clarity concerning the concept of the sound at issue than does consistently correct responding in Step 2.

Step 3 again was difficult for some children in the beginning, and therefore a procedure providing for separation of the starting sound from the rest of the word by a pause was again included, to be used when necessary. When this procedure is used, after the child names each picture but before the child indicates whether or not the name starts with the sound at issue, the tutor says the name again with a short pause after the starting sound and has the child repeat the name that way too. For example, suppose the child is working on the sound *a* and has erroneously reported many names as starting with *a* that don't and many names as not starting with *a* that do. Suppose the next picture that comes up is an apple. After the tutor has the child name it—"apple"—the tutor says, "a-pple," and has the child say, "a-pple." Only then does the tutor ask, "Does apple start with *a*?" Again, with this modification, all children were able to reach criterion, and on later letters the special help became unnecessary.

Step 4: Letter Tracing

After the child has reached criterion on Step 3 as well as on Step 2 for a given sound, the child should have a fairly well-developed concept of the sound at issue and be ready to learn to relate a letter to that sound. In order to facilitate that learning, the letter is shown to the child embedded in an "alpha-picture"—a picture of an object the name of which starts with the sound the letter is for. The twenty-six alpha-pictures are presented in Appendix B. Thus, for instance, the alpha-picture for the letter "b" is shown below:

The tutor makes sure that the child understands what the picture is supposed to be and tries to make clear to the child that the dark lines are the letter for the sound at the start of the picture's name. For example, in the case of "b," the tutor says, "This is supposed to be a bird. The dark lines here (pointing) are the letter for *b* (the tutor makes the sound), the sound at the start of 'bird.' You repeat after me, 'bird.'" After the child repeats, the tutor says "b-ird" and has the child repeat that. Finally, the tutor says the sound by itself, "*b*," and has the child repeat that as well.

The child is then given practice tracing the form of the letter along dotted lines provided on the same page as the alpha-picture itself. The tutor sees to it that the child proceeds to trace the series of dotted letters from left to right, completes one row of letters before going on to the row beneath, and traces each letter in the correct manner. The tutor continually refers to the letter by its "sound name." If the child knows the alphabet name, the tutor agrees that the alphabet name is right and says that the letter *also* is for the given sound.

Besides providing practice in printing itself, such tracing should facilitate discrimination of the letter form and association between this form and the appropriate sound. It also gives the child a sometimes welcome shift in activity.

Step 5: Letter Drawing
In Step 5 the child again is shown the alpha-picture and is asked what the picture shows, with the tutor reminding the child if necessary. Then the child is asked what the dark lines are, and if the child cannot answer by giving the sound the tutor again tries to make clear to the child that the dark lines form the letter for the sound at the start of the picture's name, using the same procedure as in Step 4.

The child then proceeds to draw the letter, again on a page also containing the alpha-picture, this time without dotted lines to trace but only the kind of horizontal guidelines typically given children who are learning to print. The tutor again provides whatever help is needed. If necessary, the tutor has the child do some tracing again as in Step 4, then try drawing the letter again, and so on, going back and forth a number of times. However, not more than a total of half an hour is to be spent on Steps 4 and 5 together, as complete mastery of printing is not necessary for the rest of the program and further time seems better spent mastering the activities that are essential.

Step 6: The Picture-Matching Game with the
Letter-Drawing Sheets
The next four steps all are games involving the matching of sounds with letter forms. In Steps 6 and 7, the letter forms still are presented embedded in the alpha-pictures; in Steps 8 and 9 they are shown by themselves. The tutor begins Step 6 by placing in front of the child three different alpha-pictures (except for "b," where only the two learned at that point can be used, and "a," where Steps 6–10 do not apply), using the sheets for drawing letters. The tutor asks in the case of each

one what the picture shows and what the dark lines are. The child is helped as in Step 5 if the child does not remember.

The tutor then shows the child, one at a time, game-pictures the names of which start with one of the three sounds corresponding to the three alpha-pictures. The tutor has the child say what the picture shows, and sees to it that the picture gets identified by its appropriate name. Then the tutor has the child say the sound that the name starts with. If the child says the wrong sound, the tutor says the name again—first normally, then once more with a pause after the starting sound—and then the tutor says the starting sound by itself. The child then repeats the name both of these ways as well as giving the starting sound by itself.

When the child has said the correct starting sound for a picture, the child is asked to put it together with the letter for that sound—the letter embedded in the alpha-picture. Again there is a specific correction procedure if the child puts the picture with a wrong letter. For example, if the child places the picture showing an apple with the "b" in the bird alpha-picture the tutor says, "That's *b*, the sound at the start of bird. Apple starts with *a*. Can you find the letter for *a*?" If necessary, the tutor points to the "a" in the alpha-picture for that letter, which is an ant, and says, "Here's *a*. Ant starts with *a* like apple does."

The child is required to match seven game-pictures in a row to the right letters without error before going on to the next step. If all the game-pictures pulled out for use have been shown before this criterion is reached, they get shuffled, the alpha-pictures get rearranged so they are in a different order as well, and the game continues.

Again in Step 6 procedures are included for the tutor to use if the child experiences too much difficulty without them. Two parts of what the child is asked to do in Step 6 constitute potential trouble spots where such help may be needed: identification of the starting sound of the game-picture's name, and matching that sound with the correct letter. If the child has a hard time giving the right starting sounds, then the following is done. After the child names the game-picture, the tutor repeats the name and has the child repeat it again. Then the tutor says the name with a pause after the starting sound and has the child repeat it that way too. Only then does the tutor ask for the starting sound; and if necessary, the tutor provides it and has the child repeat it after hearing it. If the child has trouble matching the game-pictures with the letters, then just before the child is to choose the letter for a game-picture the tutor again says the sound the name starts with and then, pointing to each of the three letters in turn, gives their sounds. These additions again made it possible for all children to reach criterion and, when needed at the outset, became unnecessary on later letters.

Steps 6, 7, 8, and 9 all involve comparisons between the letter being worked on and two other letters. The two other letters that are used in each case were chosen in such a way as to make sure practice would be provided at discriminating letters that are visually similar (such as b, d, p, q, and g) and at discriminating similar sounds (like *d* and *t*, or *g* and *k*)— although, as in earlier steps, we avoided sound contrasts which in some dialects would be almost or completely identical. We also attempted to provide for adequate rehearsal of letter-sound correspondences that already had been taught, making sure that not too much time elapsed between successive occasions on which given letters appeared.

Steps 7, 8, and 9: Further Sound-Letter Matching Games

Steps 7, 8, and 9 are all like Step 6, with minor modifications. They provide further practice at matching the sound and letter being worked on, using different sets of other sounds and letters for contrast. Step 7 is just like Step 6 except that, instead of showing the child game-pictures, the tutor simply tells the child words. For each word heard, the child is to give the starting sound of the word and to point to the letter—embedded in its alpha-picture—for that sound. Use in this way of what amounts to a sizable set of spoken words, besides the game-pictures of Step 6, removes the possibility that would otherwise exist for the child simply to memorize what is to happen with each game-picture or word individually.

Step 8 is like Step 6 but with a different modification. Now the sound that the game-picture's name starts with is to be matched to the appropriate letter as such, rather than to the letter as embedded in its alpha-picture. Thus the child is now required to remember the sound which a letter is for without the reminder provided by its alpha-picture. Finally, Step 9 is like Step 8 except that spoken words once again are used instead of game-pictures.

Each of these games continues until the child has matched the sounds to the correct letters seven times in a row without making an error. Similar correction procedures as described with Step 6 are followed if errors occur, and the same procedures are used to make the task easier if at first it is too difficult.

Step 10: Giving the Sounds for the Letters
In Step 10 the child is shown, in scrambled order, all the letters of the alphabet up to and including the one which the child is on, and is asked to give the sound each letter is for as well as a word that starts with that sound. If the child needs help with any letter, the tutor provides it, along with further practice for that letter. This step, located at the end of the series of steps for each letter, essentially constitutes a continual review of all the letters that have been worked on up to that point.

Observations on Part I
Here, and at the end of the descriptions of Parts II and III of the tutorial program that follow, we will summarize observations on how the program looked in operation during the field research. The tutors needed about three weeks of practice to get the routines of Part I down smoothly. Before starting work with the children, they role-played tutoring with each other and with one of us (L. W.) until they clearly were following all the correct procedures for the different possible contingencies. Such practice was undertaken with all the different sounds and letters in order for the tutors to become accustomed to working with all of them.

As for the children, many of them had a great deal of difficulty at the beginning. For children having such trouble, constant and rapid provision of the prescribed help by the tutors, using the special procedures for making the tasks easier, often seemed crucial. Even with those special procedures, it sometimes took one or two weeks before a child got through the first five steps for "a" and "b." After the first few letters had been gone through, however, all this changed markedly. The children picked up the idea of what was wanted, and usually did not even wait for the tutor to tell them what to do but simply went ahead and did what they were supposed to without being asked. Almost all of the children reached the point where they were averaging about a letter a session, and they generally gave correct sounds and words for all the letters they had worked on—with very few exceptions—when carrying out Step 10.

The children's attitudes also changed enormously in direct relation to their progress. In the beginning, many children "didn't think they could do anything, and didn't want to try," as one of the tutors in the field experiment put it. Some weeks later they looked like an entirely different group of children—confident, eager, and, most of the time, working hard and working well. It was clear from observing them that, despite the letter-by-letter learning required by the program, there was no need to worry that the tasks would seem tedious or boring to the children—quite the contrary. Here were children for whom the prognosis from readiness tests was that they were unlikely to learn to read in first grade, children from a group often regarded as incapable of sustained attention—and indeed their teachers often told us of their inattentiveness in class—behaving very differently than such data about them would suggest. They were, by and large, eagerly and competently working away on letter after letter, a half-hour at a time.

It also seemed clear that the problem, considered insoluble by some writers, of teaching such children to develop concepts of the sounds for letters, or phonemes, as discussed in chapter 3, is relatively easy to solve in situations like the one described here. Most of the children worked their way through all the letters of the alphabet in about two and one-half months, meeting the rigorous criteria that were established not only for learning sound concepts but also for letter-sound associations. Only four of the forty children tutored took appreciably longer. Three of these were very frequently absent from school for long periods of time, and the fourth was continually kept from tutoring by his teacher as a punishment for misbehaving in class. It should be kept in mind that the forty children we are talking about were attending inner-city public schools and had obtained the kinds of low scores on readiness tests which meant that they were expected to have trouble learning to read. Some of them had tested IQs in the 50s, and several had serious speech and/or hearing problems. Even a group of this kind, then, did not find it difficult to develop concepts of phonemes when they were given suitable instruction.

Part II. Learning to Sound Out Simple Words

In Part I of the program the child learns to recognize sounds at the beginning of words and to associate these sounds with letters. In Part II, the child learns to blend the sounds together into words. The child gains practice at recognizing and manipulating the sounds in any position in a word, transforming sounds to letters and letters to sounds, and sounding out some short, simple words with regular spelling. There are three steps in Part II, each of which is to be repeated a number of times with different specified sets of words before going on to the next step or, in the case of the last step, to the next part of the program. The child must again meet certain precise achievement criteria before leaving each set of words for what comes next. Appendix A presents complete details.

Step 1: The Which-Picture Game
Three of the game-pictures that have short names starting with the same sound are placed before the child. (The child by now knows these names well.) The first set is a ball, a bus, and a bed. The tutor tells the child she is going to say the name of one of the pictures but not in the regular way—she is going

to say the separate sounds that make up its name; the child is
to guess which picture is meant. The tutor then says the sounds
of one of the names, pronouncing each sound separately with
pauses between the sounds—for example, "*b-u-s.*" If the child
can't tell which picture is meant, the tutor has the child repeat
the sounds after her. If the child still can't tell, the tutor says
the name the regular way except for pausing after the starting
sound—for example, "*b-us.*" If necessary, the tutor repeats
the word again with a shorter pause after the starting sound;
if the child still doesn't know it, the tutor gives the name of the
picture—that is, says the word normally. The same procedure
then is repeated with another of the three pictures—for example, the bed—the tutor beginning with "*b-e-d,*" and so on.
The tutor continues in this way with the three different pictures
in the given set until the child has correctly identified each
one from the separate sounds alone. Then that set is put away
and the same procedures are followed with the next set. There
are seven different sets of three game-pictures each which are
used in this way, with the child meeting the specified performance criterion for all the sets before proceeding to Step 2.

The game-pictures used here all have short names which are
fairly different, except that the three names within a single set
always have the same starting sound. We wanted to keep the
task very easy, but since the children become very familiar
with the starting sounds of the names of the game-pictures in
Part I we could not permit the three names here to be differentiated on the basis of starting sounds or many children might
never pay any attention to anything else. This way the children
are forced to consider the later sounds and to make some
matchings between the sounds spoken separately and the
sounds blended into words. Difficulty is minimized by having
only a small number of alternative words for the child to
choose from and having the game-pictures in front of the child
as a reminder of what these alternatives are.

When the tutors first told the children what was to be done
in Step 1 and gave the separate sounds of the first name, almost
all of the children seemed to have no idea what the tutor was
talking about and to be quite at a loss. They caught on ex-

tremely fast, however. After the tutor had helped them with
the name of the first game-picture or two, almost every child
immediately chose all the other game-pictures correctly from
hearing the separate sounds alone. Very little time was needed
for Step 1 by any of the children.

*Step 2: Building and Reading the Names of Some
Game-Pictures*
In Step 1 the child is given separate sounds and blends them
together into words. In Step 2 the child builds words with
letters and reads the words by sounding them out. Again three
game-pictures are placed before the child, but now the child
also is given "letter-cards"—cards containing the separate letters needed to form their names. The first set of game-pictures
is a hat, a map, and a yam; cards with the letters "h," "a,"
"t," "m," "p," and "y" are shuffled and put out in no particular
order. The tutor places one of the pictures—for example, the
hat—directly in front of the child and has the child say its
name, "hat." The tutor repeats the name and then pronounces
each sound separately with pauses between the sounds—
"*h-a-t.*" The child tries to find the letter-card for each sound
in order and places these letter-cards underneath the picture
from left to right, receiving whatever help is needed from the
tutor. When the name has been built in this way, the tutor
points to each letter in turn, from left to right, and has the
child say the sound it is for, helping the child if necessary.
Then the tutor moves her finger a little faster across the letters
and says the sounds more blended together. Finally, she moves
her finger quite fast and says the name the regular way, having
the child repeat it after her. The point, of course, is to get the
child to realize that the letter sounds blended together make the
name. After all this has been done with one of the pictures,
the same procedures are repeated with the other two pictures
in the set.

After that, the tutor builds the name of one of the three
game-pictures by herself and has the child try to read which
one it is. She gives the child help, if needed, in sounding out
the letters from left to right and blending the sounds together

into the name. When that name has been read by the child, the tutor goes through the same procedure again with another name, and so on. The tutor keeps doing this with the names of the three pictures, in different orders, until the child has managed to read each one correctly without needing to be helped.

Then it is the child's turn to build the names, receiving only whatever help may still be needed. Some children are able at this point to build the names completely on their own, in which case all the tutor does is read the name—child and tutor thus in effect doing what they did just before but with reversed roles. Other children still need the tutor to help them with the building, in which case the children again read the names themselves after the names are built.

When all this has been carried out with one set of three game-pictures, those game-pictures and the letter-cards that go with them are put away and the complete procedure then gets repeated with the next set of three game-pictures, and so on. There are five sets of game-pictures in all for Step 2. To keep the task sufficiently easy, all the names of the game-pictures are of the form consonant-vowel-consonant with each letter corresponding to the sound taught for it in Part I, and the vowel is always the same within each set of three names. The only criterion the child must meet in Step 2 is that of once recognizing each name without help when it has been built by the tutor. This is far from a rigorous criterion, especially with the three pictures in view for the child to choose among for the name; the aim, of course, is not thorough learning of the particular words used but rather a beginning grasp of how the letters of printed words represent, in sequence from left to right, the temporal succession of the sounds in spoken words.

Step 3: Building and Reading Some More Simple Words
Step 3 is almost identical to Step 2, the purpose being to provide additional practice of a similar kind. Instead of building and reading the names of game-pictures, however, now the building and reading is done with short spoken words. There again are three words to a set, and the words are of the same

form as the names in Step 2. In selecting the words, an attempt was made to provide for practice with many different letters. As in Step 2, each set is first built by the tutor and child together; then the tutor builds the words of that set and the child reads them until managing to get each one correct without help; and finally the child builds each word in the set again.

The tutor introduces each word to be built by using it in context, saying, for example, "The first word is pan, like a pan on the stove." Then the word is pronounced again, first the regular way—"pan"—and then with each sound separately—"p-a-n." The child again finds the appropriate letter-cards for the sounds, puts them in place, and goes on as in Step 2. In order to increase the salience of letter-sound correspondence, the three words in each set in Step 3 are very similar to one another, often varying only in a single letter. For example, the first set is "pan," "man," and "fan." To facilitate the child's awareness of the similarities and the differences, the letter-cards that remain the same within the set are left in place, and only the ones that change are moved. Thus, after "pan" has been built and gone over, the tutor has the child exchange only "p" for "m" when "man" is to be built, leaving the "a" and the "n" in place. Similarly, when the tutor builds words for the child to read, she again leaves in place the letters that remain the same and only moves the ones that change. In Step 3 there are no game-pictures to remind the child of what the alternatives are, so if the child has trouble reading the word, the tutor gives the alternatives orally.

There are twenty-two sets of words to be used in Step 3. When all the sets have been gone through in the prescribed way, the child moves on to Part III of the program.

Observations on Part II
As already indicated, although most of the children were quite mystified at the beginning of Step 1, the which-picture game, they caught on rapidly. Reaching criterion with the seven sets of words in Step 1 took very little time for anyone. The other two steps, building and reading the names of some game-pictures and doing the same with some other simple words,

raised no serious difficulties either. All of Part II—including the twenty-seven sets of words in Steps 2 and 3 as well as the seven sets of words in Step 1—typically took only about two or three weeks, and no child needed appreciably longer.

The beginning of Step 2, when the first words are built with the letters and read, was marvelous to observe. The first child we happened to see at this point was a first-grade boy who had scored at the twelfth percentile of the national norms on the battery of readiness tests administered at the start of the school year and who had reportedly been having trouble in class. After the tutor and he had built one of the words together, the tutor sounding it out and the boy finding the letters and putting them in place, he suddenly fairly shouted, "You mean that's how you spell words?" He was terribly excited and extremely happy. Other children behaved in much the same way, although the insight was not always quite that sudden. Another particularly striking child was a boy in a "slow-learner" second-grade section who had scored at the thirty-sixth percentile of the national norms on the readiness tests that were for beginning first graders. He was hard of hearing, and his tutor noticed that he tended not to pronounce the last sounds in words. This boy took longer than most children to catch on to the blending in Step 1. Then, when Step 2 began, he suddenly became very excited and started snatching up the letter-cards and building the names of the pictures before the tutor even had time to pronounce the separate sounds. Almost every child seemed excited, happy, and eager when reaching the point of building and reading words.

Part III. Reading Simple Stories

In Part III the child finally begins work with actual reading materials, using whatever materials are in use in the child's classroom. While there would, of course, be certain advantages to being able to specify a particular set of materials that should be used with the program, these seem clearly outweighed by the advantages of having the child work on the same materials with the tutor as with the classroom teacher and of there being no need for any requirements as to what should be done in the classroom. As before, complete details are in Appendix A.

All words are taught separately before the child is to read them in context, according to a precisely specified procedure that builds carefully on the learning in Parts I and II and provides further help as needed. For this purpose, all the words in the reading materials are separately printed on small cards by the tutor, with the number of the page on which they first occur written on the back. (All standard readers end with a list of words they contain and the numbers of the pages where the words first occur.) Most words get printed twice per card—once with all letters in lowercase and once with the first letter capitalized. Names or other words where the first letter always is capitalized are printed only once, the way they occur.

Part III begins by finding out where in the reading materials to start with the child. From the point of view of maximum congruence between what is going on in tutoring and in class, one could argue for starting at the point the child has reached in his or her classroom work. However, given the exigencies of classroom situations, children ready to start Part III may well have been processed along in the classroom texts despite a fast-growing number of words they do not know, with the result that the task of mastering what they are supposed to be working at becomes impossibly huge. We frequently came across children who were supposed to be reading material that, in terms of the words they could recognize, seemed much beyond them. Once again, providing for cumulative mastery of the skill seemed crucial. We decided, therefore, to arrange that each child would start Part III at a point in the classroom materials where there would be very few words that the child could not already read. To determine the appropriate point, the tutor (explaining the way words are printed twice, once with the starting letter capitalized, once with the whole word lowercased) shows the child the word-cards one by one in the order that the words are first used in the reading materials.

She sees if the child can read them and stops when the child has missed three words. Part III then starts from the beginning of the story in which the child's third word was missed.

The work of Part III begins with the tutor's going over with the child all the word-cards for the first page of this story, that is, cards for each of the words that occur for the first time on that page. She shows the child the words one at a time. If the child reads a word correctly, she tells the child it is right and goes on to the next word. When the child cannot read a word correctly, the tutor follows the Procedure for Teaching Words below, stopping and telling the child the word is right if the child says the word correctly at any point before the end. The procedure is to be followed fairly rapidly, with the tutor always trying to provide help quickly enough to maintain the child's attention.

The Procedure for Teaching Words
This procedure consists of the following four steps.

a. If the word is built up from one or more simpler words, the tutor shows the child the simpler word or words in the bigger one and follows the steps below with the simpler ones first. For example, if the word is "something," the tutor covers up the second part and follows the steps below with "some," then comes back and follows them with "thing."

b. The tutor tells the child the sound of any letter or set of letters where the sound is different from what the child learned before. For example, if the word is "talk," the tutor points to the "a," "l," and says, "Instead of *a, l,* these two together are *aw.*"

c. Then the tutor points to the letters in turn from left to right and has the child give the sounds. For the letters that have different sounds than were learned, the tutor again says the sounds first and has the child repeat them after her. The child is permitted to look at a chart showing the alpha-pictures if the child can't remember the sound he or she had learned for a given letter.

d. When the child has said all the sounds, the tutor waits a moment to see if the child can recognize the word. If the child can't, the tutor, pointing to the appropriate letters, says the sounds again. Then if the child still doesn't recognize the word, the tutor, again pointing, says the first sounds blended together (for instance, for "Tom" the tutor says "*to . . .*," for "girl" "*gir . . .*," and so on) and sees if the child can finish the word. If the child can't and the word is long enough, the tutor gives the child more and more of the blended sounds (for example, for "father," after "*fa . . .*" the tutor says "*fath . . .*"; or, for "birthday," after "*bir . . .*" the tutor says "*birth . . .*" and then "*birthd . . .*"). Finally, if necessary, the tutor says the whole word and has the child say it after her.

When the child has said the word correctly, the tutor goes on to the next word until she has gone through the entire set. Then the tutor changes the order of the cards and goes through them again the same way as before, always following the Procedure for Teaching Words in the case of any word the child does not recognize. The tutor keeps going through all the words in this way until the child gets all of them right without making any mistakes and without needing any help twice in a row. If there are a sizable number of words and this task is difficult, the tutor makes it easier by first working on only two or three of the words. When the child has gotten these right without help several times in a row, the tutor then adds one or two more, and so on, continuing to increase the size of the set in this way until the child has gotten the entire group of words correct as a set without help twice in a row. After the child has met this criterion for all the words that occur for the first time on the page that the child is to start with, the tutor turns to that page and has the child read. If the child has trouble keeping the right place or doesn't understand something, such as punctuation marks, the tutor gives the child what help is needed. If the child comes to a word that the child can't read or reads wrongly without self-correction, the tutor again follows the Procedure for Teaching Words with that word. Then the tutor prints it on a small slip of paper to practice with afterwards. The tutor discusses what is happening in the story with the child a little as they go along, and, if the child does not seem to understand the meaning of what he or she was reading, then the tutor has the child read it again and discusses it further. When the child has read through the page and has indicated understanding of what was read, the tutor takes the slips she made for the words that were missed and goes over these with the child in the same way she went over the word-cards before, using the Procedure for Teaching Words whenever the child does not recognize a word correctly. Again, the tutor continues with this until the child gets all the words correct without help twice in a row. Then the tutor goes over all the word-cards for the page again, just as she did before.

If the child missed more than two words in reading the page or had any difficulty with the reading, the child now reads the page again. Slips again are made for any words the child misses. Then the tutor again goes over the slips for missed words and the word-cards for the page. If the child missed more than two words in reading this time or still did not read smoothly, the whole cycle is repeated; the repetition is continued until the child misses no more than two words and the reading is fairly smooth and easy.

When this criterion is reached, the procedure is repeated with the next page, starting with the word-cards for that page, then having the child read it, and then going over the slips for missed words and the word-cards again. (Slips for missed words and word-cards from the page before are included, if otherwise there only are one or two words to go over.) Again the cycle is repeated until the criterion is reached for this page; then the same procedure is followed with the next page; and so on. After all the pages of the story have been worked through in this way, the tutor puts all the slips for missed words from the whole story together and goes over these slips with the child, as before. Then the tutor does the same with all the word-cards for the story. If the child missed more than seven different words in reading the story, or if the reading was difficult, the entire sequence is then repeated again, starting with the word-cards for the story's first page. The story is worked over in this way until the reading is easy and the child misses no more than seven different words altogether in the reading. Then, in exactly the same way, work begins on the next story, and so on.

Succeeding sessions always start by going over the slips for words missed in the session before. This is done in the same way as has already been described, using the Procedure for Teaching Words whenever a word is not recognized and continuing until the child has gotten all words correct without help twice in a row. Then the word-cards for the story before the one the preceding session began with are gone over in the same way; then the word-cards for the story that session began with; and then the word-cards for any succeeding stories, continuing through all pages completed last time. Tutoring then proceeds with the regular cycle for the next page, starting in by going over the word-cards for that page, and so on. At the end of each week, the tutor also goes over all the word-cards for each of the last five stories again.

If the tutor feels the child has gotten too far ahead and should be further back again—for example, due to a long absence—the tutor starts the child further back, otherwise following the same procedures. Also, if Part III is particularly difficult for a child, the tutor keeps starting the regular cycle back a page or two from the page at which the last session ended. Review of the letter sounds is provided if this seems necessary.

Observations on Part III
Establishing the routines of Part III for the tutors took a fair amount of practice. It was not easy for them at first to think of individual words as a series of separate sounds, as required by the Procedure for Teaching Words, and they found it especially difficult to provide rapidly the sounds of letters that were different from the sounds that had been taught. With some practice, however, going over in advance all the word-cards they would be using with the children, the tutors were able to manage quite well.

The great amount of practice in Part III for the children on the words encountered, the great amount of review generally, and the very stringent criteria for moving forward in the texts, were arrangements instituted as a result of observing the program in action. When, in the beginning, we had less review and weaker criteria, it soon became evident that some children were accumulating more and more words which they were unable to read. This of course meant that their tasks became extremely difficult and their work very discouraging. After we increased the amount of practice and strengthened the criteria that had to be satisfied for moving on to new material, these children were able once again to make good progress. For the children who, on the other hand, already had been learning the words fairly well before, the change meant little except for providing some extra practice that was minimally time-consuming.

Like Parts I and II, Part III frequently was much more difficult at the start for the children than it became later on. A large number of the children at first kept trying to guess what the words were rather than to figure them out from the sounds, and some of these children did not abandon this strategy until they had been persistently reminded by the tutors for some time. Once they did shift to trying to decipher the words from the sounds, striking changes would take place. For example, there was one boy in a "slow-learner" second-grade section who had scored at the nineteenth percentile of the national norms on the readiness tests for children beginning first grade and was scheduled for placement in a special class for the mentally handicapped. The first three weeks he was on Part III he kept guessing the words; he would give the sounds of letters only when the tutor reminded him to do so on every word, and even after giving the sounds he would guess what the words were without considering the sounds. At this time, although he was working on a preprimer that he had already gone over in class, he was progressing at the rate of only six or seven pages every five days. Then he seemed to catch on, although for the next week or so he still sometimes slipped back into guessing. At that time one could readily observe a direct relation between his sounding out and his getting the words right: when he tried to sound out, he usually got them; when he just guessed, he almost never did. During this fourth week he advanced sixteen pages, even though he was now past the point in the book which he had reached in class. After that, he used sounding out consistently. Each of the next two weeks he worked through forty pages of text, and from then on he continued to progress rapidly.

The significance which such changes must have for the children involved can readily be imagined. The boy we just described had already accepted and become quite reconciled to the idea that he was "not able to learn." He looked and behaved like a different person when what he was doing finally made evident the falsehood of that belief. Quite a few children underwent some kind of radical transformation of this type. Another child who was particularly striking was a first-grade boy who had scored at the fourteenth percentile on the readiness tests. Although most of the children cooperated well from near the beginning of tutoring, this child's tutor had a great deal of difficulty during most of the year getting him to do his work or even to stay at his seat, and sometimes he would just not respond at all. When he was being relatively cooperative in Part III he would sometimes "pretend" to read like a very small child might, mumbling something that had little relation to the printed words. Near the end of the school year he came to realize how he actually could figure out what the real words were. He was extremely pleased and proud about this discovery and from then on worked eagerly and intensively, not wanting to stop a session when the time came for him to do so.

Almost all the tutored children in the field experiment made excellent progress on Part III. Recall that the forty children who were tutored attended two inner-city public schools and had been selected for tutoring on the basis of scoring low on a battery of readiness tests. Thirty-seven of them were beginning first graders—the other three, in "slow-learner" second-grade sections. They included children who were labelled as learning-disabled and mentally handicapped. Four of the original forty left the school they were in too late in the school year to be replaced, leaving us with thirty-six tutored through the year. Twenty-five of these thirty-six children, or slightly over two-thirds of them, were reading in books past the preprimers at the rate of about twenty pages every five days or better, for something on the order of two months or more before the end of the school year. One can get some idea of what this means when one considers the very high criteria which must be met for moving forward in Part III and the nature of the children's classroom reading books. The children had to know the words well and read fairly smoothly and with good comprehension before they were permitted to leave one story for the next. The preprimers in the series used in one of the schools cover seventy-eight words, and the preprimers in the series used in the other school cover ninety-six words. The succeeding books at each school use these words and add increasingly more. For two months or longer before the school year ended, these twenty-five children thus were reading competently (about twenty pages every five days or better, with our high criteria for progression) in books that started with from eighty to a hundred words and went up from there. Six more of the thirty-six children were reading twenty pages every five days or better in books past the preprimers, or doing almost this well, by the end of the year. This leaves only five children out of the thirty-six who were not doing well by June. Three of these were in Part III but making slower progress; two were still in the preprimers, and one had just finished them. Of the remaining two children, one was in the midst of Part II and the other had not quite finished going through Part I. It seems worthy of note that *no* child failed to make continual progress.

Of the thirty-six low-readiness children who were tutored with the program through the year, then, thirty-one, or 86 percent of the group, were reading competently before the year's end—and twenty-five of those thirty-one had been doing so for two months or longer. The remaining five of the thirty-six were making progress too, but at a slower rate. All the children learned, and most of them learned very well. They paid attention and worked hard, even though there were no "material reinforcers" given and they were children often viewed as inattentive and disruptive.

These results certainly look very encouraging. They all are restricted, however, to observations of the tutored children in their tutoring situation. One would like to know how these children performed in other reading situations and on general tests of reading as well. And in order to be sure that the tutoring really has helped them, one needs to know what they could have been expected to accomplish without it. In short, one needs an experiment in which quantitative comparisons are made of measures of reading achievement among tutored children and carefully matched controls. Our field research undertook to provide just such an experiment, and we turn now to a more extensive consideration of what the research involved.

5
Applying the Program: Community Tutors in the Schools

Experimentation under Real-World Conditions

If the approach taken in the preceding chapters is correct, it should prove possible to teach reading competence to first graders who, in the "normal" course, fail to learn—and to do so in a way that is practical for widespread implementation. How does one determine if this is the case? In our view, the answer is quite straightforward, although it is an answer that has seldom formed the basis for the design of research. The answer is: Carry out a carefully controlled experiment but conduct it under all of the actual conditions of real-world implementation that characterize how the approach is supposed to be applied in practice.

It is frequently held that "true experiments are of . . . doubtful applicability where national, politically based social action programs are concerned" (Evans and Schiller 1970, p. 219). This is said to be the case because it is believed that small-scale, technically correct experimentation "would yield information only on how a program works under very special hot-house conditions, not on how effective it is under the real conditions of mass implementation" (Evans and Schiller 1970, p. 219). We quite agree that well-controlled experimentation on intervention programs is pointless if it is conducted under artificial conditions and therefore is nongeneralizable. But while it seems crucial to look at the results of intervention attempts under real-world conditions, this does not warrant the neglect of experimental control.

A true experiment is one that makes assignments *at random* to treatment and control conditions. Only if genuinely random assignment has taken place can we unequivocally evaluate the treatment's effectiveness. If, for example, all the children to be given a treatment are at one school and all the control children are at another, differences between the schools—in teachers, programs, or student clientele—could be responsible for apparent effects of the treatment. Quite generally, if experimental and control groups are given a chance to vary systematically with the treatment, they—rather than the treatment—may contribute to or even be wholly responsible for whatever effects are obtained. Again nothing would really be learned about what could be hoped for from application of the intervention.

It may be difficult in practice to arrange for a genuine experiment with random assignment when the subject of experimentation concerns a presumptive benefit and when this benefit is to be awarded under the unruly and emotionally laden circumstances of real-life conditions. But although it takes some doing, there is no reason in principle why experiments cannot be both well controlled and realistic. This is what we attempted to bring about. We tried to carry out a genuine experiment that, instead of being artificial, faithfully contained all of the real-world characteristics—and problems—that will be present when the cumulative mastery program that we developed is in regular use. This should tell us rather clearly what the program can really deliver.

Thus, the children who were tutored in our experiment were randomly chosen from among children who would be selected for tutoring if the program were in normal operation. Recruitment of tutors, day-to-day operation of the tutoring in the schools, and so on, were carried out in the ways that would prevail under the program's normal use. In order to find out what our tutorial program can be expected to accomplish, then, we carried out neither a "hot-house" experiment under idealized conditions nor a methodologically flawed survey of something instituted on a nationwide scale. Rather, we conducted a carefully controlled experiment that sought to institute the very circumstances that would be encountered in the general operation of the program, but with random assignment to conditions and systematic measurement of outcomes. Such an approach, while it may be demanding empirically, is simple indeed in its logic. It is recommended by many—by Campbell (1969), by Gilbert and Mosteller (1972), and by Rivlin (1973)—as the obvious thing to do when feasible. But it has not often been followed.

The Schools and Their Setting

The target for the practical application of our program is the children who demonstrate, or for whom the prognosis is that they will demonstrate, low proficiency at the academic skill the program addresses. The program is a specific remedy for a specific deficiency, but a deficiency that is presumed to have rather pervasive consequences for a child's school competence. While there will be schools where almost all the first graders need our program if they are to learn to read on schedule, and schools where almost none of them need it, the most frequently encountered situation, judging from the extremely large within-school variation discussed in chapter 3, will likely be one in which some of a school's first graders need it.

As the children to be tutored in our experiment were to be randomly chosen from among children who would be tutored under the program's normal application, these children were chosen from among first graders for whom tests indicated a low probability of learning to read. These first graders were in schools which had sizable proportions of such children, along with large numbers of other children, as would typically be the case.

Our field experiment took place in two inner-city public schools on the South Side of Chicago during the 1972–73 academic year. Chicago's South Side is predominantly black in its racial composition, and the economic situation of this black population is predominantly low-income. While heavily black for some time, the area recently has undergone even greater racial homogenization in this direction. The public schools find themselves confronted with large numbers of poverty-background pupils who score low on whatever traditional tests they are given and who learn little of what the schools undertake to teach. The situation just described is comparable, of course, to that facing inner-city schools across the nation, although obviously it is not limited to such schools. If one considers performances on standardized tests by students from the various districts of the Chicago public school system, for example, the inexorable pattern is for better performances to be found in the districts around the urban perimeter, which are also the districts with the predominantly white enrollments and the higher income levels (Sellers 1972; *Chicago Daily News* 1972; Dedinsky 1972; *Chicago Today* 1972). For higher scores still, one only has to look outside the city limits at the schools in the well-to-do suburbs. As a recent newspaper article reporting on test-performance results in the Chicago public school system puts it, "in most cases a relationship could be drawn between a school or district with poor test scores and the socio-economic makeup of its attendance area" (Dedinsky 1972, p. 4).

The two schools in which our program was set up, which we shall call Cranston and Pratt, are large elementary schools with almost all of their students black. Each has a black principal, and the majority of the teachers at each school are black as well. While the buildings need attention and many windows have been broken, the schools are reasonably well equipped, the principals are effective administrators, and the teachers work hard. Although the socioeconomic makeup of Cranston's pupils is somewhat lower on the average than that of Pratt's, the basic characteristic of both schools is that their student clientele covers a socioeconomic range extending from low-income to middle-income levels. These are by no means, then, among the South Side's worst-off schools but rather are typical of a number of schools where some heterogeneity prevails as to the socioeconomic status of the students. The average performance levels on conventional tests at these schools are not very different from those for the Chicago public school system as a whole, but the latter in turn, like other urban school systems, reflects its inner-city core by lagging well behind national norms.

Thus, for example, recently released compilations of scores on nationally normed reading achievement tests for all schools in the Chicago system, based on assessments for the academic year ending June 1971, gave the following city-wide results (Sellers 1972; *Chicago Daily News* 1972; Dedinsky 1972; *Chicago Today* 1972): the median percentile ranks for the Chicago schools fell at the thirty-fourth, twenty-eighth, thirty-sixth, thirtieth, and twenty-ninth percentiles of the national samples for students in the third, sixth, eighth, ninth, and eleventh grades, respectively. This means, for instance, that the median reading achievement test-score for third graders in the Chicago schools—the score at the fiftieth percentile—was at the thirty-fourth percentile of the scores in the national sample. The reading test-score at the fiftieth percentile for eleventh graders in the Chicago schools was at the twenty-ninth percentile of the scores in the national sample. And so on. These lags, furthermore, seem in Chicago as in other urban school systems to have been on the increase in recent years.

Scores for Chicago public schools that are closest to the suburbs and hence serving socioeconomically better-off pupils make up the upper part of the distribution for the Chicago schools. Cranston and Pratt, in turn, have median scores on these reading tests that are in the general vicinity of the city-wide medians that, as we have seen, lag in terms of national norms. The problem for Cranston and Pratt is not just this lag of median scores, however, but the considerable range covered by the scores that make up the lower portions of the score distributions at such schools. In other words, many of the children in these schools do very poorly indeed, as could be expected from the large number of students from low-income backgrounds in these schools. Pratt and Cranston thus seem to reflect the kind of within-school spread in academic achievement to which the Coleman Report called attention as such a pervasive finding. The reality behind the lower parts of those score distributions is large numbers of children far behind on reading, with many unable to read at all. The goal of our approach is to identify children at the start of school who otherwise would be likely to fall into this group and to bring them to learn to read on schedule in the course of the first-grade year.

The Research Design

The basic differences between running our program at Cranston and Pratt as an experiment, and just running it, were two. First, the program was given not to all first graders who were identified at the beginning of the school year as low in academic "readiness" but to a randomly defined subset of them, so comparisons could be made. And second, extensive evaluations were carried out toward the end of the school year in order to assess how much the program had in fact helped the children thus identified. In this section we shall describe the experiment's design; in the next, we shall consider the role of community adults as tutors in the program; and after that, we shall describe the various ways in which the program was evaluated as to effectiveness.

During the first month of the school year, the children in all of the first-grade classes at Cranston and Pratt—along with the children in one second-grade section that had been set up for slow learners at each school—received the *Metropolitan Readiness Tests*, Form B (Hildreth, Griffiths, and McGauvran 1966, 1969). Most of the children were tested in groups ranging in size from twenty-three to thirty-three—their own classes, or a different class if they had been absent when their class was tested. A few of the children were tested in smaller groups. In all, 268 children received the tests. All testing was carried out by the same examiner, a woman experienced at group administration of tests. She worked with two assistants when testing all groups except the residual smaller ones. Test administration was conducted in accordance with the Metropolitan's *Manual of Directions* (Hildreth et al 1969).

The *Metropolitan Readiness Tests*, in either of their two forms, give the child six tasks to do, each involving a number of similar items (Hildreth et al. 1966, 1969): a *word meaning* test, in which the child selects the picture that illustrates a word named by the examiner; a *listening* test, in which the child selects the picture that illustrates what the examiner has described; a *matching* test, in which the child picks the visual stimulus that is the same as a given stimulus; an *alphabet* test, in which the child chooses the letter which the examiner has named; a *numbers* test, in which the child demonstrates knowledge of various facts about numbers; and a *copying* test, in which the child draws a copy of a visual stimulus. Scores on the various tests are interrelated. The total of the scores on all six tests, in turn, has been shown to correlate substantially with a range of contemporaneous assessments purporting to measure "intelligence," "mental maturity," "mental ability," and "reading readiness." For a national standardization sample of 12,225 beginning first graders who received Form A of the Metropolitan, for example, the obtained correlation with the total score from the *Murphy-Durrell Reading Readiness Analysis* (Murphy and Durrell 1965) was .80 (Hildreth et al. 1969). The Metropolitan's total score also has been shown to correlate substantially with subsequent academic achievement assessments. For example, with 9,497 or 6,561 of the national standardization sample of first graders mentioned above used in different cases, correlations between the Metropolitan administered at the start of the school year and various subtests from the Primary I Battery of the *Stanford Achievement Test* (Kelley, Madden, Gardner, and Rudman 1964) administered the following May were .63 with word reading, .60 with paragraph meaning, .63 with vocabulary, .57 with spelling, .64 with word study skills, and .67 with arithmetic (Hildreth et al. 1969). Clearly, the Metropolitan total score offers a representative assessment of what is widely viewed as indicating how successful a child will be at school tasks, and this assessment turns out to possess considerable prognostic value for academic achievement in first grade. It seems fair to assume that relatively low scorers on the Metropolitan are relatively unprepared for the demands of school and hence likely to do poorly in response to them. We used the Metropolitan total score as a means for identifying beginning first graders in this category although obviously other ways of identifying such children, ranging from other forms of standardized assessment to evaluations by teachers, can be used as well.

Total scores for all children receiving the Metropolitan were converted to percentile ranks as given in the *Manual of Directions*. The percentile ranks indicate for each score what percentage of the children in the national standardization sample earned that score or a lower score. We took as the cut-off point for defining our low academic-readiness samples total scores yielding percentile ranks up to and including the fortieth percentile. Of the 106 children at Cranston receiving the Metropolitan—in three beginning first grades and a slow-learner second-grade section—49 scored at the fortieth percentile or lower, 57 at the forty-first percentile or higher. Of the 162 children at Pratt receiving the Metropolitan—in five beginning first grades (one of those first grades subsequently was disbanded and its children redistributed among the other four) and a slow-learner second-grade section—49 scored at the fortieth percentile or lower, 113 at the forty-first percentile or higher. For both schools combined, therefore, 98 children made up the low academic-readiness group from which experimental and control children would be selected, out of a total of 268 children. The proportion of children in this low-readiness category was somewhat higher at Cranston than at Pratt, as would be expected from the somewhat lower average socioeconomic status of pupils at Cranston than at Pratt, as mentioned earlier.

To give an indication of how the Metropolitan percentile rank scores were distributed among the members of the low academic-readiness group, table 5.1 provides the breakdown by deciles for the forty-nine children in this group from each school. It is evident from table 5.1 that the children were spread reasonably evenly across the four deciles, with the exception of more children at Pratt in the fourth decile than in any of the three lower deciles at that school—again congruent with the socioeconomic difference between the two schools. Of the ninety-eight children identified for the low academic-readiness group from their Metropolitan scores, sixty-three or approximately two-thirds of them had very low scores indeed —percentile ranks at the thirtieth percentile or below. The remaining thirty-five were located in the percentile range from thirty-one to forty. These latter children fell in about the bottom quarter of what the Metropolitan's authors define as readiness level "C" and consider average. Percentile scores of thirty or below fall into what the authors of the Metropolitan define as readiness levels of "D" or "E" (Hildreth et al. 1969), which they take as signifying a quite poor academic prognosis. About two-thirds of our low academic-readiness children, then, fell within these "D" or "E" categories, and the rest were not far away.

Table 5.1. Breakdown by Percentile Rank Score Deciles of Children Scoring at or below the Fortieth Percentile on the *Metropolitan Readiness Tests* at Cranston and Pratt

School	Percentile Rank Score				
	10 or less	11–20	21–30	31–40	Total
Cranston	9	13	14	13	49
Pratt	7	11	9	22	49
Total	16	24	23	35	98

Starting from the pool of ninety-eight children scoring at or below the fortieth percentile in terms of the Metropolitan's national norms, forty children were chosen to receive the tutoring program—twenty out of the forty-nine children in this pool at each school. The remaining twenty-nine children at each school in this target pool served as controls and also provided replacements for tutoring if a tutored child left the school during the first two months of the academic year. The choice of forty as the sample size for the tutoring program was based on employing two tutors full time at each school, each tutor conducting a half-hour daily session with ten children. At each school, the twenty children to receive tutoring were

selected from the forty-nine eligible children by a random procedure that drew the twenty children from the available classes
in numbers proportionate to the number of children in each
class who were eligible. In other words, if a class contained
more children scoring at or below the fortieth percentile on the
Metropolitan, that class contributed proportionately more
children to the tutoring sample. More specifically, the selection
procedure for arriving at the tutoring sample followed these
steps at each of the two schools.

1. Find all children scoring at the fortieth percentile or below on the Metropolitan. (As we have seen, this yielded forty-
nine children at each school, and we refer to the children identified in this manner as "low-readiness" children.)

2. For each class, divide the number of low-readiness children in that class by the number of low-readiness children in
all the classes (forty-nine at each school).

3. Multiply the proportion thus obtained by twenty to find,
for each class, the quota of low-readiness children to be tutored
from that class. (These numbers were rounded so as to add to
twenty for each school.)

4. For each class, determine how many of the low-readiness
children in that class are boys and how many are girls. Divide
the number of low-readiness boys in that class by the number
of low-readiness children in that class. Multiply the proportion
thus obtained by the quota of low-readiness children to be
tutored from that class to find the quota of low-readiness boys
to be tutored from that class.

5. Find in the same way the quota of low-readiness girls to
be tutored from that class. (The numbers of low-readiness boys
and girls to be tutored from a given class were rounded to
equal the quota of low-readiness children to be tutored from
that class as found earlier.)

6. For each class, find the specific low-readiness boys to be
tutored by using the method of random choice that follows.
List, in ascending order of percentile score, the low-readiness
boys in that class. (Any score ties that occurred were broken
by using alphabetical order based on last name.) Divide the
number of low-readiness boys in that class by the quota of

low-readiness boys to be tutored from that class, and call the quotient *n*. (Each *n* was rounded to the nearest whole number; if *n* ended in .5, rounding was to the nearest odd whole number.) Take every *n*th low-readiness boy from the list for the tutoring sample. For cases where *n* turns out to be 2, in the first such class take boy 1, boy 3 . . . , in the next such class take boy 2, boy 4 . . . , in the next such class take boy 1, boy 3 . . . , and so on. For cases where *n* turns out to be 3, in the first such class take boy 1, boy 4 . . . , in the next such class take boy 2, boy 5 . . . , in the next such class take boy 3, boy 6 . . . , in the next such class take boy 1, boy 4 . . . , and so on. For cases where *n* turns out to be 4, in the first such class take boy 1, boy 5 . . . , in the next such class take boy 2, boy 6 . . . , and so on. If this procedure yields too few boys to meet the quota to be tutored from a given class, drop back to the series starting one number lower. If, on the other hand, the procedure yields too many boys to meet the tutoring quota, move up to the series starting one number higher.

7. Find in the same way the specific low-readiness girls to be tutored from each class.

The random procedure for selecting the tutoring sample of twenty at each school thus drew it from the pool of forty-nine eligible children in a manner that reflected the distribution of those forty-nine in their respective classes, taking account of sex of child as well. If a child in the tutoring sample left the school within the first two months of the school year, that child was replaced with whatever low-readiness child of the same sex in the same class had the closest Metropolitan score. The latest replacement of this kind was a child who started October 20. Such replacements occurred in three instances— one child at Cranston, and two children taught by one of the tutors at Pratt. It further was the case that four children (three boys and one girl), one from each tutor's set of ten, left the school too late in the academic year to be meaningfully replaced. The earliest child to leave the tutoring sample and not be replaced did not come back after the Christmas vacation. One of the nonreplaced tutees who left had been the one child in the tutoring sample from Pratt's slow-learner second-grade section. Since no child from that class was then being tutored, the two other low-readiness children in that class were dropped from the study. As the final entry in this listing of sources of attrition, one of the nontutored children in the low-readiness group at Cranston left school. In all, therefore, ten children were lost from the sample—four at Cranston and six at Pratt—in the course of the research: three tutored children who left and were replaced, four tutored children who left and were not replaced, two nontutored children who were dropped when their class no longer contained a tutored child, and an additional nontutored child who left.

The starting sample of ninety-eight low-readiness children hence dropped for the reasons just described to a final sample of eighty-eight. And included here was a decline in the size of the tutoring sample from forty to thirty-six, spread evenly across tutors, as it turned out, so that each tutor's number of tutees dropped from ten to nine. The eighty-eight low-readiness children came from three first grades and a slow-learner second-grade section at Cranston, and from four first grades at Pratt (recall that one of Pratt's first grades was absorbed into the other four). Table 5.2 shows the distribution of the final sample of eighty-eight by class, sex, and experimental condition. As the table indicates, almost all of these children were in first-grade sections—only five were in Cranston's slow-learner second-grade section. Each of the two tutors at a given school worked with children from two of the four classes at that school, except that one tutor also had one child from a class otherwise assigned to another tutor since the division of tutees by classes did not work out evenly in this instance.

It is evident that the tutoring sample was selected in such a way as to insure that enough low-readiness children from each class would be left untutored to permit comparisons between tutored and untutored low-readiness children taught by the same classroom teacher. Some of our evaluations specifically matched pairs of tutored and untutored children in a given classroom. Since there were thirty-six tutored children, these matched pair comparisons made use of thirty-six of the control children. In other evaluations, we made use of the full number

Table 5.2. Distribution of Final Sample of
Low-Readiness Children by Class, Sex, and Experimental
Condition

School and Class	Condition and Sex				Total
	Tutored		Untutored		
	Boys	Girls	Boys	Girls	
Cranston					
First grade	4	2	6	3	15
First grade	2	2	5	2	11
First grade	3	3	5	3	14
Slow-learner second grade	1	1	2	1	5
Pratt					
First grade	3	2	4	2	11
First grade	2	2	3	3	10
First grade	2	2	6	2	12
First grade	3	2	3	2	10
Total	20	16	34	18	88

of control children available in the study—fifty-two—comparing this control sample as a group with the experimental sample as a group. The fifty-two control children were distributed across teachers in roughly the same proportionality as the thirty-six experimental children—see table 5.2—so that in these evaluations, too, particular teachers could not be affecting outcomes differentially for experimentals versus controls. While the samples for the evaluations comparing all fifty-two control children with the thirty-six experimentals are evident from what has just been said, specification of the samples for the evaluations based on matched pairs requires further description of the process by which matching was established. Experimental and control children were matched according to the following rules, which were applied, of course, to the final sample of eighty-eight.

Match the tutored children on the basis of the Metropolitan percentile scores as closely as possible with untutored children of the same sex taught by the same teacher, so long as the discrepancy is not greater than ten percentile points. If the discrepancy is greater than ten, try first remaining untutored children of the opposite sex taught by the same teacher, and then if necessary children of the same sex taught by a different teacher within the same school. Use alphabetical closeness of last names in case of score ties.

Matching in accordance with these rules, which completely specified the matchings, was carried out on the basis of the relevant sets of Metropolitan percentile scores. All of the thirty-six matched pairs that resulted were congruent in sex— twenty pairs of boys and sixteen pairs of girls. All but three of these thirty-six pairs were congruent as to teacher. Comparisons of experimental and control group Metropolitan percentile scores for the seventy-two children in the matched-pair evaluations and for the eighty-eight children in the full-sample evaluations will be presented at the beginning of the next chapter.

Each tutor's daily half hour with a given tutee did not occur at the same time each day. The tutoring schedules were set up in such a way as to assign any tutee a different time slot for each of the five days in the school week, spreading those five slots across the hours of the school day by a rotational procedure that served to minimize and equalize any interference with regular classroom activities and any help or hindrance that different times of the day might provide. The child scheduled from 2:00 to 2:30 on Monday, for example, was scheduled from 1:00 to 1:30 on Tuesday, from 11:00 to 11:30 on Wednesday, from 10:00 to 10:30 on Thursday, and from 9:00 to 9:30 on Friday. Although each child in the tutoring sample was scheduled for a daily half-hour session, the logistics of arranging for children to be brought from and returned to their classes often meant that the actual length of daily tutoring was less than that.

The classroom teachers were to proceed with their classes without any consideration of the tutoring program except for permitting children to leave when it was their turn to be tutored. They were to teach in whatever manner they were accustomed to, with whatever materials they normally used, and with no greater or lesser degree of attention to the tutored children than they would otherwise have paid them. These points underscore, of course, the extent to which our tutorial program is explicitly supplemental, imposing no restrictions at all on what the teacher does in her classroom but simply helping with the children who are most difficult for her to reach anyway. The teachers were informed as to the general content of the tutoring, but it was made clear to them that the program proceeded quite independently of their classroom instruction. They were encouraged, therefore, to ignore its presence. By and large, this seemed to be what happened. They did have their hands full running a class, after all. The one complaint we heard from teachers was that they had other children in their classes who were every bit as badly off academically as the ones receiving tutoring, so why were not those other children being tutored too? This comment reflected, of course, the randomized design of the experiment. To the extent that this might have led teachers to work harder with those other children, the consequences simply would be to minimize obtained differences between experimentals and controls.

While use of the tutoring program roughly spanned the 1972–73 academic year, the actual duration of tutoring that would be reflected in evaluation test performances was substantially less than the full school year. With the first month of the school year devoted to administration of the Metropolitan test battery, its scoring, and the defining of the tutoring sample, tutoring did not begin until October 5. A teachers' strike closed the Chicago public schools from January 10 to January 25, although one week of this lost time was made up by cancelling spring vacation. And finally, we conducted our evaluation testing from May 1 to May 23, so that the average tutee had been tutored through only about the first third of May when evaluation tests were administered. While tutoring continued to the end of the school year in mid-June, those remaining weeks had no bearing on the tests. Apart from the normal school holidays, therefore, other time restrictions were operating on how much tutoring actually had occurred before the evaluation testing. The average tutored child had experienced in fact only about thirty weeks of tutoring before the evaluation testing, compared to a normal school year of forty weeks. At least some of those time restrictions would be removed when running the tutoring program normally rather than as an experiment.

Evaluation testing was individually administered to all eighty-eight children by the same examiner. The examiner, a woman experienced at test administration and not the same woman who administered the Metropolitan battery, did not know which children were experimentals and which were controls. She was supplied with lists which established for her the order in which children would be tested. With a few exceptions, a given child's testing took place in a single session. All low-readiness children in one classroom were tested before moving on to the next, and they were taken from the class for testing in alphabetical order. This process was completed for all four of the classrooms that contained low-readiness children at one school before moving on to the other school. The sequence in which the four classes at a school were worked with was chosen randomly, with the restriction that the two classes from which a given tutor had drawn tutees should be in ABBA sequence (that is, the two classes should be tested first and fourth or second and third). Which of the two schools came first for testing was decided on the basis that one school could accommodate the testing in early May more readily than the other.

It is evident from what has been said about the tutorial program and from the design of this evaluation research that, in our view, the program's basic function is use with low academic-readiness first graders for the first-grade year. As our inclusion of a few slow-learner second graders who scored equally low on the Metropolitan suggests, however, there is no reason in principle why it cannot also be used with second graders who haven't learned to read in first grade. Other non-reading children—somewhat older ones who still have not begun to read and kindergartners for whom the prognosis from their socioeconomic level would be a low likelihood of academic success in first grade—also seem relevant for it. Nor is there any necessary requirement that the time-length for tutoring be one school year. Children who can move faster through the program may need less, while children who move through it very slowly could profit from more. These flexibilities of usage seem appropriate to keep in mind, therefore, even though the modal forms of application that we envision for the program involve identifying low-readiness first graders at the start of the first-grade year and carrying them through the tutorial program until that year is over.

As a final point in this discussion of the research design, a word is in order concerning the definition of the control condition. A critic could argue that we are confounding two factors in our evaluation of the program—the nature of the tutorial program itself, and the use of a one-to-one tutoring situation—because we are comparing it to a control condition consisting of normal classroom instruction. Two answers seem relevant in response to this charge. The first is that the real-world question we are addressing concerns precisely the comparison that is being made: namely, how much does this particular tutorial program, with the one-to-one tutoring that it needs in order to be carried out, help low-readiness children learn to read? Since the question of real-world application is the one we are trying to answer in this research, it is appropriate to compare the program's presence and its absence for equally low-readiness children taught by the same classroom teachers.

If the above were the only answer we could offer, however, we would not have designed the research the way we did. We noted in chapter 3 that research on the use of nonprofessionals as tutors for beginning reading instruction was conducted by Ellson and his collaborators (Ellson et al. 1965, 1968). Some of their work is parallel to ours in all major respects *except* the nature of the curriculum. As in our program, the Ellson group's major experiment (Ellson et al. 1968) included conditions where a total of half an hour's daily tutoring during the first-grade year was conducted by adults with minimal formal educational credentials who received on-the-job training in the tutoring procedures to be followed. This experiment, which has been complimented as "what may be the finest example of product oriented research in the literature" (Bausell,

Moody, and Walzl 1972, p. 592), gives us, therefore, baseline information on how much can be expected when the same kind of tutoring is tried for the same amount of time but with other curriculum materials. Used with some of the children in this 1968 study was "programed tutoring," which refers to a set of procedures developed by Ellson and his collaborators tied from the start to the classroom reading instruction and emphasizing from the outset the reading of whole words in continuous prose; used with other children was "directed tutoring," which refers to procedures adapted from classroom teaching materials by an experienced reading specialist for application by tutors. If the attention and expectations generated by one-to-one tutoring of a serious sort were the pivotal factor, either of these carefully conducted tutorial approaches should have done the job quite well. The results, however, were that neither of them was able to show clear effects, compared to untutored controls, on tests of general reading achievement— the crucial issue. Effects of any substance at all, comparing experimentals and untutored controls, were shown only on tests of what had been specifically taught, not on tests of general reading skill, and then only for "programed tutoring," not for "directed tutoring." Approaches comparable to ours, in terms of who does the tutoring and how much tutoring is carried out, therefore have been of no utility in the case of "directed tutoring" and of only moderate utility, yielding specific but not general effects, in the case of "programed tutoring." If our tutorial program does much better than the best of these findings from Ellson et al. (1968), the reason must primarily have to do with the nature of our tutorial materials and the theorizing behind them rather than with the use of one-to-one tutoring.

Community Adults as Tutors

From disciplines concerned with mental health, medicine, and education, interest has been on the rise in recent years concerning the roles that people lacking professional or educational certification of kinds formerly viewed as necessary for all aspects of client contact can play in delivering needed services to clients. Variously known as "nonprofessionals," "paraprofessionals," "mental health aides," "paramedical personnel," "physicians' assistants," or "teachers' aides," and sometimes working as volunteers and sometimes as paid employees, such individuals have turned out to be capable of helping clients in ways that used to be reserved for credentialed professionals. What seems, broadly speaking, to be occurring in these instances is that having to specify in relatively concrete terms what is to occur between helper and client is leading to the realization that many of the activities called for are within the competence of many more people than had been viewed as qualified to do them.

We will not undertake here a survey of the already extensive literature on utilizing nonprofessionals in various client-contact roles. Much of this effort has concerned medical- or mental health-related functions, such as the carrying out of therapeutic work. Some of it has tended to assume a middle-class background on the part of the nonprofessional, but some of it has tapped a much broader population base. For illustrative overviews of such work, see Pearl and Riessman (1965), Cowen, Gardner, and Zax (1967), Grosser, Henry, and Kelly (1968), Arnhoff, Rubenstein, and Speisman (1969), Guerney (1969), Sobey (1970), and Gartner (1971). For a recent example of the provision of predominantly therapy-oriented services by nonprofessionals to elementary schoolchildren, see Cowen, Dorr, Izzo, Madonia, and Trost (1971), Cowen, Dorr, Trost, and Izzo (1972), and Dorr, Cowen, Sandler, and Pratt (1973). As a term like "teacher's aide" or "tutor" suggests, however, utilization of nonprofessionals has taken place not only with mental health or medical objectives but also more specifically educational ones. The tutoring research by Ellson and his collaborators is an example in this regard. Increasing numbers of schools these days seem to have teachers' aides on the payroll. A recent article by Bereiter (1972) goes so far as to recommend a virtually exclusive dependence on appropriately supervised nonprofessionals for the carrying out of training in basic academic skills. While one can disagree with the extremeness of such a proposal, that it can be advocated at all suggests how awareness has been on the upswing as to services that nonprofessionals can be taught to perform.

The concept of community adults functioning as nonprofessionals in such roles as have been described—whether full-time or part-time, and whether paid or unpaid—thus already enjoys a certain degree of acceptance and emerges as part of a general trend toward broadening the categories of individuals viewed as relevant or potentially qualified for helping clients in various ways. Our aim was to unite this concept with the cumulative mastery tutorial program for basic reading that we developed, expecting in this way to show not only that low academic-readiness children can be effectively taught to read by using it but that this can be accomplished by tutors who do not have to meet formal requirements of education or certification. In particular, it seemed quite feasible to recruit as tutors adults from the same communities as the children who need the help in learning, utilizing the "teacher's aide" or similarly named positions in the schools for this purpose. While paid positions obviously are not a necessity for such tutoring, many of the community adults we are talking about need remunerative employment, and the "teacher's aide" or "paraprofessional" type of position offers a relevant job opportunity for them.

Community adults were recruited for tutoring in our field experiment by asking the principals of Cranston and Pratt each to suggest two individuals from the neighborhood served by the school who in their view would be appropriate for the two full-time, salaried tutor positions that would be available at the given school. The salaries, which were paid by outside funds, were set at the level that coincided with what was offered for similar positions within the school system. As guidelines to consider in making their suggestions, the principals were told that, besides knowing how to read, the only attributes of importance for the job were (1) liking and being able to work well with children; (2) responsibility—being conscientious and dependable in fulfilling assigned tasks; and (3) patience. Nothing by way of formal educational credentials was to be taken into account. The principals each recommended two persons of their acquaintance who were deemed appropriate in terms of these guidelines. All four persons thus referred were accepted as tutors.

What is obvious from the guidelines set forth for tutor selection is that large numbers of potential tutors are available in any community where our program would be utilized. The method of tutor recruitment that was followed in our field experiment is quite representative of what could be done in general. It should be evident that any recruitment approach which is mindful of the preceding guidelines will do the job; there is no one best way to fulfill such guidelines, and the most practical way to do so will no doubt vary from one setting to another. In one setting, for example, there may be no need to recruit because paid or volunteer teachers' aides may already be on hand, most or all of whom would qualify to become tutors. In another, some recommendations for tutor recruitment may come from local ministers. In another, selection of tutors may include consideration of actual performance in a tutoring situation in order to sample how the person does at a task of that kind. The point to emphasize is that the attributes needed for success as a tutor are widely distributed among any community's adults. The principals at Cranston and Pratt, for example, found it easy to think of people to recommend as tutors.

All of the tutors recruited for our research were black mothers. One of the four, after about a month of tutoring, was offered a permanent job—in contrast to the tutor position, which was to last only for the academic year. Since the principal readily suggested another black mother as a replacement for her, and since it obviously was in her financial interest to take the permanent job, we encouraged her to make the switch. She largely single-handedly trained her replacement by having the new tutor observe her, imitate her behavior, and role-play child or tutor with her. The numbers of children in the families of the various tutors ranged from three to five. The tutors' ages ranged from the mid-thirties to the mid-fifties. Previous jobs they had held included food-server in a cafeteria, messenger, cashier, and temporary clerk.

The initial training of the tutors took place during about three weeks at the start of the school year. In the course of this period, one of us as tutor supervisor (L. W.) went over Part I of the *Tutor's Manual* with them, role-played the various activities and routines in Part I with them—a tutor sometimes would play the role of child while the supervisor played the role of tutor, and vice versa—and had the pair of tutors located at each school role-play child and tutor alternately with each other. When the tutors began working with the children, apart from some further observations for the purposes of development of the program, they were monitored by the supervisor on approximately a once-weekly basis through the school year. In the course of such monitoring, the supervisor dealt with whatever problems and questions arose and provided training—similar to that for Part I—in Parts II and III of the *Tutor's Manual* as they became relevant to the tutor's work.

The function of tutor supervisor is one which we envision any of a wide range of professionals as performing when the tutorial program operates on a widespread basis. It can be carried out by anyone who has mastered the tutorial program and possesses in addition sufficient skills of organization and communication. As with specific recruitment approaches for tutors, so also the specifics of who will serve as tutor supervisors is expected to vary from setting to setting. Among the professionals who would be relevant for taking on the tutor supervisor role are reading specialists, school psychologists, clinical psychologists, and teachers themselves. What is necessary is that the individual who is to do such supervision must be in a position to provide several weeks of intensive training before the tutors begin work and ongoing monitoring of their activities with sufficient frequency during the school year. As the use of our tutorial program becomes institutionalized within a school or school system, some of these responsibilities can be delegated to already trained tutors. As we saw in the case of a tutor who trained her successor in our research study, once trained tutors are on hand they can help train new tutors. In the program's regular operation, of course, many tutors would be working who had learned the program one or more years before.

Evaluating the Program

Our evaluation of the tutorial program involved three kinds of tests: (1) reading of words and sentences based on the vocabularies in the reading texts that were used in the children's classes; (2) reading the words and sentences in a standardized reading achievement test; and (3) tests of the children's knowledge of the sounds that letters stand for and that words start with. We shall consider each of these three kinds of assessments in turn, taking up the various tests in the order in which they were administered to the children.

1. Reading Words and Sentences Based on Classroom Text Vocabularies

In order to obtain indices as to how much of the vocabularies in their classroom reading texts the children could read and utilize in reading, we devised tests of word recognition and sentence reading involving words from the texts used in their classrooms. Since Part III of the tutorial program uses material from the classroom reading texts, that much of the tutoring— but not Parts I and II—would involve some help specific to what the tests concerned. It should, however, be borne in mind that we attempted to devise sentences for the sentence-reading test which the children had never seen before in their classroom texts, even though the sentences were based on classroom text vocabularies. To the extent that they could read and comprehend such sentences, therefore, they were going beyond the specifics of what was in the classroom reading materials.

Pratt and Cranston used different sets of reading texts: at Pratt the reading texts were levels 3–6 of the *Reading 360* program published by Ginn (Clymer 1969*a*, 1969*b*; Clymer and Gates 1969; Clymer and Jones 1969); while at Cranston the preprimers, primer, and first and second readers of the *Basic*

Reading Program published by Harper and Row were the reading texts (O'Donnell 1966*a* through 1966*g*). Since it seemed desirable to be able to treat the whole sample as a unit, we formulated tests in such a way as to contain vocabulary entries that were common to both series of texts.

a. Word recognition test based on classroom text vocabularies. The child was to read words aloud from a list of twenty-five words typed with a primary typewriter. Here is the list of words in the order in which they were given: not, the, and, little, do, like, something, but, what, go, eat, up, help, new, am, oh, work, fun, looked, time, around, way, trip, under, answer.

The twenty-five words for our list were chosen in the following manner. For both the Ginn and the Harper-Row programs of reading texts, vocabulary words were grouped into sets of twenty-five according to the order in which they were introduced as new words in the books of each program. Thus, we had one series of sets of twenty-five words each for the Ginn texts, and another series of such sets for the Harper-Row texts. For each parallel pair of sets in the sequence—the first set of twenty-five new words for each program, the second set of twenty-five new words for each program, the third set, and so on—we could determine which new words the two reading programs had in common. The first six words on the word recognition list came from among the words common to the Ginn and Harper-Row programs in their first and second sets; the next three words on the word recognition list were chosen from words common to both programs in their third sets, or in the third set for one program and in as recent a set as possible for the other; the next two words on the list were chosen from words common to both programs in their fourth sets, or in the fourth set for one program and in as recent a set as possible for the other; and so on, taking in like manner two additional words for the list by considering each additional set up to the seventh set, and then by considering each two additional sets up to the fourteenth and fifteenth sets. In fulfilling the above criteria, words were never taken from further than five sets back; use of the Ginn and Harper-Row vocabularies, when words had to be picked from back sets, was approximately balanced; and, insofar as possible, the specific words chosen for the word recognition list were different from the words chosen for the sentence-reading test to be described below.

The examiner was asked to administer our word recognition test by following the instructions for a comparable word recognition test devised by Spache (1963a, pp. 25–26) that was used later on in the testing sequence. Besides the list typed with a primary typewriter for the child to read, the examiner was equipped with the same list reproduced on scoring sheets for making tallies. Specifically, our instructions to the examiner were these:

Follow Spache's instructions for the Spache Word Recognition test. The following states what is to be done when this is not entirely specified by Spache.

Tell the child, "I have some things I want you to do for me. The first thing I want you to do is to read some words out loud. Start at the top and read the words you can." Offer him a marker. If it seems helpful, point to the word the child is to try to read.

If he does not know a word, ask him if he can figure it out, unless it becomes evident he is not able to do so. (Do not ask if he can sound it out since this might favor the tutored children.) If it is not clear whether he is saying the correct word or not, ask him if he has ever seen the word before. If he says yes, ask him to repeat the word.

Check at the left those words he reads correctly. If it is clear he cannot read a word, or if he reads it incorrectly, tell him the word and move on. Stop after the child misses five consecutive words.

The child's score was the number of words correctly read before missing five words in a row, a score that could range from 0 to 25.

b. Sentence-reading test based on classroom text vocabularies. The child was to read sentences aloud from cards typed with a primary typewriter and to answer comprehension questions about the sentences. Besides those cards with the sentences for the child to read, the examiner had the sentences reproduced along with the comprehension questions and their answers on scoring sheets for her use. There were thirteen cards in all, eleven with one sentence to read per card and two with two sentences to read. Two comprehension questions were asked concerning the material on each card, except for one card where a single question was asked, thus totaling twenty-five comprehension questions. As mentioned before, in devising the sentences we attempted to avoid using sentences included in the classroom texts, although utilizing classroom text vocabularies. The comprehension questions were designed to indicate whether the literal meaning of what was read had been understood. The various sentences to be read, their comprehension questions, and the correct answers, are as follows.

Card 1
Come here.

Question 1.   What does it say to do? (*Come.*)
Question 2.   Come where? (*Here.*)

Card 2
Stop and look.

Question 3.   What does it say to do? (*Stop.*)
                   (If the child says "look," ask "Anything else?")
Question 4.   Stop and what? (*Look.*)

Card 3
Ride with me.

Question 5.   What does it say to do? (*Ride.*)
Question 6.   Ride with who? (*Me.*)

Card 4
You are not little.

Question 7.   What does it say you are? (*Not little.*)

Card 5
Mother said, "You can play."

Question 8.   Who said something? (*Mother.*)
Question 9.   What did Mother say? (*You can play.*)

Card 6
We want to play ball.
We will get a big ball to play with.

Question 10.   What do they want to do? (*Play ball.*)
                (If the child says "play," ask "Play what?")
Question 11.   What are they going to get? (*A big ball.*)
                (If the child says "a ball," ask "What kind of
                ball?")

Card 7
We are going home now.

Question 12.   Where are they going? (*Home.*)
Question 13.   When are they going home? (*Now.*)

Card 8
The bear ran to the tree.

Question 14.   Who ran somewhere? (*The bear.*)
Question 15.   Where did he run to? (*The tree.*)

Card 9
The frog will hop on me.

Question 16.   What is the frog going to do? (*Hop.*)
Question 17.   Where will he hop? (*On me.*)

Card 10
The boys made a surprise for Mother.

Question 18.   What did the boys do? (*Made a surprise.*)
                (If the child says "made something," ask
                "Made what?")
Question 19.   Who was the surprise for? (*Mother.*)

Card 11
The girls are looking for the duck.
He is lost.

Question 20.   What are the girls doing? (*Looking for the
                duck.*)
Question 21.   Why do they have to look for him? (*He is
                lost.*)

Card 12
The boys walked on the street.

Question 22.   What did the boys do? (*Walked.*)
Question 23.   Where did they walk? (*On the street.*)

Card 13
The rabbit had red eyes.

Question 24.   What was red? (*The eyes.*)
Question 25.   Who had red eyes? (*The rabbit.*)

The words for the sentence-reading test were chosen by essentially the same kind of procedure as was used for constructing the word recognition test described before. Thus, the sentences to be read for the first six questions used words that came from among those common to the Ginn and Harper-Row programs of reading texts in their first and second sets of twenty-five new words; the sentences to be read for the next three questions used some words that came from among those common to both programs in their third sets of twenty-five new words, or in the third set for one program and in as recent a set as possible for the other; the sentences to be read for the next two questions used some words that came from among those common to both programs in their fourth sets of twenty-five, or in the fourth set for one program and in as recent a set as possible for the other; and so on, adding in like fashion some words for the sentence materials to be read for each two additional questions by considering each additional set up to the seventh set, and then by considering each two additional sets up to the fourteenth and fifteenth sets. Words for fulfilling the above criteria were never taken from further than five sets back, and use of the Ginn and Harper-Row vocabularies when having to select words from back sets for these criteria was approximately balanced. Thus, in moving from earlier to later sentences on the test, some words from new portions of the common vocabulary kept making their appearance. Besides such new words, sentences also of necessity contained some words from earlier parts of the common vocabulary. As mentioned before, the specific words chosen for the sentences we constructed were different, insofar as possible, from the words picked for the word recognition test.

The examiner's instructions for administering our sentence reading test were as follows:

Say, "I'm going to show you some sentences to read. Then I'll ask you some questions about them. You read the sentences out loud, and then see if you can answer the questions." Answer any questions the child may have.

Proceed to give the child the first card and give him time to read it. Point to the words if it seems helpful. If the child has trouble reading, encourage him to do what he can.

Then ask the first question. Mark it with a check at the left if he answers it correctly.

Permit the child to continue looking at the card while he tries to answer the questions. (Note: this is unlike Spache.) A question needs to be fully answered to be counted as correct, but reasonable paraphrases of the given answers are permitted. If the child begins to fantasize in answer to the question, redirect his attention to the sentences.

If the child fails to answer the first question, tell him the answer as indicated. (The first question should be answered before the second is asked.) If the child already includes the answer to the second question in his answer to the first, don't ask the second, and count him as correct on it.

Then, unless the child already answered the second question, ask it now. Again mark it with a check if he answers it correctly. If he answers the second question incorrectly, do not correct him. If he does not respond to the second question, ask him if he knows the answer.

Then proceed similarly with the other cards. (When there is only one question, treat it like the second question.)

If it is clear from the child's performance on the word list that he is likely to be a nonreader, skip the directions initially and just ask him to read the first sentence. If he cannot read either word, try him on cards two and three. If he can read any of the substantive words on any of the cards, ask him the first question for that card and continue as stated above. If he cannot read any of the substantive words on the first three cards, move on to the Spache Word Recognition test.

Stop when he fails to answer any question on three successive cards.

The child's score was the number of questions correctly answered before failing all questions for the sentences on three cards in a row. The possible score range was from 0 to 25.

2. Reading the Words and Sentences in a Standardized Reading Achievement Battery

To provide yardsticks of general reading competence quite apart from any reference to the vocabularies in the classroom texts, we administered standardized tests of word- and sentence-reading developed by Spache and presented along with certain phonics tests as the *Diagnostic Reading Scales*, which comprises an *Examiner's Manual* (Spache 1963*a*; 1972*a*), *Examiner's Record Booklet* (Spache 1963*b*; 1972*b*), and child's *Test Book* (Spache 1963*c*; 1972*c*). The Spache scales here to be described assess the child's ability to recognize words and to read unfamiliar passages in such a way as to derive their meaning accurately. These measurements seemed to offer a good representative sampling of what competence at basic reading means—indeed, the most adequate evaluation of actual reading behavior for beginning readers that seemed available in the test literature. We chose the Spache scales for this reason, even though their standardization data for arriving at grade norms are less extensive than would really be desirable.

The Spache scales were revised in 1972, too late for us to arrange to utilize the revised version in toto. The test of word recognition is essentially unchanged in the later version, but there are some changes in the test of reading passages. To the extent it was possible, we modified the 1963 version of that test to fit the 1972 version, in a manner to be described below. The norms for both versions of the word recognition and reading-passages tests are the same, although the dividing lines for the word recognition test norms are more clearly specified in the 1972 version.

a. Spache Word Recognition lists. Spache's word recognition lists (Spache 1963*b*, 1963*c*) present words to be read aloud by the child. The words on each of the Spache lists—fifty words on the first list and forty words on each of two additional lists—are graduated as to difficulty. The lists themselves are of ordered difficulty also, ranging up to material appropriate for sixth graders. Beginning with the first list, the child reads words aloud until failing at five consecutive words. If the first list is completed without missing five words in a row, the child moves on to the next list. Spache's instructions were followed for administering and scoring the lists, as presented in the 1963 editions of the *Examiner's Manual* and *Examiner's Record Booklet* (Spache 1963*a*, 1963*b*), together with the further amplifications that were presented for the word recognition test that we developed based on classroom text vocabularies, as described before.

Two scores were obtained from these data. The first was the total number of words which the child succeeded in reading, regardless of list. The second was the grade placement level as given by Spache for particular numbers of words correct on the recognition lists (table 1 on page 14 in Spache 1972*a*). These grade placement levels, which can only be taken as approximate, were the following discrete steps as to grade year and number of months: 1.3, 1.6, 1.8, 2.3, 2.8, 3.3, and then higher levels which are beyond our range of concern. The month indications of 3, 6, and 8 essentially suggest whether the child's achievement level can be pegged at one-third, two-thirds, or all of the way through the given school year's reading demands.

b. Spache reading-passages and comprehension questions. Spache's reading-passages are a series of reading selections ordered as to difficulty. A given passage is to be read aloud by the child and is followed by comprehension questions asked by the examiner to reveal how well the child has understood what he or she has just read. Choice of which passage to start the child on is determined by the child's performance level on the Spache word recognition lists: the child starts one level below his or her word recognition test level. As the child reads a passage, reading errors are scored by various criteria; after the passage has been read, the examiner asks various comprehension questions and determines the correctness of the child's responses by using stipulated rules as to acceptable answers. Norms as to allowable maximum numbers of reading errors and required minimum numbers of correct answers to comprehension questions have been set for each passage. If a child makes too many reading errors or shows insufficient comprehension in reading the first passage tried, the examiner drops back to the passage that is one level easier; if the child does not exceed the reading error norm and does meet the comprehension norm in reading that passage, the examiner moves up to the next harder passage. If the child has passed the first passage in the *Test Book* both by reading error and comprehension yardsticks, testing continues until reaching a passage which is failed either in terms of reading errors or comprehension. The child's score, called the "instructional level," is the grade level for the passage just below the failed passage in difficulty.

Spache has two equivalent sets of graded passages with their respective comprehension questions and specifications of acceptable answers, an "AC" set and a "BD" set. We used the "AC" set in our testing. The children read from the 1963 edition of the *Test Book* (Spache 1963*c*). The 1972 version of the *Examiner's Record Booklet* (Spache 1972*b*) includes some minor changes in the comprehension questions and acceptable answers from the 1963 version. As we indicated earlier, the norms were the same. Since these changes appeared to be improvements, we incorporated them, so that question 6 for passage 2A and acceptable answers to question 3 for passage 1A, question 7 for passage 2C, and questions 3, 4, 5, 6, and 8 for passage 3A were all taken from the 1972 version. Other than that, for administration of the passages, comprehension questions to ask, and criteria for scoring of answers to the comprehension questions, the examiner followed the 1963 editions of the *Examiner's Manual* and *Examiner's Record Booklet* (Spache 1963*a*, 1963*b*)—except for not recording time, and utilizing the following additional instructions which were given to augment those of Spache and fit the procedure into our overall testing sequence.

Begin with the first passage one level below the level
achieved on the Spache Word Recognition test, except begin
with the first passage on the lowest level if the child reaches
the 1.3 or 1.6 level on the Word Recognition test. If his level
on the Word Recognition test is less than 1.3 skip the passages
and move on to the Spache Consonant Sounds test.

Start by telling the child, "Now I'm going to give you a story
to read. You read the story" (indicate what he is to read)
"and then I'll ask you some questions about it. But this time,
after you read it I'll cover it up" (illustrate by covering the
story with your hand) "so you can't look at it when I ask the
questions."

Be certain the child understands the directions before
proceeding. Offer him a marker. Do *not* point to the words as
the child reads since this deters omissions and Spache scores
omissions as errors.

Tell the child the word when it is clear he cannot read it.
(Allow about five seconds for an attempt.) Correct all errors
that affect comprehension. (The omission of an article, for
example, will not affect comprehension, and correction would
probably only serve to break the child's train of thought.)

Pronunciations or alterations which may, on a liberal
interpretation, be attributed to dialect are not scored as errors.
(For example, "He live" for "He lives.")

If the child skips a line, score this as an error and point out
the mistake. Any mistakes he makes in reading the line when
he returns to it are also scored as errors.

If the child reads a phrase correctly and repeats it
incorrectly, this is scored as one error of repetition.

If a reversal within a word results in the addition of an extra
word, the entire phrase (reversal and addition) is scored as
one error of reversal. (This parallels what Spache says is to be
done with substitutions.)

If a repetition can be attributed to a problem that is already
scored as an error, don't score it as another error.

When the child has finished reading, cover up the story and
ask the questions. If the child fails to respond, ask the question
again, prefacing it with "Do you know" or "Do you remember."
If he says no, or if he has answered incorrectly, simply move
on to the next question. Do not supply the correct answer
except for question 5 of passage 2A, question 2 of passage 2C,

and question 1 of passage 3A. (The questions that follow these make sense only after these have been answered.)

If the child's reading errors exceed the standard or if his comprehension score is below the standard, go to the first passage of the next level down, unless you started at the lowest level, in which case you go on to the Spache Consonant Sounds test. If the child's reading errors are lower than or equal to the standard, and his comprehension score is higher than or equal to the standard, proceed in the same way with the first passage of the next level up. Continue in the same way, proceeding to further passages as called for.

The measure obtained from the Spache reading-passages was the grade placement level expressing the child's "instructional level" as defined before—the grade level given by Spache as corresponding to the passage just below the passage on which the child failed. The grade placement levels for the passages within our range of concern were grade years and months of 1.6, 1.8, 2.3, 2.8, and 3.3, for passages 1A, 1C, 2A, 2C, and 3A, respectively (table 2 on page 15 in Spache 1972a). As noted when discussing the Spache word recognition lists, these grade levels should be viewed as approximate, the month notations of 3, 6, and 8 indicating essentially whether the child's achievement suggests a degree of performance about one-third, two-thirds, or all of the way through what is wanted for a given school year.

3. Knowing the Sounds that Letters Stand for and That Words Start with

Our final set of evaluation tests sought information on certain sound identification skills implicated in reading. The first test was from the Spache battery; two additional tests were of our own devising.

a. Spache Consonant Sounds test. In the Spache consonant sounds test, the child is shown every letter of the alphabet except "a," "e," "i," "o," and "u," and is asked in the case of each how the letter sounds, what the letter says. Alternate sounds for a given letter are accepted where appropriate. Test administration and scoring followed the 1963 editions of the *Examiner's Manual* and *Examiner's Record Booklet* (Spache 1963*a*, 1963*b*), and the children were shown the letters from the 1963 edition of the *Test Book* (Spache 1963*c*). Spache's instructions were augmented by the following additional instructions to the examiner:

Again, essentially follow the Spache instructions. Start by telling the child, "I'm going to point to a letter and you tell me what sound the letter makes, what the letter says." Point to the letter, give its name, and ask the child what the letter says. If the child says a word, tell him, "That's a word. I need to know what sound the letter makes." If the child does not respond, restate the question, asking, "Do you know what sound this letter makes?" If he says "no" or answers incorrectly, circle the letter and proceed to the next one.

The child's score on this test was the number of letters for which a correct sound was given, with a possible score range from 0 to 21.

b. Starting-sounds test with paired words. For each of eight pairs of words, the examiner spoke the two words and asked the child whether they started with the same sound. Some paired words did, some did not. We selected the words so as to include both easy and difficult starting sounds and made some effort not to use words that appear in Part I of the tutorial program. The word pairs, which were reproduced on scoring sheets for the examiner, are as follows in the order in which they were administered: borrow, let (different); ugly, underneath (same); wish, Vincent (different); mask, napkin (different); bank, biscuit (same); arrow, road (different); take, pick (different); draw, dance (same). The examiner's instructions were the following:

Say, "Now I'm going to say two words and you tell me if they start with the same sound. Let's try some for practice. Big, baby—do they start with the same sound?" After the child answers, indicate he is right if he is, or correct his answer if he is wrong. Then say, "Big and baby start with the same sound. They start with *b*."

Then go on to the next practice words, asking, "Cat, sit—do they start with the same sound?" Again, indicate that the child is right or correct the child's answer, and explain, "Cat and sit don't start with the same sound. Cat starts with *k* and sit starts with *s*."

If at any point the child doesn't seem to understand something, restate it using the word "begin" in place of "start." Also, if at any point the child refers to the letter with which a word starts, point out that it is the *sound*, not the *letter*, you are asking about. The instructions may be given again if necessary, using the practice words as examples.

After completing the instructions and practice words, say, "Now I'm going to say the first two words. Tell me if they start with the same sound. Borrow, let—do they start with the same sound?" Mark them with a check at the left if the child answers correctly. Do not correct incorrect answers. Proceed in the prescribed manner with all eight questions.

The measure obtained from this test was the number of word pairs for which the correct answer was given. The possible score range was from 0 to 8.

c. Starting-sounds test with single words. Identification of the sounds that words start with was again at issue here, but this time with the child asked to give starting sounds for spoken words. The examiner spoke each of five words, asking the child in each case to give the sound the word starts with. Once again we chose words for the test such that both easy and difficult starting sounds would be included and made some effort not to use words appearing in Part I of the tutorial program. The words were reproduced on scoring sheets for the examiner's tallies. In the order of their administration, the words are as follows: car (k), rose (r), name (n), you (y), sleep (s). These were the instructions given to the examiner.

Tell the child, "Now I'm going to say a word and you tell me what sound the word starts with. Let's try one for practice. 'Jack.' What sound does 'Jack' start with?"

If the child gives the name of a letter instead of giving a sound, say, "That's a *letter*. Can you tell me the sound 'Jack' starts with?" (Don't ask for the sound of the letter "J.")

When the child gives a sound, indicate whether he is right or wrong. Then in either case, or also if he gives no sound at all, say, " 'Jack' starts with the sound *j*."

Then ask: " 'Car' starts with the sound ___?"

Again, if the child gives the name of a letter, say the same as above.

Mark the word with a check at the left if the child answers correctly. Do not correct incorrect answers. Proceed in the same way with all five questions.

The child's score was the number of words for which the correct starting sound was given, with a possible score range from 0 to 5.

Report card information. Besides the seven evaluation tests just described, we also recorded the grades for reading and mathematics given by the teachers on the children's report cards. These can, of course, be treated as no more than supplementary data since teacher grades are subjective and, in addition, were open here to possible bias effects from the teachers' knowledge of which children were being tutored. Despite such hazards, these report card grades seemed of interest for whatever they could tell us concerning ways in which tutored and control children turned out to be comparable as well as ways in which they turned out to be different.

In the case of both reading and mathematics achievement, the report card nomenclature expresses the child's attainment in terms of which of several possible levels the child is at, together with how well the child is doing within that level. By the end of the school year, grades for reading and mathematics spanned from "level A" to "level E," and each level was further differentiated into the subcategories of "U" (unsatisfactory), "F" (fair), "G" (good), and "E" (excellent). This essentially gave us, therefore, a twenty-category scale for either reading or mathematics achievement, running from U to F to G to E at level A; to U to F to G to E at level B; and so on, to U to F to G to E at level E. For reading, the levels of A to E are defined as follows: level A is "readiness," level B is "preprimers," level C is "primer," level D is "first reader," and level E is "second reader, part one." For mathematics the levels A to E have the following definitions: level A is "readiness," level B is "basic number concepts," level C is "first year, part one," level D is "first year, part two," and level E is "second year, part one."

We recorded reading grades from the report cards for each of the four quarters of the school year, while we recorded mathematics grades for the first and last quarters. Number of days absent during each of the four quarters also was recorded (in days and half days) so that experimental and control children could be compared in amount of school attendance.

In this chapter we have considered, then, the design of a field experiment to evaluate our tutorial program under actual conditions of intended usage. We talked about the training of community adults to function as tutors for carrying out the program with low academic readiness children—children for whom the prognosis is that they will not, on the average, learn basic reading competence in first grade. More often than not, these are children from low-income and minority group backgrounds. Our hypothesis is that these children simply have not acquired certain component masteries that, according to our analysis of the skill of reading, are necessary for its achievement and can be readily taught by nonprofessionals. If one fashions a tutorial program that systematically builds up these component masteries for low-readiness children, and if community adults without any particular educational credentials are trained to provide the requisite tutoring with this program, do these children learn to read? We turn next to the results that permit us to answer this question.

6
Results of the Field Research

Our first order of business must be to check whether experimental and control children in fact were equally low in academic readiness. Our system of random assignment to the two conditions should, of course, have made them so, but clearly the matter must be explicitly examined. Once assured about their comparability, we can then ask whether and in what degree low-readiness children experiencing the tutorial program benefit over those who do not. If benefits are found, these should be typical of what is to be expected from the standard operation of the program, rather than atypical products of special "hothouse" conditions, because the research was carried out in a manner that approximates the real-life circumstances that would prevail under its general application. In this chapter we will consider, therefore, what the consequences are for the reading competence of low-readiness first graders when they are tutored under our program.

Percentile Rank Scores on the Metropolitan Readiness Tests for Experimentals and Controls

We begin with the question of equivalence between experimentals and controls on the yardstick used to define low academic readiness. Table 6.1 presents percentile rank scores on the *Metropolitan Readiness Tests* earned at the start of the academic year by the final sample of low-readiness children, com-

146

Table 6.1. Metropolitan Readiness Tests—
Percentile Rank Scores for Total Control Group, Experimental
Group, and Matched Control Group

	TC (N = 52)	E (N = 36)	MC (N = 36)
Mean	23.46	24.03	24.81
Standard deviation	11.26	12.40	11.33
1st quartile	15.5	15	16.5
Median	25	25	25
3rd quartile	33	37	35
2-sample t test	t = 0.22 df = 86 p = n.s.		
Difference score t test		t = 0.99 df = 35 p = n.s.	
Mann-Whitney test	z = 0.37 p = n.s.		
Wilcoxon test		T = 113 N = 24 p = n.s.	

paring the experimental group of thirty-six with the total
control group of fifty-two on the one hand and with the
matched control group of thirty-six on the other. The scores
express each child's standing in relation to the Metropolitan's
national norms, and, of course, no score was higher than the
cutoff percentile of 40 used to define low academic readiness.
As is apparent from the table, the experimental group's percentile scores are quite comparable to those of the total control
group and matched control group. The mean percentile scores
for these groups are all in the vicinity of 24, with standard
deviations all on the order of 11 or 12. The median percentile
scores, in turn, are 25 for each group, with the first quartile
falling about 10 percentile points below the median and the
third quartile about 10 above it. The middle half of the scores
in each group, therefore, are to be found between about 15
and the mid-30s. Three-quarters of the scores in each group
are located below or in the mid-30s; half of the scores in each

group are located below or at 25. We see from such indications that the three groups have similar distributions indeed, and that, in terms of national norms, these scores are quite low.

The statistical tests summarized in the lower portions of table 6.1 document further the comparability of the groups. Two tests evaluate the experimental group in relation to the total control group, while two other tests consider the difference scores between matched pairs of members of the experimental group and the matched control group. Of the two tests in each case, one is parametric and the other nonparametric. All four tests agree in finding no differences in Metropolitan scores between experimentals and controls. For comparing the experimental and total control groups, the parametric test is a two-sample t test, while the nonparametric test is the Mann-Whitney U test computed as described by Siegel (1956), using the formula for large samples with correction for ties. For evaluating the difference scores between matched pairs in the experimental and matched control groups, the parametric test is a one-sample t test for difference scores, while the nonparametric test is the Wilcoxon matched-pairs signed-ranks test, again computed as described by Siegel (1956). For the Wilcoxon test, the N used in the analysis is not the full number of pairs but the number of pairs whose difference score is not zero, with the result that in some applications of this test we had what Siegel defines as small samples and in others large samples; we followed Siegel accordingly for the samples of each kind. Any reader wishing still more specific information about results can consult Appendix C, where key data from the research have been set forth on a child-by-child basis.

The four kinds of statistical tests just described will appear in later tables as well. Inclusion of these four tests permits the reader to compare the tutored children with each of two differently defined control groups and to do so in each case with both a parametric and a nonparametric type of test. Consistency of outcomes across the four tests thus can be examined. To the extent that a result is clear, it should produce similar outcomes across the various tests.

We conclude from the results of table 6.1, then, that our system of random assignment of low academic-readiness children to experimental and control conditions resulted in highly comparable groups. Whether compared with the total control group or with the matched control group, the children of the experimental group are indistinguishable from the control children in their percentile rank scores on the *Metropolitan Readiness Tests*. The scores for all three groups are low, centering around a median that places them at the twenty-fifth percentile of beginning first graders across the nation. Armed with this information, we can proceed now to evaluate the tutored children against the yardstick provided by the control children's accomplishment. In doing so, we shall take up the various assessments in the same order in which they were described in chapter 5.

Reading Words and Sentences Based on Classroom Text Vocabularies

Word Recognition Test Based on Classroom Text Vocabularies Consider first the word recognition test that we built on the basis of vocabulary entries in the classroom reading materials. Recall that there were twenty-five words on the test, becoming more difficult as one progressed down the list, and that the child's score was the number of words read correctly before missing five in a row. Table 6.2 shows central tendencies and variabilities on these scores for the total control group, the experimental group, and the matched control group. The mean number of words correct for the experimental group approaches fourteen, while for the control children it is seven or eight. This difference is large enough to be almost a whole standard deviation in size, as we see from the standard deviation entries in the table. The median numbers of words correct, in turn, are fifteen for the experimental group and seven for each of the two control groups. This striking contrast in medians has its reflection at the first and third quartiles as well. Perhaps especially intriguing are the results for the first quartile, where children in the total control and matched control groups get no words correct at all while experimental group children get nine words correct—a first quartile figure for the experimentals which already exceeds the median for both control groups.

Table 6.2. Word Recognition Test Based on Classroom Text Vocabularies—Number of Words Correct

	TC (N = 52)	E (N = 36)	MC (N = 36)
Mean	7.44	13.56	8.11
Standard deviation	7.26	6.64	7.56
1st quartile	0	9	0
Median	7	15	7
3rd quartile	13	18	15.5
2-sample t test		$t = 4.09$ $df = 86$ $p < .0005$	
Difference score t test			$t = 4.52$ $df = 35$ $p < .0005$
Mann-Whitney test		$z = 3.69$ $p = .0001$	
Wilcoxon test			$T = 85, N = 34$ $z = 3.63$ $p = .0001$

Not only, then, do these data suggest that the tutored children have much higher score distributions than the controls but also that large numbers of control children get no words correct at all or very few words correct, while this is seldom the case for the experimentals. The frequency distributions presented in table 6.3 for the total control group and the experimental group offer further documentation for this last point. We find a preponderance of the controls at relatively low scores, including a pileup of eighteen controls getting zero or one word correct, while the experimentals have few children at the lower scores and a good representation of children toward the upper end of the score dimension.

Table 6.3. Word Recognition Test Based on Classroom Text Vocabularies—Frequency Distributions of Number of Words Correct for TC and E Groups

Words Correct	TC Group (N = 52)	E Group (N = 36)
0-1	18	3
2-3	1	0
4-5	4	2
6-7	7	3
8-9	6	2
10-11	2	1
12-13	1	5
14-15	3	2
16-17	3	8
18-19	3	4
20-21	2	2
22-23	1	2
24-25	1	2

Since, as described in chapter 5, the words on the test were taken from specific groups of words in the children's reading books, it is possible to provide some idea of the absolute meaning of the scores attained. Since the first nine words on the test came from the first seventy-five words in the books, the score of nine words correct, which was the tutored children's first quartile score, can—very roughly—be translated as the ability to recognize on the order of something like seventy-five words. The score of zero words correct, which was the untutored children's first quartile score, of course gives no evidence of ability to recognize any words at all. As, in turn, the first fifteen words on the test were taken from the first 150 in the books, the median score of fifteen words correct for the tutored children represents the ability to recognize something like 150 words. By the same sort of translation, the median score of seven words correct for the untutored children represents the ability to recognize only a little over fifty words or so. The upper quartile score of eighteen words correct for the tutored children represents the ability to recognize about two hundred words—"upper-first-grade achievement," according to Chall (1967 p. 199)—while the upper quartile scores of 13 to 15.5 for the untutored children represent between about 125 and a little over 150 words. By these rough estimates, then, experimental and control children compare as follows regarding the absolute numbers of words they can recognize: at the first quartile, about 75 versus 0; at the median, about 150 versus a little over 50; and at the third quartile, about 200 versus somewhere between 125 and 150.

Turning to the statistical evaluation of the effects described, we find in table 6.2 that all four of the statistical tests—whether comparing the experimentals with the total control group or with the matched control group, and whether parametric or nonparametric—yield extremely high significance levels. The effects found for the two-sample t test, difference score t test, Mann-Whitney test, and Wilcoxon test, all are significant well beyond the .001 level. The significance levels cited in this and subsequent tables for these statistical tests all will be one-tailed since, obviously, the direction of the difference between experimentals and controls was predicted. In sum, tables 6.2 and 6.3 tell us that, for the word recognition test based on classroom text vocabularies, the performance of tutored children is vastly superior to that of controls.

Sentence-Reading Test Based on Classroom Text Vocabularies
How do the children do at reading and comprehending sentences that draw on classroom text vocabularies but, insofar as possible, are being seen for the first time on the test? With the sentences becoming more difficult and including words from later and later in the children's books as one progresses to later sentences in the series, recall that twenty-five comprehension questions were asked about sentence materials read from thirteen cards. Testing continued until the child failed all questions pertaining to the sentences on three cards in succession. Table 6.4 presents measures of central tendency and variability, along with statistical tests, for the number of comprehension questions answered correctly by experimental and control children. The experimentals show a mean of about

Table 6.4. Sentence-Reading Test Based on
Classroom Text Vocabularies—Number of Questions Correct

	TC (N = 52)	E (N = 36)	MC (N = 36)
Mean	9.06	16.08	9.97
Standard deviation	7.98	7.84	8.39
1st quartile	0	10	0
Median	7.5	19.5	9
3rd quartile	14.5	22.5	18
2-sample t test	t = 4.11 df = 86 p < .0005		
Difference score t test		t = 4.83 df = 35 p < .0005	
Mann-Whitney test	z = 3.79 p = .0001		
Wilcoxon test		T = 74, N = 34 z = 3.82 p = .0001	

sixteen questions correct, the controls a mean of about nine or ten—a difference representing on the order of three-quarters of a standard deviation, and hence substantial. The median number of questions correct for the experimentals is 19.5, compared to medians of 7.5 for the total control group and nine for the matched control group. With a maximum possible score of twenty-five, this is a striking difference: the median for the experimentals is not far from the score ceiling, while the medians for the control groups are way below. Indeed, as the third quartile results indicate, the score at the seventy-fifth percentile for the experimentals is 22.5, which is very close to the ceiling of twenty-five. In other words, the upper quarter of the experimental sample answers all or almost all of the questions correctly. The first quartile results in turn show that, as for the last section's word recognition test, for the sentence-reading test as well large numbers of control children get scores of zero. While the experimental group's score at the first quartile is ten, that for both control groups is

zero. Large numbers of tutored children are clustered near the
score ceiling, therefore, and large numbers of control children
are clustered at the score floor.

Table 6.5 amplifies the basis for the preceding generalization
by presenting the frequency distributions as to number of
questions correct on the sentence reading test for the experimental group and the total control group. Eighteen of the
thirty-six members of the experimental group—half the sample
—have scores between twenty and twenty-five; something
achieved by only 17 percent of the total control group. At
the other end, 27 percent of the total control group, but only
6 percent of the experimental group, have scores of zero or
one. As these results and those described before would lead us
to expect, table 6.4 indicates that all four of the statistical tests
carried out on the scores from the sentence-reading task—the
two-sample t test, difference score t test, Mann-Whitney test,
and Wilcoxon test—yield effects that are significant well beyond the .001 level. Thus, the tutored children show themselves
to be much more capable than the controls not only at reading
words, as we saw in the last section, but also at reading sentences with comprehension.

The evaluation tests considered thus far are ones that draw
upon vocabulary entries from the classroom text materials,
although, as we have noted, we attempted for the sentence-
reading test discussed in the present section to compose sentences which the children had never seen before. What happens
when we evaluate the children's reading competence in terms
of standardized reading achievement tests that have nothing at
all to do with the classroom text vocabularies? We turn to this
question next.

Reading the Words and Sentences in a
Standardized Reading Achievement Battery

Spache Word Recognition Lists
Performance on Spache's word recognition lists tells us how
the child does at reading words of increasing difficulty on a
test that is fully independent of classroom reading materials.

Table 6.5. Sentence-Reading Test Based on Classroom Text Vocabularies—Frequency Distributions of Number of Questions Correct for TC and E Groups

Questions Correct	TC Group (N = 52)	E Group (N = 36)
0-1	14	2
2-3	2	1
4-5	5	2
6-7	5	3
8-9	2	0
10-11	5	3
12-13	4	1
14-15	4	3
16-17	1	1
18-19	1	2
20-21	5	6
22-23	1	7
24-25	3	5

The test continues, it will be recalled, until the child misses five words in a row. Tables 6.6, 6.7, and 6.8 present the findings on this test for experimentals and controls. Consider first the measures of central tendency and variability for number of words correct as shown in table 6.6. The mean for the tutored children is over twenty-three, while the means for the controls are on the order of thirteen or fourteen, a difference of sizable proportions representing about three-quarters of a standard deviation. The medians, in turn, show a stark separation between experimentals and controls: twenty-six for the experimental group, compared to eight or nine for the controls. This separation is also found to be strong at the first and third quartiles of the distributions. At the first quartile, the experimental group's score is 7.5, while for both the total control and the matched control groups the score is 1.5, again indicating a large pileup of very low scores for the controls. At the third quartile, the experimental group gets thirty-three words correct—a very large number—while for the total control and matched control groups the figures are sixteen and twenty-one, respectively.

Table 6.6. Spache Word Recognition Lists—
Number of Words Correct

	TC (N = 52)	E (N = 36)	MC (N = 36)
Mean	12.65	23.47	14.00
Standard deviation	14.25	16.11	14.87
1st quartile	1.5	7.5	1.5
Median	8	26	9.5
3rd quartile	16	33	21
2-sample t test	t = 3.25		
	df = 86		
	p < .005		
Difference score t test			t = 3.27
			df = 35
			p < .005
Mann-Whitney test	z = 3.04		
	p = .001		
Wilcoxon test			T = 116.5
			N = 34
			z = 3.09
			p = .001

Table 6.7. Spache Word Recognition Lists—
Frequency Distributions of Number of Words Correct for
TC and E Groups

Words Correct	TC Group (N = 52)	E Group (N = 36)
0-4	17	6
5-9	13	6
10-14	7	0
15-19	4	2
20-24	2	0
25-29	0	8
30-34	5	6
35-39	0	4
40-44	0	1
45-49	2	2
50-54	2	0
55-59	0	0
60-64	0	0
65-69	0	1

Table 6.8. Spache Word Recognition Lists—
Grade Placement Level

	TC (N = 52)	E (N = 36)	MC (N = 36)
< 1.3	33	12	21
1.3	3	0	2
1.6	6	2	4
1.8	3	13	3
2.3	6	8	6
2.8	1	0	0
3.3	0	1	0
% at 1.6 or better	31%	67%	36%
% at 1.8 or better	19%	61%	25%
Mann-Whitney test	z = 3.13		
	p = .0009		
Wilcoxon test			T = 35.5
			N = 22
			p < .005

The frequency distributions for number of words correct on the Spache lists as shown in table 6.7 make quite graphic how different the performances are of the experimentals and controls. There is indeed a pileup of the controls at the low end—71 percent of the total control group earning scores of fourteen or less, compared to one-third of the experimental group. By contrast, only 17 percent of the total control group receives scores of twenty-five or higher, compared to 61 percent of the experimental group. The statistical tests summarized in the lower portions of table 6.6 confirm the striking differences between tutored and control children on number of words correct that we have been describing. All four of the tests that were run—the two-sample t test, difference score t test, Mann-Whitney test, and Wilcoxon test—produce effects that are significant beyond the .005 level.

Recall that the Spache word recognition lists provided grade placement norms for various numbers of words correctly read. We translated the children's scores as to number of words correct into the grade placement levels given by Spache, with the results shown in table 6.8. Keeping in mind that these levels can only be viewed as approximate, they nevertheless do show striking differences in grade locations for experimentals and controls. The distributions of children over the various grade placement levels indicate that a large proportion of the controls fail to reach the 1.3 level—63 percent of the total control group and 58 percent of the matched control group—compared to 33 percent of the experimental group. On the other hand, the proportions of the groups functioning at the 1.6 level (and hence about two-thirds of the way through the demands of first grade), or better, are 31 percent of the total control group and 36 percent of the matched control group, in contrast to 67 percent of the experimental group. So too, the proportions functioning at the 1.8 level (and hence all of the way through the demands of first grade), or better, are 19 percent of the total control group and 25 percent of the matched control group, in contrast to 61 percent of the experimental group. About two-thirds of the tutored children, then, are performing near grade level, or beyond, on the Spache word recognition lists, that is, doing what would be expected for about two-thirds of the way through the first-grade year (the 1.6 level), or doing better than that, on a test that preceded the end of the first-grade year by a number of weeks. On the other hand, this is the case for only about one-third of the control children.

The bottom two sections of table 6.8 present the statistical tests pertaining to these grade placement level results. For the grade level data, only nonparametric tests were run since the grade level categories cannot be said to constitute more than an ordinal scale, and parametric tests can be justified only if it is at least fair to entertain the view that a given measure can be considered an interval scale. Both tests, the Mann-Whitney and the Wilcoxon, yield highly significant effects. Whether we use Spache's grade level categories or simply take number of words correct directly, the statistical evaluations for performances on the Spache word recognition lists find the tutored children vastly superior to the controls.

Spache Reading-Passages and Comprehension Questions
Next we turn to the reading and understanding of the sentences
that comprise Spache's reading-passages, once again a test that
is fully independent of classroom reading materials. Recall that
a child had to demonstrate competence both in reading and
comprehension of a given passage in order to proceed to a
more difficult passage in the series, and that the grade placement level score earned by a child was the grade level for the
passage just below the one that the child failed either by reading or comprehension yardsticks. This grade-level score was
the measure derived from the test, and as we have noted, these
grade placement norms should be taken as approximate. Table
6.9 shows the numbers of children in the total control group,
experimental group, and matched control group earning the
various grade placement level scores. Most of the control children—85 percent of the total control group and 83 percent
of the matched control group—scored below the 1.6 grade
level, compared to half the experimentals. This means that we
find 50 percent of the experimental group, but only 15 percent
of the total control group and 17 percent of the matched control group, scoring at the 1.6 grade level or better. If in turn
we look at children scoring at the 1.8 grade level or better,
this is true for 25 percent of the experimental group, but for
only 10 percent of the total control group and 11 percent of
the matched control group. Half of the tutored children thus
are performing near grade level or beyond on the Spache
reading-passages—that is to say, meeting what is expected for
about two-thirds of the way through the first-grade year (the
1.6 level), or surpassing that level, on a test administered a
number of weeks before the end of the first-grade year. By
contrast, only about 15 or 17 percent of the control children
reach this point.

Turning to the nonparametric tests of these findings shown
in the lower portions of table 6.9—again only nonparametric
tests were carried out since the grade-level categories constitute
no more than an ordinal scale—both the Mann-Whitney and

the Wilcoxon tests show significant effects. Indeed, in the case of the Mann-Whitney test, the effect obtained is significant beyond the .001 level. On a standardized test of the reading and comprehension of paragraphs, therefore, as well as on a standardized test of word recognition, tutored children are much superior to control children.

Table 6.9. Spache Reading-Passages—Grade Placement Level

	TC (N = 52)	E (N = 36)	MC (N = 36)
< 1.6	44	18	30
1.6	3	9	2
1.8	1	4	1
2.3	2	5	2
2.8	2	0	1
% at 1.6 or better	15%	50%	17%
% at 1.8 or better	10%	25%	11%
Mann-Whitney test	z = 3.21		
	p = .0007		
Wilcoxon test		T = 22	
		N = 15	
		p < .025	

Whether using reading achievement tests of our own devising or the reading achievement tests developed by Spache, we have found the children of the experimental group to show considerable competence at a reasonable ecological sampling of reading activities: they can read words; they can read and comprehend the meaning of sentences that they are seeing for the first time. And they demonstrate these achievements with materials that range over into a fair degree of difficulty. One-half to two-thirds of these children, depending on the criterion used, perform near grade level or better—some considerably better. But these are children all of whom showed low academic readiness as judged from their low standing on the *Metropolitan Readiness Tests* back in the first month of the school year. Indeed, the control children, equally low in academic readiness as judged from their Metropolitan scores, by and large fulfill their prognosis and do very poorly on these reading achievement tests. The question posed at the end of the last chapter thus receives an affirmative answer: low-readiness children tutored by community adults who are trained in the use of our program do learn to read. Next we turn to the results on evaluation tests that sought to assess some sound-identification skills that should be implicated in reading competence.

Knowing the Sounds That Letters Stand for and That Words Start with

Spache Consonant Sounds Test
The first of the three tests on sound-identification skills that we administered was the consonant sounds test from the Spache battery. Recall that in this test the child was to give a sound for every letter of the alphabet except the five vowels. Findings on the number of letters for which a correct sound was given, a score which, of course, could go up to twenty-one, are shown in tables 6.10 and 6.11. We see from table 6.10 that the mean number correct for the experimental group is almost seventeen, while for the controls it is about eleven or twelve—a difference substantial enough to represent not much less than a standard deviation. The table also indicates that the biggest difference between experimentals and controls is to be found among the low scorers. The first quartile score is 16.5 for the experimental group, but only 3.5 for the total control and 4.5 for the matched control groups. This is, obviously, a huge contrast. At the median, the experimentals score eighteen and each of the control groups fourteen; while at the third quartile, the score for the Experimental Group is 19.5 and that for each of the control groups is eighteen. The difference, then, is very large at the first quartile, substantial but smaller at the median, and smaller still at the third quartile. Large numbers of control children, therefore, get low scores—while this is very seldom the case for experimentals.

Table 6.10. Spache Consonant-Sounds Test—
Number Correct

	TC (N = 52)	E (N = 36)	MC (N = 36)
Mean	11.44	16.78	11.92
Standard deviation	7.26	4.79	7.31
1st quartile	3.5	16.5	4.5
Median	14	18	14
3rd quartile	18	19.5	18
2-sample t test	t = 4.15 df = 86 p < .0005		
Difference score t test			t = 3.94 df = 35 p < .0005
Mann-Whitney test	z = 3.78 p = .0001		
Wilcoxon test			T = 86, N = 33 z = 3.48 p = .0003

Table 6.11. Spache Consonant-Sounds Test—
Frequency Distributions of Number Correct for TC and E
Groups

Number Correct	TC Group (N = 52)	E Group (N = 36)
0-1	8	2
2-3	5	0
4-5	3	0
6-7	2	0
8-9	2	0
10-11	1	2
12-13	2	0
14-15	9	2
16-17	4	6
18-19	12	15
20-21	4	9

The frequency distributions presented in table 6.11 for the total control group and the experimental group amplify the basis for what has just been said. Only two of the thirty-six experimentals—6 percent of them—get less than ten letters correct. On the other hand, twenty of the fifty-two members of the total control group—38 percent of them—get less than ten letters correct. Similarly, only 17 percent of the experimental group, compared to 62 percent of the total control group, get less than sixteen letters correct. We see rather directly from these figures that most of the tutored children know most of the consonant sounds, while many of the control children know few of the consonant sounds.

The lower portions of table 6.10 give the results for statistical tests of these comparisons between experimentals and controls. The two-sample t test, difference score t test, Mann-Whitney test, and Wilcoxon test, all yield effects that are significant well beyond the .001 level. Knowledge of consonant sounds, then, constitutes a strong basis of differentiation between tutored and control children.

Starting Sounds Test with Paired Words
The two remaining tests concerned with sound-identification skills assessed the child's knowledge of the starting sounds of words. In the present test, recall that the child was to indicate whether, for each of eight pairs of spoken words, some of which started with the same and others with different sounds, the words did or did not begin with the same sound—thus giving a score range up to eight and the possibility of a large number correct by chance. We see from tables 6.12 and 6.13 that experimentals once again were superior to controls, whether judging from means or medians. By comparing results for the first quartile, median, and third quartile, we note that the major difference between controls and experimentals is found at the lower scores. At the first quartile, the experimental group scores five, while each of the two control groups score three—a larger score difference than is found at the median. As

Table 6.12. Starting-Sounds Test with Paired Words—Number Correct

	TC (N = 52)	E (N = 36)	MC (N = 36)
Mean	4.83	5.64	4.94
Standard deviation	1.73	1.50	1.84
1st quartile	3	5	3
Median	5	6	5
3rd quartile	6	7	7
2-sample t test	t = 2.35 df = 86 p < .025		
Difference score t test			t = 1.87 df = 35 p < .05
Mann-Whitney test	z = 2.04 p = .02		
Wilcoxon test			T = 111.5 N = 26 z = 1.63 p = .05

Table 6.13. Starting-Sounds Test with Paired Words—Frequency Distributions of Number Correct for TC and E Groups

Number Correct	TC Group (N = 52)	E Group (N = 36)
1	1	0
2	3	1
3	12	3
4	6	3
5	8	8
6	10	10
7	12	8
8	0	3

on the Spache consonant-sounds test, many control children earn quite low scores on the present starting sounds test also. Table 6.13 makes this point clear with its frequency distributions, where we find 31 percent of the total control group, compared to 11 percent of the experimental group, with scores of three or less.

The statistical tests summarized in table 6.12 indicate that, by all four of the kinds of tests that were carried out, experimentals are found to be superior to controls at the .05 level or better—the conventional level for calling effects statistically significant—but not strikingly superior. The test is probably not a very sensitive one, however, both because it allows chance guessing to play a sizable role and also because, like the auditory discrimination tests discussed in chapter 3, it asks children to make a kind of judgment ("same" or "different") which may be difficult for many of them quite apart from the recognition of sounds. These factors may well have resulted in the differences between the experimental and control groups being smaller than would otherwise have been the case.

Starting-Sounds Test with Single Words
This last point receives direct corroboration when we turn to the other starting-sounds test that was conducted, this one calling not for judgments of "same" or "different" but for the child to produce the starting sound for each of five spoken words: a more direct task, and one in which chance guessing will not help. Findings on the number of words for which the correct starting sound was given—which could range, of course, from zero to five—are shown in tables 6.14 and 6.15. Very strong contrasts between experimentals and controls are in evidence. The means are about four for the experimentals and about two for each of the control groups, a difference representing approximately a standard deviation. The median for the experimentals is four, and their first quartile score also is four. By the third quartile, the experimentals are scoring five, the highest possible score. For the controls, on the other hand, a very different picture emerges. In the case of the total control group, the first quartile score is zero, the median two, and the third quartile score four. Results for the matched control group are similar—a first quartile score of zero, median of 2.5, and third quartile score of four. What these numbers indicate is that

Table 6.14. Starting-Sounds Test with Single Words—Number Correct

	TC (N = 52)	E (N = 36)	MC (N = 36)
Mean	2.31	4.11	2.33
Standard deviation	2.02	1.17	2.04
1st quartile	0	4	0
Median	2	4	2.5
3rd quartile	4	5	4
2-sample t test		t = 5.30 df = 86 p < .0005	
Difference score t test			t = 4.75 df = 35 p < .0005
Mann-Whitney test		z = 3.99 p = .0000	
Wilcoxon test			T = 29, N = 26 z = 3.72 p = .0001

Table 6.15. Starting-Sounds Test with Single Words—Frequency Distributions of Number Correct for TC and E Groups

Number Correct	TC Group (N = 52)	E Group (N = 36)
0	17	1
1	6	1
2	4	1
3	4	3
4	11	14
5	10	16

almost all of the experimentals are getting all or almost all of the starting sounds correct, while large numbers of the controls are getting none or only a small number of the starting sounds correct.

The frequency distributions in table 6.15 point up just how pervasive these differences are. Thirty of the thirty-six members of the experimental group—83 percent of them—get four or five of the starting sounds correct, compared to 40 percent of the total control group. At the other end, only three of the thirty-six experimentals—8 percent of them—get two or less of the starting sounds correct, compared to 52 percent of the total control group. Indeed, only one of the thirty-six experimentals gets absolutely none of the starting sounds correct at all, while this is true for seventeen of the fifty-two children in the total control group.

Turning to the statistical evaluations of these results, we find in table 6.14 that the two-sample t test, difference score t test, Mann-Whitney test, and Wilcoxon test all yield effects that are significant well beyond the .001 level. Indeed, the significance level for the Mann-Whitney test is so high that its value is .0000 to four places. Clearly, the experimentals are considerably superior to the controls in their performance on this starting-sounds test.

In knowledge of the sounds that words start with as well as knowledge of the sounds that letters represent, therefore, the experimentals do much better than the control children. Not only degree of reading competence as such, but possession of these sound-identification skills as well, strongly differentiate the tutored children from the controls. It seems likely, therefore, that enhancement of sound-identification skills of these kinds is at least one factor that has contributed to the reading achievement of the tutored children.

We should further note that on all seven of the evaluation tests that were conducted—the word- and sentence-reading tests that we devised on the basis of classroom text vocabularies, the word- and sentence-reading tests developed by Spache, and the three tests concerned with sound-identification skills—the results were quite comparable across tutors and schools. The close similarity can be illustrated by the fact that on the Spache word recognition test, three of the four tutors had four children scoring below the 1.8 grade level and five children scoring at or above that level; the remaining tutor had two children below and seven children at or above 1.8. Not only was the tutoring with our program found to be effective, therefore, but it was effective with each of the tutors at the two different schools and there were no great differences in effectiveness among them. Since, of course, the tutors inevitably varied among themselves in diverse ways and the schools were characterized by differences too, this means that the tutorial program's attributes were explicit and prominent enough to override differences from tutor to tutor or school to school. These results are important, of course, in supporting the general applicability of the program, since they indicate that the kinds and amounts of training and supervision provided to these nonprofessionals were sufficient to bring them all to a comparable degree of effectiveness in their work with the children, regardless of the ways in which they differed among themselves and of differences in the contexts in which they worked. We might also note that boys and girls were very comparable in their responsiveness to the tutoring.

Report Card Information

The results of the evaluation tests reviewed in this chapter let us conclude that use of our tutorial program with nonprofessionals as tutors brings low academic-readiness first graders to a substantial degree of reading competence by the spring of the first-grade year. Nontutored children who start the year equally low in academic readiness are vastly inferior to the tutored children as assessed on the evaluation tests. And, viewed in absolute terms, what the tutored children can do in the line of reading seems impressive, especially when keeping in mind their poor academic prognosis at the beginning of the year.

How much of these substantial superiorities in reading competence for the experimentals compared to the controls gets reflected in the report card grades for reading given by the teachers? Recall that we recorded the teachers' quarterly report card grades for reading and that these grades categorized the child both as to reading level ("readiness," "preprimers," "primer," "first reader," and "second reader, part one") and quality of performance within the given level (unsatisfactory, fair, good, excellent). While there are problems in how to interpret such grades for purposes of analysis, they seem most appropriately viewed as constituting an ordinal scale running from the poorest performance at the lowest level to the best performance at the highest level. We proceeded accordingly, assigning numbers one through four to unsatisfactory, fair, good, and excellent, respectively, at level A, the lowest level; numbers five through eight for unsatisfactory, fair, good, and excellent at level B, the next level; and so on to numbers seventeen through twenty for unsatisfactory, fair, good, and excellent at level E.

Table 6.16 presents the report card grades for the total control group, experimental group, and matched control group in terms of these numbers, showing first quartile, median, and third quartile grades during each of the four marking periods.

Table 6.16. Grades for Reading on Each of the Quarterly Report Cards—First Quartile, Median, and Third Quartile

	TC	E	MC
10th week (N)	(50)	(34)	(34)
1st quartile	2	2	2
Median	6	6	6
3rd quartile	6	6	6
20th week (N)	(49)	(34)	(33)
1st quartile	6	6	6
Median	6	6	6
3rd quartile	6	7	7
30th week (N)	(48)	(34)	(32)
1st quartile	6	6	6
Median	7	10	10
3rd quartile	10.5	14	11
40th week (N)	(51)	(35)	(35)
1st quartile	6	6	6
Median	10	11	10
3rd quartile	11	15	14

NOTE: The numbers 1 through 20 have been assigned to the grade categories, running from unsatisfactory at level A to excellent at level E.

Sample sizes vary somewhat from one quarterly report card to another and are somewhat lower than the full sizes of the groups in question, because of missing entries on report cards. The numbers suggest a relatively clear story. During the first and second quarters of the school year, report cards show virtually no differentiation between experimentals and controls in teacher grades for reading. During the third and fourth quarters, on the other hand, report cards show the experimentals receiving higher reading grades than the controls. This superiority of the tutored children found during the last half of the school year is most evident at the third quartiles of the distributions, is also to be seen at the medians, and is not in evidence at the first quartiles.

Table 6.17. Grades for Reading on Each of the Quarterly Report Cards—Statistical Tests

	Mann-Whitney Test		Wilcoxon Test	
	TC	E	E	MC
10th week (N)	(50)	(34)	(32)	(32)
	z = 0.38		T = 74	
	p = n.s.		N = 20	
			p = n.s.	
20th week (N)	(49)	(34)	(31)	(31)
	z = 1.07		T = 51	
	p = n.s.		N = 15	
			p = n.s.	
30th week (N)	(48)	(34)	(30)	(30)
	z = 2.16		T = 119.5	
	p = .02		N = 26	
			z = 1.42	
			p = .08	
40th week (N)	(51)	(35)	(34)	(34)
	z = 1.95		T = 114.5	
	p = .03		N = 28	
			z = 2.02	
			p = .02	

Before discussing these trends in reading grades further, we should note their statistical confirmation in table 6.17, which shows the results of nonparametric tests for these ordinal data. The sample sizes shown for the Mann-Whitney tests are the same as given for the total control group and the experimental group for each quarter on table 6.16. In the case of the Wilcoxon tests, however, matched pairs are at issue, and therefore the sample sizes given for these tests are the number of matched pairs in the experimental group and the matched control group where report card entries were found for both members of the pair. For the first quarter and also for the second quarter, neither the Mann-Whitney nor the Wilcoxon test yields a significant effect. For the third quarter, on the other hand, the experimentals show a superiority to the controls at the .02 level on the Mann-Whitney test and the .08 level—thus failing to meet the conventional .05 level but still near it—on the Wilcoxon. And for the fourth quarter, the experimentals show a superiority to the controls at the .03 level on the Mann-Whitney test and the .02 level on the Wilcoxon. These statistical evaluations thus support what was suggested on the basis of the results in table 6.16: that the report card grades for reading are no different for experimentals and controls during the first and second quarters but favor experimentals over controls during the third and fourth quarters. Armed with this statistical corroboration, let us return now to the data of table 6.16.

If we translate the table's numbers back to the grade categories that they represent, we find that the teacher grades for reading at the third quartiles of the distributions work up by the fourth report card to "good" at the first-reader level for the experimentals, compared to "good" at the primer level for the total control group and "fair" at the first-reader level for the matched control group. On the third report card, these grades were "fair" at the first-reader level for the experimentals, compared to between "fair" and "good" at the primer level for the total control group and "good" at the primer level for the matched control group. There is little differentiation on earlier report cards. At the medians of the distributions, in turn, the grades by the fourth report card work up to "good" at the primer level for the experimentals, compared to "fair" at the primer level for each of the two control groups, with the differentiation between experimentals and controls trailing off as one goes back toward earlier report cards. At the first quartiles of the distributions, finally, no distinction between experimentals and controls is found at all; they rise no higher than "fair" at the preprimer level.

Thus the teachers' grades reflect to some degree, albeit a limited one, the greater reading competence of the experimentals as the year proceeds. Since superior report-card grades for experimentals compared to controls don't emerge until the latter part of the school year, it seems unlikely that they have anything to do with teachers' knowledge of which children were receiving tutoring, rather than being a direct reflection of teacher perceptions of performance. But since we know from the objective evaluation tests that the experimentals are much more competent than the controls at reading, why are the report card effects not stronger than they turn out? We suspect that the answer lies in the reading groups to which the children are assigned. All the children in a given group remain together in terms of where they are reading in their books—a child's "reading level" thus is simply a function of whether that child's group is in the preprimers, primer, first reader, and so on. The only way a child can move ahead of the other members of that child's group in reading level is to be placed in a different group. But there is a strong tendency for reading groups to be entities that stabilize early in the school year, with shifts in group membership as the year proceeds much more the exception than the rule. Thus, it was not unheard of for children who were doing well at reading the first reader with their tutors, still to be reading a preprimer in their classrooms. It is obvious, then, that the report card grades cannot adequately reflect the actual reading competence of children who have been held back by their reading groups in this way.

Report card grades for mathematics are presented for the first and last report cards in table 6.18, with nonparametric statistical tests for these data shown in table 6.19. The same

Table 6.18. Grades for Mathematics on the First and Last Report Cards—First Quartile, Median, and Third Quartile

	TC	E	MC
10th week (N)	(50)	(33)	(34)
1st quartile	5	6	5
Median	6	6	6
3rd quartile	7	7	7
40th week (N)	(51)	(34)	(35)
1st quartile	9	10	10
Median	10	10.5	10
3rd quartile	14	14	14

NOTE: The numbers 1 through 20 have been assigned to the grade categories, running from unsatisfactory at level A to excellent at level E.

Table 6.19. Grades for Mathematics on the First and Last Report Cards—Statistical Tests

	Mann-Whitney Test		Wilcoxon Test	
	TC	E	E	MC
10th week (N)	(50)	(33)	(31)	(31)
	z = 0.42		T = 56	
	p = n.s.		N = 17	
			p = n.s.	
40th week (N)	(51)	(34)	(33)	(33)
	z = 1.09		T = 83.5	
	p = n.s.		N = 21	
			p = n.s.	

kind of ordinal scale was set up as with the reading grades, the five levels here being defined on the report cards as "readiness," "basic number concepts," "first year, part one," "first year, part two," and "second year, part one," and each level being further differentiated into quality designations of unsatisfactory, fair, good, and excellent. The sample sizes shown on tables 6.18 and 6.19 vary for the same reasons as were dis-

cussed in connection with tables 6.16 and 6.17. In contrast to
the report card results for reading, those for mathematics show
no difference between experimentals and controls either early
or late in the school year. All four statistical tests—the two
for the last report card as well as the two for the first report
card—yield nonsignificant effects. This outcome of no superiority of grades for experimentals on mathematics, in contrast
to the superiority that emerges by the end of the year for the
experimentals on reading, supports what a skill-centered view
of the meaning of our tutoring program would lead us to expect: tutoring that establishes competence at reading bears
upon reading-related activities. There is no clear basis for
expecting it to promote competence at mathematics, because
the child was not taught mathematics by the tutor.

Consider finally the report card information as to number
of days absent during each quarter, which permits us to check
whether there was any differential amount of school attendance
for experimentals and controls. If there was and it favored the
tutored children, then sheer school attendance would constitute
an uncontrolled variable that could play a role in the greater
reading competence of the experimentals. We see from tables
6.20 and 6.21 that this was not the case. If anything, the means
for number of days absent during each marking period as
shown in table 6.20 reflect somewhat more absences for the
experimentals than the controls. In seven of the eight possible
comparisons, experimentals exceed controls in mean number
of days absent. As the standard deviations in table 6.20 indicate, however, variabilities are rather high. The two-sample t
tests and difference score t tests summarized in table 6.21 for
each of the quarterly report cards indicate no significant differences between the experimental group and the total control
group, or between the experimental group and the matched
control group, in number of days absent at any point during
the school year. Once again, the sample sizes shown in tables
6.20 and 6.21 vary for the same kinds of reasons as were
mentioned in the discussion of tables 6.16 and 6.17. The tutored children were not at school any more often, therefore,
than the controls.

Table 6.20. Number of Days Absent on Each
of the Quarterly Report Cards—Mean and Standard Deviation

	TC	E	MC
10th week (N)	(51)	(36)	(35)
Mean	2.44	2.86	2.96
Standard deviation	3.49	3.33	3.94
20th week (N)	(51)	(36)	(35)
Mean	3.91	4.92	3.96
Standard deviation	4.65	4.54	4.69
30th week (N)	(50)	(36)	(34)
Mean	2.97	3.71	2.87
Standard deviation	3.31	3.50	3.05
40th week (N)	(51)	(35)	(35)
Mean	2.69	3.93	2.89
Standard deviation	5.35	3.99	6.25

Table 6.21. Number of Days Absent on Each
of the Quarterly Report Cards—Statistical Tests

	2-Sample t Test		Difference Score t Test	
	TC	E	E	MC
10th week (N)	(51)	(36)	(35)	(35)
	t = 0.57		t = 0.07	
	df = 85		df = 34	
	p = n.s.		p = n.s.	
20th week (N)	(51)	(36)	(35)	(35)
	t = 1.01		t = 0.81	
	df = 85		df = 34	
	p = n.s.		p = n.s.	
30th week (N)	(50)	(36)	(34)	(34)
	t = 0.99		t = 1.01	
	df = 84		df = 33	
	p = n.s.		p = n.s.	
40th week (N)	(51)	(35)	(34)	(34)
	t = 1.23		t = 0.92	
	df = 84		df = 33	
	p = n.s.		p = n.s.	

If nonprofessionals are trained to carry out the cumulative mastery tutorial program that we developed, children who begin school scoring low in academic readiness acquire a considerable degree of reading competence by the following spring. Children who start out equally low in academic readiness but do not receive such tutoring, on the other hand, do poorly at reading. These generalizations have been supported by the results of a range of evaluation tests, including the reading and comprehension of sentences and paragraphs as well as the recognition of words, and including performances on standardized reading achievement tests as well as tests of our own devising. These findings were obtained, furthermore, not under "hothouse" conditions but under real-world circumstances of utilization representative of what is feasible to arrange in practice. It seems fair to come away from this chapter's evidence, then, with two conclusions. One is that systematic cumulation of the component skills that, according to our analysis, are needed for basic reading competence brings such competence about for large numbers of children who otherwise fail to acquire it on schedule during the first-grade year. The other is that the kind of instruction called for can be capably provided by community adults without professional or educational credentials who receive appropriate training and supervision.

7
Implications for Theory and Practice

The work presented in this volume arose from our concern over the educational problems faced by low-income children in America and our belief that the approaches heretofore undertaken toward dealing with those problems were missing some important psychological possibilities that could produce powerful beneficial effects if taken into account. The field research just described suggests that we were correct in this belief. What we have tried to do here is break down what seems to us an often artificial and misleading barrier in psychology erected between "pure" and "applied" research by showing how attention to real-world problems can spark theoretical insights that lead to findings which are of practical significance. Perhaps it is time to turn Lewin's dictum to the effect that there is nothing so practical as a good theory upside down and assert instead that a careful examination of real-life events in order to solve a practical problem such as the failure of poverty children to learn to read in first grade can become a significant means for advancing theoretical understanding, in this case our knowledge about the nature of cognitive competence and its development.

Our recommended reversal of the Lewinian dictum may, in fact, be in the wind. Bronfenbrenner (1974), among others, has inveighed against a tendency for psychological research to proceed in a manner that stays locked within some paradigm that is far from the reality one ultimately hopes to illuminate. He has noted that one can learn a great deal about the paradigm while learning nothing new about the reality—that the research can be quite lacking in "ecological validity"—and that much of the time this is exactly what goes on without its seeming to bother the researcher or those with whom the researcher communicates. Clearly they should be bothered, but the crucial question is how one translates such dissatisfaction into better strategies for research. What seems necessary is to take as one's focus not some academically based paradigm but a real-world phenomenon, and there are all kinds of phenomena in the real world that fairly cry out for greater understanding and better means of coping with them. Why not, then, try to understand such phenomena and test one's presumptive understanding by means of activities designed to influence them, carried out in the target-setting itself? One can start out with a question like why children from low-income backgrounds are not learning to read in first grade and test what one thinks are the causes by trying to bring such learning about.

We have, in turn, tried to apply our understanding of how to affect this particular real-world phenomenon in a way that would not only work but be practical as well. Once we thought we saw the reasons why these children were not learning, it was evident to us that, if we were correct, the solution would be amenable to widespread implementation because nothing esoteric was called for. We could envision fashioning a tool which, placed in the hands of noncredentialed adults trained to use it as tutors, would be expected to establish basic reading competence in a timely manner for a large proportion of the hundreds of thousands of children each year who presently fail to learn when they go through first grade. The preceding chapters document how our approach worked out in practice. In this concluding chapter we begin with an overview of what those chapters contain and then move on to consider where one goes from here.

The Argument in Outline

The major stratagems that gained momentum in the 60s for helping poor children do better at school have yielded disappointing results. Among the diverse kinds of responses currently abroad in the land to this apparent failure of the compensatory education movement are the Jensen and Herrnstein view that genetic inferiorities of intellect form the root of the trouble and thus limit what can be hoped for from education; the Jencks view that help for poor children will not be forthcoming from the schools but only from such direct means as government-arranged redistribution of the nation's wealth; and the view of Hunt and others that extreme intervention in the early lives of poor children with the aim of improving their intellects is the only kind of psychological intervention likely to work. Still another response, often heard from those looking to "open education" for an answer, is to say that the seat of the problem is not intellective at all but attitudinal and motivational, so that poor children will learn if schools will only give them a proper sense of self-regard and personal worth. Then there are those who simply want to intensify or continue the kinds of compensatory attempts carried out thus far through the schools, in effect denying that the picture is as bad as all that or arguing that, whether it is or not, the most practical course is to persevere with more of the same.

Each of these responses seemed, in our estimation, to be problematical. According to the Jensen position, the schools deserve little blame, which in effect relieves them from any responsibility for constructive change. According to the Jencks position, meaningful help requires a redistribution of income within the society, something which does not seem about to take place. According to the Hunt position, drastic interference with the ways in which some citizens raise their children must take place, which is highly questionable on civil libertarian grounds, would be impractical in its expense, and has not looked particularly effective in its bearing on poor children's academic accomplishment anyway. When it comes to responses that seek to work by means of the schools, attempts to affect low-income children's attitudes or motives through what can be done in school have not seemed to help their academic achievement in any clear way. And continued or intensified use of the compensatory educational tools, resources, and approaches currently favored by educators seems, on the basis of the data available for analysis and projection, to be unlikely to offer much prospect of academic improvement to low-income children either. If these various lines of response seem questionable, is there anything better to do? We believed that an affirmative answer to this question could be provided and that the lack of payoff for poor children's educational progress from the kinds of reforms now being tried could be understood in terms of certain basic errors in people's views as to what is wrong.

One such error is the belief that the seat of the problem for poor children is inferiority of intellect. If intelligence is viewed as deficient, the problem of improving school achievement becomes seen as one of making low-income children more intelligent, of improving their thinking or problem-solving abilities. But it is questionable whether genuine deficiencies of intellect exist for poor children; and even if they did, it is unclear how to jack up intellect in such a way as to bring about increased academic achievement, the realm we really care about. It is also an error, however, to believe that, if their intelligence is not deficient, then low-income children's difficulty with school must be motivational or attitudinal in its nature. If seen this way, the task becomes one of getting poor children to be more motivated to learn in school. Sometimes it is felt that school needs to be made more interesting or relevant to them; often it is argued that poor children must be made more confident about their academic potential. But how such efforts should suffice for causing achievements that are not found otherwise remains unclear once again, while we have no trouble understanding the reverse causal direction, namely, that actual establishment of greater school competence would bring in its wake more positive expectations about school success and greater motivation.

The two errors just described share a model of the child's functioning which essentially sees school success as depending on no more than two types of determinants—intelligence and motivation. According to this conception, academic achievement will be a relatively straightforward matter if a child is sufficiently intelligent and appropriately motivated; no more is called for than instructional procedures that are familiar stocks in the educator's trade. As we see it, however, sufficient intelligence and appropriate motivation *by no means* guarantee the easy acquisition of academic competences. Rather, there is a third type of determinant, quite apart from intelligence and motivation, that is crucially important as well; it is precisely in this third area that poor children's problems with school reside. This third type of determinant consists of the specific skills that underlie competence at school tasks. It is generally presumed that, given sufficient intelligence and motivation, the needed skills are learned from standard classroom instructional procedures. We submit, however, that the lion's share of the learning of these skills by middle-class children is provided not by the schools but by their homes, and that these skills receive little attention in the homes of poor children. That middle-class children can, by and large, readily attain the desired academic achievements with use of the standard procedures has meant that the sufficiency of these procedures has not been called into question. But if we are correct in asserting that attainment of the needed skills by middle-class children rests heavily upon the contribution of their homes, then attention must be paid to arranging for these skills to be explicitly developed at school in the case of children whose homes do not make this kind of contribution.

The issue that in our view needed to be addressed, then, is how to deliver to poverty-background children mastery of the basic skills necessary for coping with school—in a way that not only works but also is practical. Because such mastery has typically been viewed as relatively nonproblematical, given enough intelligence and motivation, what should properly be the very focus of concern has in fact largely been bypassed. The most significant skill to provide for seemed rather clearly to be reading, since reading competence underlies so much of schoolwork. We suspected that large numbers of poverty-background children were failing to develop basic reading competence on schedule in first grade simply because the customary modes of instruction, modeled as they have been on the needs of middle-class children, assumed possession of mundane but crucial subskills that poor children did not have. In other words, unless one had already learned these component ingredients of reading skill to a fairly substantial degree at home, the kind of instruction generally available at school was insufficient to establish them. And we suspected as well that what was needed could be built up in a straightforward manner if a program was designed that would really start from where the child is at, give enough practice every step of the way, and assure prior mastery of whatever the child had to know how to do in order to handle what was asked for next. The routines of such a program could, we believed, be readily taught to nonprofessionals who would function as tutors in carrying them out with the children who needed the help. No particular educational or professional certification would be necessary to equip someone to function in this kind of tutor role; rather, the program would be spelled out in enough detail so that a wide range of people could learn to apply it, working in "teachers' aides" or "paraprofessional" positions from a variety of possible bases.

But what are the ingredient subskills that such a program would need to establish? Before considering our answer to this question, let us underscore the importance of asking it by noting in a bit more detail what some current directions of thinking about compensatory education have been like. Major effort has been aimed at the preschool years, taking the form, in its earlier phase, of trying to raise poor children's scores on customary psychometric assessors of intelligence; its more recent phase, after largely disappointing results came in from attempts to raise traditional intelligence test scores, has taken the form of trying to enhance such children's functioning on tests reflecting Piagetian rather than psychometric conceptions of intelligence. Indeed, the switch from psychometric to Piaget-based ways of understanding intelligence has been widely heralded as promising a new era of clarity concerning how to evaluate and improve the cognitive functions that will help a child later with schoolwork. Thus, the assumption is kept that poor children are deficient intellectually, but instead of defining such deficiency in, say, IQ terms, the preference now is to define it in terms of crippled powers of categorization, abstraction, symbolic representation, causal understanding, or sense of environmental stability.

The particular appeal to Hunt (1968, 1969) and others behind such a Piaget-inspired redefinition of the intelligence concept was that it indicated a strong role for early experience in the development of intelligence and hence seemed to suggest that there would be ways to alter the early experiences of poverty-background children so as to make them more intelligent, with improved academic achievement presumed to follow as a natural consequence. Forgotten in all this was the point that Piaget, when seeing early experience as crucial to the development of a child's intellect, was referring, by and large, to forms of experience so basic as to be available to almost all children by virtue of the human condition, not just to children who are sufficiently well-off economically. It should come as no surprise, then, that trying to "enrich" such preschool experiences according to Piagetian formulas has not helped poor children do any better in school than has trying to raise their IQ scores.

This apparent failure of the Piaget-based preschool intervention strategy has not led to its abandonment, however. Instead, there has been a resultant emphasis on starting the task of repairing intelligence even earlier in the child's life and carrying it out in even more intensive—and intrusive—forms (see Blank 1972; Hunt 1973; Sigel, Sechrist, and Forman 1973). The possibility that the entire strategy may be in error —that there are no significant deficiencies of intellect for low-income children and that their problems in school lie in a quite different direction—receives little consideration. Whether invoking Piagetian or more traditional psychometric-test-oriented conceptions of intelligence, then, the major answer offered to the problems low-income children have with school is to try to remedy presumed deficiencies of intellect during the years before schooling begins—while both the existence of these deficiencies and just how remedying them should lead to greater academic achievement remain highly questionable.

Compensatory education attempts also have been made, of course, during the actual years of schooling. What has usually taken place along these lines, however, despite the rhetoric of innovation that may accompany the effort, is increased usage of tools, approaches, or remedies already in the armamentarium of techniques that the educator has ready at hand when larger budgets become available. More teachers may be hired, more days added to the school year, newer textbooks bought, more books acquired by the school library, team teaching instituted, ungraded classrooms arranged for, higher levels of certification required of incoming teachers, more reading specialists hired, more school psychologists hired, and so on. What in fact gets done pedagogically for poverty-background children as a result of such enhancements of "school resource quality" is not very different from what gets done already, although the programs will be costly and often carry fancy names.

Once again it should come as no surprise when evidence arrives suggesting that variations in such school-quality factors as these have little bearing on educational outcomes for the students, compared to the pervasive significance of social class or family background (see Coleman 1966; Jencks 1972a; Mosteller and Moynihan 1972a; Thorndike 1973). By now it seems clear that however one analyzes the data that the Coleman Report and analogous surveys are based on (see Armor 1972; Smith 1972), the picture is one of little impact on student achievement from increasing the resources schools know how to bring to bear on the pupils. If any hope for educational compensation is still held out when such negative evidence is accepted, it usually is attached to earlier and more pervasive intervention, asking in effect that low-income families raise their children from infancy in ways that the experts will prescribe for improving the children's minds. Once more, then, attention gets further deflected from the task of acquiring school skills; the answer to poor children's school difficulties is assumed to lie elsewhere than in figuring out how to teach them more effectively.

Those who question the early intervention premise that low-income children suffer from deficits of intellect usually assume that if intelligence is not the problem, then motivation must be. Frequently it is held that the child must get to feel better about his or her ability to cope with school; the child must be made to feel more confident, more in control. Most often, the teacher has been held responsible for such presumed impairments of motivation or attitude; it is argued that, if the teacher expected poor children to learn, then they would. When poor children fail in school, therefore, a self-fulfilling prophecy on the teacher's part is thought to be taking place: she communicates her expectations in various ways to the child, who comes to feel less or more competent accordingly.

While teachers do tend to expect greater success or failure at school learning as a function of the social-class background of their students, and interact differently with these students as a result, this is of course not enough to document the view of the self-fulfilling prophecy, although it has indeed been construed this way (see Rist 1971). Such prophecies on the teachers' part are in fact highly veridical and thus need not be self-fulfilling at all. The question is whether these different expectations, and any consequent differences in treatment, are *causing* the contrasting academic outcomes for the pupils. Attempts have been made to vary teachers' expectancies experimentally through manipulating information about the academic potential of their pupils. Although high hopes had been held for such work, the appropriate conclusion seems to be that teacher expectancies in themselves have little power to cause different outcomes for the students (see Thorndike 1968, 1969; Claiborn 1969; Elashoff and Snow 1971; Fleming and Anttonen 1971; Dusek and O'Connell 1973; Mendels and Flanders 1973). Yet blaming the teacher for causing poor children's learning difficulties through insufficient support and encouragement on her part has remained a popular viewpoint (see Stein 1971), made plausible by the error of believing that this is the only kind of possibility remaining if the children's problem does not stem from inadequate intelligence. Lost sight of is the idea that teachers can have the best of intentions and yet not be equipped to help children who lack the preparation regarding basic academic skill development that a middle-class background provides.

Sometimes those who look to the child's motivation or attitudes for the answer recommend direct attempts to improve the learner's self-concept. If, somehow, one raises the child's self-esteem or sense of competence as such, it is proposed that better learning will result. Evidence that such is the case, however, is hard to come by; simply finding a correlation between sense of competence and academic achievement will not do, of course, since it can well mean that those who learn more feel more competent as a result rather than the other way around. Yet some even go so far as to suggest that the *primary* issue for a child who has not learned a needed skill like reading is not to learn the skill but to come to feel greater self-confidence and sense of control (see Elkind 1972; Stephens and Delys 1973). Such an approach seems indirect indeed, when there is every reason to expect that, if learning of the skill could be brought about, the child would feel greater self-esteem as a result—in other words, that *feeling* more competent is a natural by-product of *becoming* so. Making refurbishing of the self-concept the focus can only imply the view that little can be wrong with how the skill is taught. Or as a proponent of open education like Ginsburg (1972) would put it, the poor child in fact does not need to be taught at all but simply needs a hospitable and encouraging environment.

Suppose instead that how the skill is taught is precisely the problem for poor children. Suppose that their difficulty with academic achievement stems neither from intellects impaired by experiential deficits during the early years nor from inadequate motivation but from instruction that does not teach what they need to learn. In other words, suppose that middle-class homes contribute substantially (though implicitly) to the elaboration of reading skill before formal schooling begins and that instruction at school unknowingly takes for granted this contribution—one which is lacking for children from poverty backgrounds. If this were the case, one would have to look afresh at the issue of what it really would mean to teach a skill like reading from scratch—what it would mean to avoid presupposing in one's instruction all the acquisitions that the middle-class child typically already has under control but the low-income child does not. This was what we undertook to do in the tutorial program that we developed.

Tutoring in reading by nonprofessionals for poverty-background children had, of course, been tried before but not in ways that went much beyond what regular classroom procedures provide as regards the nature of the training offered. Some of this work has been spelled out in detail and has given evidence of a certain degree of success (see Ellson, Harris, and Barber 1968; Staats, Minke, and Butts 1970). The benefits found have been largely limited, however, to the specific content of the tutoring. Benefits of a general kind for reading competence have not been demonstrable with any clarity. We took such work as our point of departure, wondering if the limitation on its degree of success arose from its failure to provide for systematic skill development in what the tutor did with the child. If some success could be obtained even under those circumstances, perhaps the degree of success from carrying out systematic skill development would be striking.

What, then, is the nature of the subskill elaboration that must take place if reading competence is to come about? It would seem crucially important to know the relations between letters and sounds and to be able to make use of those relations in turning printed material into the familiar spoken form of the language one already knows. Without this, each word has to be learned de novo, calling for an inordinate amount of rote memorization that is made all the more difficult by the negative transfer resulting from the continual recurrence of the same letters in different words. If a child had to learn each word anew in this manner, learning to read would clearly be an extremely difficult task. Although some beginning reading programs largely proceed as if each word were indeed to be learned as a whole and no help could be obtained by considering the letters it contains, any child who reads well knows letter-sound correspondences and makes use of that knowledge. Yet even programs that do concern themselves with letter-sound relations fall far short of providing anything like what would be required for developing the needed skills in the case of a child who is starting from scratch. On the basis of home experiences, middle-class children typically start school with a good bit of knowledge about letters and sounds, and thus these children can generally make use of letter-sound correspondences in learning to read even when this receives little explicit attention in the classroom. Poor children, on the other hand, are far less likely to have had the home experiences that deliver the needed subskills. They are thus most unlikely, without explicit tuition, to pick up in a timely manner the relations between letters and sounds and to make use of those relations in learning to read. When explicit attempts are made to teach these matters, poor children are still unlikely to pick up these relations and to use them because such instruction generally does not provide the skills in sound recognition and manipulation that they need. In light of what we saw as the significance of having and using knowledge of letter-sound relationships, therefore, it seemed clear to us where tutoring ought to begin.

Some object to an emphasis on letter-sound relationships by pointing out that there are irregularities in these relationships (see Smith 1973). The relationships are hardly random, however, and there is no need for them to be completely regular in order to be of help to the child. The objection also has been raised that concern with deciphering letter-sound correspondences takes the beginning reader's mind away from the task of comprehension. As Chall (1967) points out, however, beginning readers' difficulties in comprehending printed material typically seem to come not from too much concern with letter-sound correspondences but from incompetence at deciphering sounds from letters—and to disappear when the child learns how to do this better. But the most crucial objection that has been raised to an emphasis on teaching letter-sound relationships is the disarmingly simple point that some children—usually, but not only, poor children—do not profit from it. They do not profit because—as we have just noted is often the case for poor children—they do not recognize the sounds in words and are not able to blend sounds together. It is widely believed that children who have difficulty doing these things cannot be taught them and that one must wait until their readiness has matured (see Roswell and Chall, 1956–59; Kavanagh and Mattingly 1972, p. 328). This belief, it seems to us, is quite misguided.

Why is this belief so strong? Its major basis seems to be the failure of such children to learn about sounds from the teaching attempts that have standardly been made. But the kinds of rhyming and sound matching tasks that have been tried already presuppose a fair amount of skill at sound recognition and manipulation! The belief also seems based on the view that the children in question are deficient in auditory discrimination ability, as presumably indicated by their low scores on standard tests of auditory discrimination (see Wepman 1960; Deutsch 1964; Plumer 1970). It turns out, however, that those low scores were artifacts of irrelevant sources of difficulty (see Berlin and Dill 1967; Blank 1968) and did not arise from impaired auditory discrimination ability at all. The grounds for believing there was a sizable group of first graders, particularly from poverty backgrounds, who simply could not learn to recognize and blend sounds, thus seemed to evaporate on closer inspection. The situation appeared rather to be one of their not having been provided with the kinds of experiences that would do the job. Low-income children, then, needed to acquire certain subskills if they were to learn to read efficiently. They were failing in large numbers to develop reading competence on schedule in first grade simply because adequate provision had not been made for teaching them these subskills. Rather than being limited to memorization of whole words by rote, with the huge burden of learning each word anew and the problems of negative transfer—and rather than having to wait until enough time passes for readiness to "mature" (which makes sense only if the subskills in question really are not teachable)—these children needed instruction of a quite different order than they were getting.

What we believe such children need to get by instruction are easily accessible and manipulable concepts of the sounds to which letters are related, or phonemes. Unlike most middle-class children in first grade, the children we are talking about, although they can make the necessary auditory discriminations, do not seem to possess such concepts. For instance, they can distinguish between "ill" and "in," but they do not realize that each of these words is made up of two sounds and that the first sounds are alike in the two words and the second sounds are different. They are not able to deal with phonemes in abstraction from their contexts (see Gleitman and Rozin 1973; Venezky in press). Although phonemes are not simple concepts, there seemed to be no reason for thinking that systematic, step-by-step instruction could not bring about the necessary skills in recognizing and manipulating them.

Ways were needed in which to call attention to phonemes and to the features differentiating one phoneme from another, so that a child would have a usable concept of a given phoneme before the child was asked to learn a letter corresponding to it. Various ways seemed feasible for establishing these concepts, such as "concept formation" or "concept attainment" tasks where the child would learn to differentiate between exemplars and nonexemplars of words that start with a particular sound. The child could be helped, if necessary, by such methods as having the tutor segment the words and then having the child do it. And then, ways were needed in which to bring the child to the ability to blend phonemes together into words. Again, there seemed to be possible techniques for accomplishing this, such as having the child try to identify a word pronounced sound by sound and doing some blending oneself if necessary.

In sum, procedures for providing the skills needed seemed feasible; the procedures were straightforward enough that non-professionals could readily carry them out with the children who needed them; and, because the procedures were to be applied in a tutoring framework, it could be assured that a given child had mastered one activity before moving on to another activity that presupposed it.

The considerations just reviewed, then, determined the form that our tutoring program took. The aim was to provide what first graders not able to learn to read from customary class-room teaching would need in order to achieve basic reading competence on schedule. And the intent was to do this with highly specific, step-by-step materials that anyone who was literate, liked working with children, was responsible, and was patient could readily be taught to apply as a tutor. Mastery of one step would be assured before the child passed on to the next. Intended to be used on a half an hour per school day basis during the first-grade year, independently of the class-room teacher's reading instruction, our program was divided into three parts. In Part I, the child learns to recognize sounds at the start of words, to recognize letter shapes, and to connect the sounds to the letters. In Part II, the child learns to synthe-size words from the sounds represented by the letters. And in Part III, the child learns to apply these skills in reading class-room materials.

Part I consists of ten steps that are followed with each letter of the alphabet in turn. In Step 1, "introduction to the sound," tutor and child work on isolating the starting sounds in exam-ples of words which start with the sound a given letter usually is for. In Step 2, "the two-picture game," the tutor uses pic-tures—"game-pictures"—depicting objects the names of which start with the sound for the letter in question, pairs them with game-pictures starting with other sounds, and teaches the child to choose the former. In Step 3, "the yes-no game," the tutor uses a shuffled pile of game-pictures some of which do and some of which do not have names that start with the sound for the given letter, and the child learns to differentiate the two groups. In Step 4, "letter tracing," the given letter's form is introduced through an "alpha-picture"—the letter is embedded in a visually compelling way in a picture the name of which starts with the letter's sound, with the child learning that the letter represents the starting sound of the alpha-picture's name and also learning to trace the letter. Step 5, "letter drawing," presents the alpha-picture again and now teaches the child to draw the letter without tracing. In Step 6, "the picture-matching game with the letter-drawing sheets," the child learns to place game-pictures the names of which start with the sound being worked on or with certain other sounds on the correct alpha-pictures for those sounds. Step 7, "the word-matching game with the letter-drawing sheets," is like Step 6 except now the tutor says words instead of giving game-pictures, with the child learning to point to the correct alpha-picture for the starting sound of each word that the tutor presents. Step 8, "the picture-matching game with the letter-cards," and Step 9, "the word-matching game with the letter-cards," are like Steps 6 and 7, respectively, except now the child learns to link up game-pictures or words with "letter-cards"—cards showing letters only—instead of with the alpha-pictures, thus eliminating the reminder of each letter's sound that the alpha-picture provides. And finally in Step 10, "giving the sounds for the letters," the child is shown in shuffled order the letter-cards for the current letter and all letters worked on already, giving for each the letter's sound name and a word starting with that sound.

Part II of the program involves three steps, each of which is completed with all materials that are given for it before the next step is undertaken. In Step 1, "the which-picture game," the child learns to identify each game-picture in successive sets of three from hearing the tutor say the separate sounds that, when blended, make up its name. Pauses between sounds get decreased if the child has too much difficulty, but ultimately the child must make correct identifications from hearing the separate sounds alone. In Step 2, "building and reading the names of some game-pictures," the child learns to build and read the names of successive sets of game-pictures from letter-cards. For each game-picture in a given set, the child with the tutor's help finds the letter-card for each sound in the picture's name, builds up these letter-cards in sequence, says the sounds they are for, and hears them blended by the tutor. Then the tutor assembles the letter-cards for each picture's name and has the child read the word, giving help in sounding out if necessary until the child can accomplish this reading without help. Finally the child does the assembling of each picture's name from the letter-cards. Step 3, "building and reading some more simple words," is similar to Step 2 except that no game-pictures are used, the words to be built and read only being spoken. For each of a large number of sets of words, the tutor first builds words with the child, then the tutor builds words for the child to read until the child can do so without help, and finally the child builds the words. After completion of Step 3, the child moves on to Part III of the program.

In Part III, the tutor systematically goes through the classroom reading materials with the child, using precisely spelled out instructional procedures. The child first reads all the new words introduced on a given page of text from word-cards that the tutor has prepared, with the tutor following explicit routines for teaching words that the child fails to get. These routines utilize the letter-sound regularities the child knows already and present exceptions to them as necessary, the child sounding out letters and, if needed, receiving help with blending. Then the child reads the page of text itself, with the tutor again following routines for the teaching of words missed by the child. Practice continues until the child makes no more than a specified number of errors and follows the meaning of what is read. Then this process is repeated with the next page of text, and so on until the story is completed. When the story has been read with few enough errors and sufficient comprehension to meet certain criteria, the tutor proceeds to the next story. Further review procedures are included as well.

Our tutorial program, then, is highly systematic and cumulative, making sure that a child is asked at a given point in time to learn no more than is feasible in terms of what the child knows already. Explicit procedures are provided to help the child when trouble is encountered and mastery criteria must be met as the child proceeds; since the program really *does* start from scratch, all prerequisite component skills that the child needs are in fact taught rather than presupposed. The tutor works independently of the teacher, who has no new responsibilities or obligations introduced as a result of the program's use but simply proceeds with her classroom instruction in whatever way and with whatever materials she wishes. While basically intended for the first-grade year, the tutorial program also is suited for second graders who have not learned to read and kindergartners who seem headed that way. Its function is to catch children at the start of school who are not able to learn basic reading competence on schedule from what goes on in the classroom and to get that skill established for them before all the negative effects of failure have had a chance to mount from successive years of falling further behind.

To evaluate the program's efficacy, we applied it in field research at two predominantly black inner-city public schools on Chicago's South Side. The program was run just as it would be under conditions of normal operation, rather than in an idealized "hothouse" version, so we could expect our results to indicate what the program could accomplish if put into regular use. Children were chosen for tutoring and tutors were recruited from the community in ways no different than could generally apply, and the program's operation was exposed to the kinds of real-life problems that will be found at public schools with an inner-city location.

The target population for the program's application is, of course, children for whom the prognosis is that they will not learn to read on schedule with customary classroom instruction. To define this population at the schools in which we worked, we administered standard tests—the *Metropolitan Readiness Tests* (Hildreth, Griffiths, and McGauvran 1966, 1969)—low scores on which indicate a low probability of learning to read in first grade. The ninety-eight children who scored within the bottom 40 percent in terms of national norms on the Metropolitan at the start of the year were taken as our target group of "low academic-readiness" children. Their median score was at the twenty-fifth percentile for the national sample. There are, of course, various ways one could define the target group, and this represented just one of many different possibilities.

What made our work an experiment rather than simply the normal, intended operation of the tutorial program was that not all of these low-readiness children but only a randomly selected subset of them received the program, thus permitting comparisons with control children; and that extensive evaluation testing to assess the program's utility was given to tutored and control children near the end of the school year. We were hoping to demonstrate strong benefits of a general kind for reading competence as a result of our program—the kind of benefits that other tutoring work had failed to find. Such work gave us essentially a benchmark indicating what tutoring of a comparable type but with other materials was able to accomplish. If we found the sort of benefits for general reading skill that we expected, it thus would be evident that not tutoring per se but the nature of our tutorial materials in particular was making the difference.

The low-readiness children in each of the eight classrooms making up the study's sample were randomly assigned to experimental and control conditions on a within-classroom basis, thus taking account of any teacher differences. Those children in the experimental condition received daily tutoring with our program from community adults who were recommended by the principals of the two schools where the work was to take place. No educational credentials or requirements were stipulated for these tutor jobs; the principals were to think only in terms of neighborhood adults who, besides knowing how to read, seemed to like and work well with children, were responsible, and were patient. Obviously there is more than one way to locate community adults who meet these criteria; indeed, they may be on hand already in teachers' aides or paraprofessional positions. The point is that people readily able to become successful tutors with our program are abundantly available in the same communities that contain large numbers of children who fail to learn to read in first grade.

Our tutors all were black mothers, ranging in age from the mid-thirties to the mid-fifties, with previous jobs that had included such work as food server in a cafeteria and cashier. They received about three weeks of training at the beginning of the school year and monitoring on about a once-weekly basis thereafter. Such supervision, provided here by one of us, can in the general utilization of the program come from any of various types of personnel—for instance, reading specialists, school psychologists, or particular teachers. All it takes is mastery of the program's specifics together with sufficient administrative skills. Indeed, as time goes on, some tutors themselves should come to know the ropes well enough to take on much of this role.

What, then, does this approach accomplish? Consider first what happened in the tutoring situation. All of the children who were tutored made progress, and practically all of them —86 percent—learned to read quite competently within the year, as judged from what their reading came to be like in Part III of the program. We had been warned that low-income, minority-group first graders such as we were working with would get quickly bored with all the repetitive elements in the tutorial program, that they would not pay attention for anything like the half-hour period of the tutoring session, and that there would be frequent "behavior problems." Quite to the contrary, however, we found that almost all of the tutored children paid close attention and worked very hard during the sessions. And this was without any use of "material reinforcers" or other extrinsic inducements of the kinds sometimes thought necessary to keep poverty-background children working on school tasks. In our view, a major reason for whatever disruptive behavior these children may show in school is that they are being asked to carry out tasks that make no sense to them, tasks for which they lack the prerequisite skills. When, instead, they are asked to do something that is within their competence to master, they work hard to do so and find the resultant knowledge of their accomplishment a sufficient reward to keep them energetically forging ahead. Rather than being a *cause* of poor learning, then, disruptive behavior from such children seems more likely to be an *effect* of demands that are incomprehensible to them and which they therefore cannot hope to meet.

What about evidence apart from observations made in the tutoring itself? How do the tutored children compare to the controls? Individual evaluation testing of the target group of low-readiness children—eighty-eight in all, down from the starting sample of ninety-eight—was carried out in the spring of the year by an examiner who was unaware of the children's status as experimentals or controls. A substantial battery of

tests was used, aimed at providing as ecologically representative a sampling as feasible of what is meant by competence
at basic reading, along with some information about sound-
identification skills.

Tests of our own devising assessed the reading of words
and of sentences based on classroom text vocabularies. The
words and the sentences were ordered to reflect increasingly
difficult vocabulary entries. In the case of sentence reading,
we tried to develop sentences that, while drawing on classroom
text vocabularies, were new to the children, that is, were not in
their classroom texts. The sentence-reading task required the
child to answer comprehension questions indicating whether
what was read had been understood. Standardized reading
achievement tests, in turn, were used to provide word-reading
and passage-reading yardsticks that had been constructed without any reference to the classroom text materials—the word
recognition lists and reading passages of Spache's *Diagnostic
Reading Scales* (Spache 1963*a*, 1963*b*, 1963*c*, 1972*a*, 1972*b*,
1972*c*). Here again, the materials are sequenced to reflect
increasing levels of difficulty. As in the sentence-reading task
of our own devising, Spache's passage-reading scales include
comprehension questions indicating whether the child understands what he or she reads. The passages were, of course,
quite unfamiliar to the child. These various tests taken together, then, provided a fairly extensive sampling of the child's
actual reading behavior: skill at recognizing words, and skill
at reading sentences and passages with comprehension of their
meaning. The Spache tests, furthermore, were built quite apart
from any reference to the classroom texts. If tutored children
did better than controls at these Spache tests, therefore, it
would be appropriate to conclude that the tutorial program
produced benefits of a quite general kind for reading competence. Also included in our test battery were tests from Spache
and of our own devising assessing the children's knowledge of
the sounds that letters represent and that words start with.

The tutored and control samples of low-readiness children
looked strikingly different in reading competence as judged
from the evaluation tests. Both samples begin the year with a

median score at the twenty-fifth percentile of the national norms for the *Metropolitan Readiness Tests*; the median child in these groups scores within the bottom quarter of beginning first graders given the Metropolitan nationally. Yet by the spring of that year the two groups have diverged sharply in reading skill. For example, in terms of the reading of words on the test derived from classroom text vocabularies, estimates based on the test scores indicate that the median tutored child can recognize on the order of 150 words, while the median control child can recognize a little over fifty words. As to the reading and comprehending of increasingly difficult sentences that draw on classroom text vocabularies but insofar as possible have never been seen before, the median tutored child correctly answers 19.5 comprehension questions while the median for control children is less than half that—out of a maximum possible score of twenty-five questions correct. The tutored children—but not the controls—are, by and large, reading and comprehending even the more difficult of the sentences they were given.

Turning to the reading of words and sentences that make up standardized reading achievement tests and thus are developed without reference to the classroom text vocabularies, consider first the reading of words on the word recognition lists from Spache's *Diagnostic Reading Scales*—words calibrated for increasing levels of difficulty. The median tutored child correctly reads twenty-six of these words—the median control child, eight or nine. In terms of estimated grade placement levels, about two-thirds of the tutored children are performing near grade level or beyond on the Spache word recognition lists, compared to about one-third of the controls. Consider next the Spache reading-passages, where the child attempts to read passages of increasing difficulty and must not only read but also demonstrate comprehension of a given passage in order to receive credit for it. Grade placement levels estimated on the basis of the results indicate that half of the tutored children perform near grade level or beyond on Spache's reading-passages, compared to about one-sixth of the controls.

The findings just reviewed add up to a rather clear picture. The tutored children, by and large, demonstrate considerable competence of a quite generalized sort at reading; the control children, by and large, do not. And this competence has been achieved within a matter of months for children who are "bad bets" academically—children who usually fail to learn in the classroom situation. What it takes is neighborhood adults without professional credentials who are trained to function as tutors with a completely explicit tutorial program that systematically establishes and cumulates the mastery of component skills which these children have not been learning at home and which they need for reading competence. Low academic-readiness children who have received this help find themselves by the spring of the year able to read even fairly difficult words and able to read and understand the meaning of even fairly difficult sentences and passages that they confront for the first time. By one criterion, two-thirds of the tutored children compared to one-third of the controls are performing near grade level or better than that; by another criterion, the respective proportions are one-half versus one-sixth. Pervasive differences between tutored and control children also were found in their performances on the sound-identification skills tests they received. And in all of this, we are talking not just about effects that are highly significant statistically by diverse kinds of tests but also are of magnitudes that testify directly to their practical utility. They are, furthermore, effects that turn out to be comparable for the different tutors and schools, which means that the tutorial program is sufficiently clear and sharp to have its impact regardless of the inevitable kinds of variability that will occur across tutors and schools where it is used.

Teaching low-income, minority-group children to read by the end of first grade may not solve all of their problems with life or even with school—but it should help. Just how much it helps awaits further follow-up studies. What we have demonstrated is an approach that should bring about timely competence at basic reading for most such children who do not otherwise learn on schedule, an approach that is eminently feasible for general implementation. Its form was dictated by some new perspectives on the development of cognitive competence, and its relevance for grappling with the real-world phenomenon of poor children's school failure was shown under representative conditions of actual use in the field. Next we turn to some further considerations bearing on the nature of the approach and its application.

Teaching What Needs to Be Learned

You would think that the first order of business in trying to help low-income children do better at school would be to analyze the instructional process in cognitive terms so as to determine whether they are being taught what they need to learn. Since the children's problem is the failure to learn certain desired school competences like reading, the first question would seem to be whether the instruction they receive supplies all the cognitive elements needed for elaborating the given academic attainment and does so in a sequence that makes sure knowledge is not presupposed which has not yet been provided. Yet, as we have seen, this is not the question that usually gets asked. The assumption is widespread that the trouble lies elsewhere—in deficiencies of intellect or problems of motivation. The reality, however, seems to be quite simply that no one is teaching these children what they need to learn if the given academic goal is to be attained on a reasonable time schedule.

There can, of course, be a perfectly good reason for not teaching what needs to be learned—one may want to but not know how. Sometimes the significance of the kinds of component skills we have been talking about is recognized but it is believed that these skills simply cannot be taught. This position has been put forth with particular clarity recently by Gleitman and Rozin (1973), who are quite well aware both that the child who is trying to learn to read needs to deal with phonemes and that the ability to do so is frequently lacking. But, given the complicated nature of phonemes and the way they overlap in speech, Gleitman and Rozin believe that the needed skill cannot be taught: "The barrier to acquisition of alphabetic units appears to be purely psychoacoustic: the child has difficulty in segmenting the sound-stream into phonemic chunks and therefore cannot map the discrete alphabetic units onto equivalently discrete speech units. . . . There is no known practical procedure for solving [this difficulty] for the child, nor is there any adequate theoretical position that points to such a procedure" (1973, p. 479).

Gleitman and Rozin rightly inveigh against the tendency to conclude from the problems surrounding decoding that decoding doesn't matter. Teaching a child to decode, they stress, "is teaching him a major essential of reading" (1973, p. 479). What then do they suggest? Dealing with phonemes, they believe, cannot be taught, but dealing with syllables is relatively easy. Hence what they would have us do is teach children to read by starting with visual symbols for syllables rather than phonemes. The children are in this way to be brought to understand how visual symbols correspond to sounds. As the authors themselves point out, however, this learning cannot replace learning of the alphabetic code. The children are still going to have to learn to recognize and manipulate phonemes and relate them to letters if they are to gain competence at reading. Initial use of the syllables only makes this task easier, it is hoped, by providing the child beforehand with a grasp of the principle of orthography mapping sound.

Gleitman and Rozin do not say much about just why they believe it is impossible to teach directly the needed skills in recognition and manipulation of phonemes. They seem to be influenced both by the complexity of phonemes and by the fact that, when standard methods of teaching these skills are used, many children fail to learn. However, as we have argued, the standard instructional methods largely presuppose the very skills they are intended to deliver; and although the complicated nature of phonemes does account for the problems children have in phoneme recognition and manipulation, it does not imply that these skills cannot be taught. As our research has shown, there *are* ways of teaching these skills quite successfully and by methods capable of wide application. Contrary to what Gleitman and Rozin believe, then, we have found that there is nothing to keep one from teaching children directly the skills in dealing with phonemes that they need to learn; this, it would seem, is clearly what ought to be done.

In the case of Gleitman and Rozin, of course, there is considerable concern about trying to teach children what needs to be learned. As we see it, they simply fail to recognize what the possibilities of instruction really are in the domain under consideration. Unlike Gleitman and Rozin, however, the great majority of experts giving advice on how to ameliorate the academic difficulties children are having in the public schools do not look at the instructional process at all. For the most part, the need for teaching to supply the cognitive ingredients required for the development of academic skills is not really taken seriously. That some children, especially those from poverty backgrounds, may merely lack certain prerequisite skills that ought to be taught them, is a point that does not get considered. It is not considered even by such writers as Cole, Gay, Glick, and Sharp (1971), who have been much concerned to counter the "deficit" view of intellectual development among minority groups and who also recognize that minority group children who are motivated and try to work hard in school still are likely to have trouble.

Cole, Gay, Glick, and Sharp (1971), working with members of a tribal group in West Africa, found that, although uneducated group members sometimes would fail to use concepts and relationships in learning or problem solving, with certain changes in the situations such use would become evident. For example, although these subjects did not transpose relationally in a task involving brightness differences, they did do so in a task involving size differences. Similarly, although they had difficulty solving certain logical problems, changes in the particular content of the problems led to the feasibility of solution. Cole et al. (1971) conclude that "cultural differences in cognition reside more in the situations to which particular cognitive processes are applied than in the existence of a process in one cultural group and its absence in another" (p. 233). What they take this to imply for the school problems of minority group children in America is that further research should be done on the nature of the children's activities on the streets and in school, in order to figure out how to get the children to apply in school the requisite learning and problem-solving abilities they are demonstrating on the streets.

We are, of course, in wholehearted agreement with Cole et al. on the point that no cultural group has deficits in broad cognitive processes such as the utilization of concepts or relations; indeed we find it difficult, given the kinds of behavior exhibited by human beings everywhere, even to entertain the idea of such deficits as a serious possibility. But we cannot agree with Cole et al. when they attribute the low academic achievement of minority group children simply to their failure to apply in school situations the cognitive processes of which they are capable. Again, the question never gets asked whether school instruction supplies what is needed without presupposing prior skills that low-income children, because of their background, have not yet developed. Academic achievement involves specific skills that are not just a matter of the application of broad cognitive abilities but require particular experiences for their development. It seems crucially important for the schools to see to it that these experiences get provided and not simply to take for granted those that may be typical for children of the dominant subculture but not for other children. As we pointed out earlier, middle-class children, before they ever enter first grade, typically have already developed a good bit of skill in dealing with sounds and letters, while poor children have much less frequently had the experiences required to develop these skills. It is little wonder, then, that when—as is typically the case—school instruction does not insure that these skills are acquired, minority group children and poor children more generally experience difficulties in learning to read. Further research on the nature of their activities on the streets and in school does not seem likely to do much for these children. What *will* help them is to make provisions for their acquiring the skills they need to learn.

Experts who have directly immersed themselves in the American public school with the aim of helping children who have trouble learning still can completely ignore the simple idea of teaching children the skills which the academic achievement requires. An example that underlines the contrast between what we believe is needed and what can be recommended instead is provided by Furth and Wachs (1974), whose answer to the problem of children for whom school presents difficulties is to have them go to "schools for thinking" in which they play Piaget-inspired "thinking games." Concerned with the prevention of school failures, particularly failures in learning how to read, Furth and Wachs propose an extensive collection of tasks for the teacher to carry out with the class which are to "help develop a child whose intelligence and personality are sufficiently mature and articulated so that he becomes capable of reading-based learning" (1974, p. 274). The games cover a broad range of activities: creeping, rolling, balancing, hopping, and skipping; crossing one's eyes, and following visual targets; tearing paper, and moving one's tongue; block matching, pegboards, and puzzles; discriminating pitch, loudness, and duration of sounds; feeling with one's fingers, and drawing; classifying and ordering; pretending; and a great deal more. With few exceptions, the activities have no direct relationship to academic skills; they are largely perceptual-motor activities thought to be of significance for the child's overall intellectual development.

But what children must acquire in school if they are to cope with its demands are basic academic skills like reading, not skill in hopping or solving puzzles or tearing paper. To urge schools to work with children on such games makes sense only if one assumes that the games will facilitate development of a far more general sort. Furth and Wachs, of course, believe that this is the case; they hold that their games provide the prerequisites a child needs for school learning. This seems largely a matter of faith, however, with little ground for support other than Piaget's general view that thinking develops from the coordination of external actions, a view which hardly can be said to imply the specific utility of the games they suggest for primary school children. The only other kind of basis provided is a statement here and there pointing out, for instance, that a six-year-old with insufficient movement control will have a hard time scanning a page, gripping a pencil, looking up and down from chalkboard to paper, and competing in games with other children. Is one really to believe, however, that the reason such vast numbers of children are failing to learn to read is that they can not move their eyes across a page, or look up and down, or compete in play? On the street or in the playground, children who fail to learn in school often seem extremely proficient at all sorts of activities involving highly elaborate sensorimotor control.

Furth and Wachs's games, then, are supposed to facilitate the child's "readiness" to learn school skills, but there seems little reason to believe that children who have trouble in school are lacking in what the games will provide. Once again, the problem these children have is seen as one of some general kind of deficiency: they are not "ready," their "intelligence" is not developed sufficiently, they have not yet reached the necessary "level of thinking." Once again, it is completely taken for granted that, if some such general deficiency were not present, these children would be learning from the instruction they receive. Furth and Wachs do not pay any attention to the teaching of academic skills like reading; they treat instruction in such matters as nonproblematical. When children are not learning to read, however, the obvious question to ask before any other would seem to be what the specific skills are that are required for learning and how instruction can provide those which the children do not possess. Why assume that the only thing which might keep a child from learning to read is some general lack that is to be remedied by activities far removed from the arena of concern? Why isn't "readiness to read" a function of particular subskills like the recognition and manipulation of phonemes, and why isn't "lack of readiness" to be remedied by systematic instruction in the specific subskills needed?

How the recommendations of Furth and Wachs work out in a concrete instance is most revealing. A first-grade boy they describe as "not able to attend to a task," toward the end of the year "requested on several occasions to participate in formal reading activities. The teacher suggested to him that he was not ready for formal reading instruction but he persisted. Finally the teacher brought him over to observe the reading group and showed him how he would have to sit still at the table, listen quietly, and attend. The boy reflected for a while and said, 'I guess you are right. I am not ready yet!' " (1974, p. 63). What Furth and Wachs prescribe for such a child is activities like use of a balance board, walking on a rail, and hopping—activities, in short, that have nothing to do with reading. Gaining better control at such activities, they feel, is what a child like this needs to prepare him for classroom learning, although no evidence for such a claim is provided. Rather than let such a child fall still further behind on reading through spending his time on activities that do not demonstrably help with that skill, what we would do with him, of course, is give him training in directly relevant subskills. The inattentiveness and flightiness evinced by so many of the low academic-readiness children with whom we worked disappeared when they were presented with tasks that they could make sense of and master. Such "behavior problems" turned out not to be fundamental and persistent traits at all but merely the consequence of continually being in a situation where what the children were asked to do was impossible for them to fulfill.

Despite Furth and Wachs's strong claims to the effect that the way to avoid learning failures in school is through a curriculum like theirs, which presumably stimulates general thinking capacities, they give no evidence that this is the case. Indeed, after completely taking over a classroom for a year and a half, the most that could be said was that children in their program did no worse academically than comparable children not in the program. But the impetus for trying the program in the first place was the high incidence of poor academic performance found among these children! Furth and Wachs, however, never question their belief that the problem for children who do not learn a skill like reading at school lies in lack of general intellectual readiness rather than in anything about how the skill is taught. From their point of view, "It is an illusion to conceive of the educational process, particularly at the primary school age, as a cumulative addition of learned performances that can be programmed and controlled at will" (1974, p. 289). The programming of such cumulation is, of course, precisely what we seem to have achieved for the skill of reading, with the consequence that children of the kind Furth and Wachs fail to help academically learn reading on schedule. Rather than being an illusion, such cumulation seems to be at the very heart of what needs to take place, with its absence being responsible for much of the troubles that children have with school learning.

There are, of course, other recent efforts besides our own to provide for the acquisition of skills children need for school achievement. Educational television has made efforts along such lines in the case of "Sesame Street" and "The Electric Company." These programs certainly try to focus on the teaching of needed academic skills and try to do so in a manner that will catch and hold children's attention. Although television does have the potential to reach large numbers of children, it does not enable them to engage in any kind of activity of their own which can be subjected to monitoring and evaluation. Nor, of course, can it in any way be adapted to individual learning needs. These would seem to be crucial limitations on what it can do for the low academic-readiness children who constitute our target of concern.

A different kind of hardware, on the other hand—the computer—can readily be programmed to provide feedback concerning a learner's activity, and in a highly individualized fashion. Some of the advocates of "computer assisted instruction" (CAI) such as Atkinson and his collaborators (see Atkinson 1968, 1972, 1974; Atkinson and Paulson 1972; Fletcher and Atkinson 1972) believe that computers are exactly what is needed for the problem with which we are concerned: "Significant progress in dealing with the nation's problem of teaching reading will require individually prescribed programs, and sophisticated programs will necessitate some degree of computer intervention" (Atkinson 1972, p. 929).

With the computer's potential for appropriately sequencing instruction that will meet the individual learner's needs, is not hardware of the CAI type the answer?

The appropriate reply seems to be no, at least for the problem we are concerned with—teaching basic reading competence to first graders who do not learn in the classroom. As we have argued, the crucial difficulty for most of these children seems to center on sound recognition and blending. These children need to learn to work with phonemes, the sounds that letters represent—to analyze words into constituent phonemes, to assemble phonemes into words. The categories of sounds involved in these activities are, as we noted in chapter 3, highly complex in physical terms. So are the categories of meaning involved in much of what gets read in regular textual materials. If CAI might ever be able to handle such matters satisfactorily —which is questionable—it clearly cannot do so now. In contrast to the great physical complexities involved in these matters, however, stands the simplicity in psychological terms of what is involved. This is just the kind of situation where human beings should serve eminently well as the instructional vehicle. And that, of course, is exactly what we found to be the case, since community adults without any particular educational credentials were readily trainable as tutors for our program. Thus, a large pool of qualified personnel stands available to carry out what needs doing pedagogically and is eager for work opportunities of just such kinds. Having tutors from the same neighborhoods as the children who need help would seem to provide two further instructional benefits over CAI, namely, a common language background shared by tutors and tutees and the compellingness of direct interaction between people.

Quite apart from the pedagogical advantages of individualized subskill cumulation mediated by a human tutor rather than by CAI, use of a tutorial program like ours also seems more feasible for widespread application than is CAI. Use of CAI at best is restricted to schools that have established the needed kind of terminal equipment and time-sharing computer access, and it is difficult to imagine this readily taking place for all the schools containing any first graders not learning to read on schedule in class. Even if CAI were installed, computers are in no sense foolproof. Computers break down, they malfunction in various ways, they do not readily achieve the reliability of working on a day-in day-out basis despite tough and relentless usage. Human beings trained to follow the easy-to-learn steps of our tutorial program are, we would submit, much more dependable means for the delivery of instructional services to children. Tutoring by nonprofessionals with a program like ours also is usable in all kinds of settings that computer terminals would never reach—community centers, neighborhood churches, and any other places where activities serving to promote community welfare might take place. It can even go on at home! In contrast, then, to Atkinson's conviction that CAI offers the only means for effectively individualizing instruction in beginning reading, we would propose that use of our tutorial program for children who do not learn with customary classroom arrangements not only is more cogent pedagogically than CAI but more practical as well.

Besides issues of pedagogy and practicality, there is a third point that bears mentioning in comparing CAI with our tutorial program as tools for individualized instruction in basic reading. Even if the grounds just reviewed failed to give our type of tutorial approach the edge over CAI, we would argue that our approach remains preferable in sheer value terms. It seems more desirable for children to learn things from another person than from a piece of machinery. Especially in a society that drifts toward more and more automation, it seems important to expand rather than contract the occasions and settings where meaningful human interaction takes place. A child and a responsive adult doing things together for their mutual benefit constitutes, we submit, more of a social good than CAI. It also seems better to create the kind of meaning for adult lives that work as a tutor provides than to devote more resources to automation. The role of tutor with our type of program makes constructive use of large numbers of human beings who are looking for activities that will help and contribute to the well-being of others. Work with a program like ours produces for tutors a valid sense of accomplishment, for they know that they are critically important in helping these children learn to read. Both in the case of people seeking paying jobs and people looking for volunteer work, tutoring with our type of program can be a highly fulfilling role for many noncredentialed adults who are perfectly capable of learning it. It is better to put more meaning into these people's lives than to create more electronic hardware.

We have concentrated in our work on what it takes to establish basic reading competence on schedule in first grade for disadvantaged children, the category to which the majority of the children not learning in the classroom belong. But not all the children who fail to learn reading in the first-grade classroom are from minority groups or poverty backgrounds. Sometimes this happens with middle-class white children too. When the children are low-income blacks, Puerto Ricans, or other minority group members, they may be labeled "mentally retarded," and little effort may be made to push their progress in academic skills—as, for example, Mercer (1974) has pointed out. When the children are middle-class whites, however, the label they receive is more likely to be something like "learning disability," "reading disability," or "dyslexia." We feel that for many such children the situation is comparable to the one we have described for poverty children who do not learn, and that our tutorial program should be helpful in their case too.

There has been increasing concern recently with learning disabilities or learning disorders. Sizable numbers of children fail to learn normally in school even though they are of apparently normal intelligence, have apparently normal sensory and motor functions, and are not from disadvantaged backgrounds. The emotional difficulties some of these children have are sometimes viewed as the source of their learning problems, but frequently the emotional difficulties seem more likely to be the result of learning problems than to be their cause. Very often it is assumed that such children have some kind of brain dysfunction. While sometimes there may be direct evidence for this, frequently there is not, the inference to brain dysfunction simply being based, in the absence of other apparent causes, on the fact of inadequate school learning.

We suspect that the trouble for many of the children categorized as having learning disabilities or learning disorders is a much simpler one than either brain dysfunction or emotional difficulties. The very concept of learning disability implies the assumption that if a child is normal—if, that is to say, there is "nothing the matter" with the child—the standard educational opportunities provided at school will suffice to bring about learning. But why should we assume this? There are other reasons besides something the matter with the child why conventional classroom arrangements need not automatically lead to learning, even if the child comes from a middle-class home. One possibility is that, once again, the child may lack crucial prerequisite skills that are needed to make sense of the classroom instruction. This may happen because the child simply had different experiences from most middle-class children or happened to fall into certain cognitive strategies that precluded the development of particular skills under conditions typically fostering them. Another possibility is that, despite the best of intentions on the part of both teacher and child, the communication between them went awry, as it frequently does between any two human beings. It is all too easy when one is in the position of trying to explain something or give instruction to assume that one is providing all the necessary information, whereas in fact one is always taking a great deal for granted. A child's failure to learn, then, may simply mean that the instructor unwittingly has failed to transmit needed information or that the child lacks the prerequisite skills needed for benefitting from what is taught, rather than anything being physiologically or psychologically the matter with the child.

Some of the children regarded as having learning disabilities are provided help by highly trained specialists in special education. Such a specialist, in working with a child, attempts to analyze that child's particular sources of learning difficulty and to design procedures that will overcome them, exercising professional judgment regarding diagnosis, preparation of specific procedures and materials and how they are to be administered to the child. This can indeed be of benefit, but often there are not enough specialists available for all the children who need help, and, sometimes, even when specialists are available, their analyses or procedures are inadequate. But if the problems of these children are as we see them, then effective help may not require this kind of idiosyncratic shaping to the individual case. What seems called for is insuring the development of whatever skills are implicated in achieving a given academic objective. What the child is to learn is specified by the school curriculum, and in order to learn it the child needs to develop those skills required for the learning and not already in the child's possession. Analysis of a given academic goal lets one spell these skills out, along with procedures for developing each one—or, more precisely, lets one formulate hypotheses about these matters which receive verification if they bring about learning for children who otherwise fail to learn. With such procedures once in hand, they can be applied as needed for individual children; quite simply, the child receives training in whichever skills cannot readily be performed.

Such a spelling out of skills and procedures is, of course, exactly what we have attempted for the task of learning to read. The procedures are in fact related to the kinds of suggestions that get made for specialists in learning disabilities. Many of the suggestions appearing in the textbook by Johnson and Myklebust (1967) on learning disabilities, for example, pertain to principles utilized in our program. Johnson and Myklebust, of course, expect the specialist first to analyze the nature of a child's learning disability and then to prescribe and adapt particular activities from among those suggested. Our program, by contrast, presents in fully specified form a complete set of procedures in sequence which adapts itself automatically to each child's situation. It is set up in such a way that each child receives further training in whatever activities that child needs, since each task must be continued until mastery. While on the one hand doing away with the need for diagnosis and individual tailoring of procedures by a professional, our program on the other hand gives greater assurance of covering the skills that the child has to have.

There seems every reason to expect, then, that our tutorial program should be able to bring about reading competence for many—perhaps even most—of the primary-school children currently viewed as having learning disabilities or disorders in the area of reading. Once again, paraprofessionals or teachers' aides in the schools could conduct the actual tutoring; another possibility would be for parents of children with reading disabilities to learn to tutor their children themselves. The highly trained learning-disabilities specialists could train and supervise nonprofessionals in the use of the program, as well as providing further help when problems arose. Without calling for a larger number of learning-disabilities specialists than are available, the consequence of their supervising tutors in this way could be that many more of the children needing help would get it and that the help would be of a more thorough kind.

The major import our work possesses beyond the topic of its direct concern—helping disadvantaged children learn to read on schedule in first grade—is its implications for those middle-class children who end up with such labels as "reading disability" or "dyslexia." There are also certain implications about instruction more generally, which were discussed in chapter 3. As described there, we believe the teaching of reading in first-grade classrooms ought to be considerably more systematic and less eclectic, paying much more attention to establishing competence at recognition and manipulation of sounds and use of the alphabetic code. Systematic cumulation of mastery of component subskills should similarly be provided for in instruction in arithmetic and other complex skills.

Implicit in what we have been saying is also a general point about how to deal with individual differences in learning abilities, learning styles, or other characteristics, when teaching. It is often held that different children need to be taught by different methods; that, for example, in the case of learning to read, certain children can not be taught by phonic methods. We would argue that what a child is to learn largely determines the skills needed to learn it; therefore all children have to develop the skills at issue. Their individual differences will mean that some children will have more difficulty with given skills than with others and will therefore need more help in mastering those skills. But these individual differences will hardly ever, if at all, mean that particular skills can be by-passed and others substituted.

The popularity of the view that different children need to be taught by different methods may, indeed, once again be due to the frequency with which teaching takes for granted pre-requisite skills which some children do not have. The idea that a child needs to be taught by a different method usually is inferred from the child's failure to learn by a given one. When that failure occurs simply because the child lacks certain pre-requisite skills—such as sound recognition and manipulation skills in the case of learning to read—the more helpful ap-proach, in our estimation, is to devise procedures that will train the child in those skills rather than try to find a method which circumvents them. This would even seem to hold when, in the case of learning to read, we are talking about a child who is partially deaf or has a speech problem, impairments that many writers (for example, Olsen 1968, p. 282) consider obvious grounds for ruling out instruction based on sound-letter relationships. Rather than needing something different, such children seem to us to need training in sound recognition, manipulation, and blending skills all the more. This certainly seemed to be the case for the children with problems of this kind that we had in our tutored sample.

Our position can be put briefly in the form of two assertions: (1) In seeking to help someone develop a given form of com-petence, a careful analysis of the prerequisite skills that must be acquired en route to the full-blown competence is needed, along with instructional arrangements that insure the learner is not asked to do anything for which he or she has not already been taught the prerequisites. (2) Many children, especially but not only from underprivileged backgrounds, have trouble learning to read because they lack certain necessary prerequi-site skills that concern the recognition, manipulation, and blending of particular kinds of sounds—phonemes. We have demonstrated that these skills are teachable if the appropriate sorts of procedures are provided, that this can be done on a practical basis, and that, if it is done, the children can learn to read. As near as we can tell, this is in direct opposition to all the major current views, which hold either that these skills are not important for learning to read, or that they cannot be taught to the children at issue, or both.

The Practicality of the Program

Keeping practicality in mind has been an abiding concern for us at all points in our work. The goal from the start was to bring theory to bear on fashioning a practical solution to a pressing educational and social problem. The nature of the tutorial program, and the nature of the field research that evaluated it, both reflected the idea that realities of intended usage be kept in focus. Thus, the program is designed for beginning schoolchildren who are unlikely to learn to read during the first-grade year; the program is sufficiently simple and straightforward that a wide range of people can readily learn to apply it effectively as tutors without regard to educational credentials or background; supervision of these tutors can be easily arranged for by various sorts of professionals; and the testing of the program's efficacy took place under representative conditions of intended usage rather than nongeneralizable "hothouse" conditions. We are at the point now where the next step with our program is to get it into more general use. While matters of practicality have been brought up throughout the book, some further examination of the practicality question thus seems an appropriate note on which to close this chapter.

Whether or not we agree with someone like Bereiter (1973) that the teaching of definable skills constitutes the *only* thing schools should undertake to do educationally, we can certainly agree with him that for schools to *fail* to teach basic academic skills—of which reading heads the list—to large numbers of children is inexcusable. But survey after survey keeps appearing documenting the prevalence of such failure. Delivering basic reading competence on schedule to all children when they start school should be a top priority, and utilization of nonprofessionals as tutors with the kind of program we have developed seems a readily feasible way to provide non-learning children with the skills they need.

These nonprofessionals could easily be brought to bear on the children who need the help through teachers' aides or paraprofessional roles in the schools. Many community adults already have paid positions of these kinds, often with little or no yield for children's learning. Where these personnel exist, it is often the teachers who have the added responsibility of thinking of things for them to do, and the consequence sometimes can be, ironically enough, teachers feeling that the teachers' aides are a burden rather than a help—while the children we are talking about still fail to learn. Our tutorial program gives neighborhood adults a highly meaningful task to fulfill in the schools, and one which functions without giving teachers any new responsibilities. They teach their class as they wish, using whatever reading materials they would anyway. The effectiveness of the program does not depend on anything that particular teachers may or may not do. All that is required of the teachers is to let particular children leave the room once a day for tutoring, children whom they find it difficult in any case to help much in class. Then, as a result of the tutoring, the children also become more amenable to instruction by the teacher. There is thus every reason to expect that, like the teachers in our field research, teachers generally should be pleased to have children tutored with our program.

The tutors do need to be supervised, of course, but various kinds of professionals can take this task on, depending on who is available in a given school setting. In one school or school system it may be a reading specialist, in another a school psychologist, and so on. As discussed earlier, all it requires is someone's having learned the program thoroughly and possessing suitable administrative skills. Even the start-up requirements when use of the tutorial program is just beginning are modest: the three weeks of initial practice needed for neophyte tutors before they start working with the children do not involve a solid block of the supervisor's time, only some time periodically; the tutors spend the rest of the time role-playing with each other. And, of course, once a tutor has been trained to the point of having learned what is necessary to apply the program through one school year, that tutor's supervision needs drop drastically for all future years. Some of the tutors in fact, after they have been on the job long enough, should themselves be able to help with much of the supervision. Once the use of the tutorial program catches on in a school, then, it should develop its own momentum and function with increasing ease.

What this adds up to for a professional like a reading specialist is more efficient—and more effective—utilization of the professional's time. Through performing a minimally time-consuming function of tutor supervisor, a reading specialist should, with our program, be able to make sure most low-readiness first graders learn basic reading competence on schedule rather than fall behind at the outset. This supervisory role lets the reading specialist nip in the bud problems that otherwise compound and accumulate by the time two or three years go by. Rather than trying to cope with the intractable consequences of such accumulated negative experiences from reading failure in third or fourth graders, a difficult task at best and one that spreads the reading specialist too thin anyway, she can, through supervision of the tutorial program, enable the children in question to have their problems caught and remedied before negative transfer has a chance to mount. Not only do these children receive more effective help, but the reading specialist can spend much more time giving individual attention to that small minority of children who need something only she can provide.

While there of course is nothing to prevent neighborhood adults from working on an unpaid volunteer basis as tutors with our program, what we would most like to see is the utilization and expansion of remunerative job opportunities for such work. Since teachers' aides or paraprofessional job categories already exist on a widespread basis in school systems and are exactly suited to the role of reading tutor with our program, this would seem to be a quite realistic expectation. Adults from the same communities as the children who need help are perfectly well qualified to perform such tutoring and need paying jobs, and federal and state monies exist which are earmarked for this kind of use. Perhaps it is appropriate at this point, then, to take a look at the monetary expenditure involved if nonprofessionals tutor with our program as a paying job.

On a full-time basis as a paraprofessional or teacher's aide, such a tutor would work with ten children whom she would tutor individually for half an hour each day. (This was the load used in our field research, and it was found to be entirely suitable.) Primarily, such children would be first graders chosen at the start of the year on the basis of tests and/or teacher referrals as unlikely to learn basic reading competence in the course of the first-grade year from classroom instruction. Tutoring with our program should put most of these children on their feet with regard to reading competence by the end of that year. A few may need more than a year's work with the program, but some others will need less than a year. The cost on a per-pupil basis of establishing competence at basic reading in a timely manner for first graders who otherwise do not achieve it (apart from negligible amounts reflecting supervisor time and tutorial program materials) thus is a full-time tutor's salary for the academic year divided by ten.

This salary will be whatever the going ten-month salary is for paraprofessionals or teachers' aides in a given school system. If the teachers' aides are paid a ten-month salary of $4000, the per-pupil cost will be $400; if the salary for the teachers' aides is $5000, the per-pupil cost will be $500; and so on. This is not very much as a one-time expenditure that serves to bring about basic reading competence in a first grader otherwise not expected to learn. It is an especially small cost when viewed in the context of much larger expenditures often fruitlessly made on some of the same children several years later in attempts to remedy what by then are massive and generalized academic failure problems.

The tutorial program we have developed can, in short, be applied within the framework of public schooling as it exists. It does not require the kind of massive infusion of money and resources that something like the Fernald School program described by Feshbach and Adelman (1974) calls for, a level of outlay that clearly is far beyond what society is prepared to pay. Nor does it require the kind of massive upheaval in how schools are run and what teachers do that something like the token economy regime described by Rollins, McCandless, Thompson, and Brassell (1974) calls for, an approach that demands a thoroughgoing ideological conversion on the part of the teachers and administrators and in any case can be questioned on ethical grounds. What we do, by contrast, sets in motion a specific solution to a specific problem in a way that is realistic in financial terms and encroaches as little as possible on the freedom of teachers and administrators—and does not add to their burdens either.

As we have seen, our tutorial program's major intended target population is low academic-readiness first graders. Second graders who did not learn to read in first grade would also seem to be appropriate for it, along with those kindergartners for whom academic readiness again seems low. Most of the children we are talking about, but not all, will tend to be from low-income backgrounds. We have concentrated in this book on what seemed like the most efficient arrangement for delivering the tutorial program to the children who need it, namely, community adults utilizing paraprofessional or teacher's aide roles to work, under appropriate supervision, as tutors in the public schools. The relevant nonprofessional roles exist for these tutors within the public school framework; relevant professionals are on hand in public schools to provide the requisite supervisory functions; and the children who need this kind of help can be found at school with sufficient reliability that it offers an obvious site for the tutoring. But there are other arrangements that can be suggested for delivering the tutorial program's instruction to children who need it. Although less efficient than the one we have emphasized, they may be quite suitable under particular circumstances. Two such further possibilities, for example, would be the following.

Community adults can work as tutors through other organizational auspices than those of schools. Community centers of one kind or another which can receive children for tutoring after school hours provide settings that may be appropriate. Such community centers are in some instances supported by a city or town, may be sponsored by a local industry or a local union or a local neighborhood association, may be part of a public recreational facility, may be part of a mental health services facility, and so on. Churches, too, may offer a highly relevant setting for such work. What it takes is a place where children will come regularly for the tutoring, as regularly as they would to school; where neighborhood adults will reliably provide tutoring, whether on a paid or unpaid basis; and where suitable supervision is available to make sure that tutors learn and follow the program. Such supervision might come, for example, from a community psychologist, a minister, a teacher, or a reading specialist working on a volunteer basis after hours —the alternatives are plentiful. In addition to community adults, high school students from the community might also be relevant for taking on the tutor role—if they have the necessary attributes of patience, responsibility, and ability to work well with children. If one tutor could see three or four children for half-hour sessions each afternoon, three or four tutors working out of a church or community center could help a dozen or so six-year-olds learn to read each year who would not learn otherwise.

Another possibility is for parents to tutor their own children with the program. If a mother tutors her own child rather than working as a nonprofessional at a school or at a community center or church, appropriate supervision is, of course, much harder to come by, though for a reading or learning disabilities specialist to provide such supervision would still be considerably more efficient than for the specialist to work directly with all the children herself. It also may well be easier to tutor other people's children than one's own. Nevertheless, tutoring by parents of their own children certainly is a possible way of applying the program, one that seems most relevant, perhaps, for middle-class parents who have children experiencing trouble learning to read.

There is, then, more than one way for the program to be used by nonprofessionals, even though the simplest route does seem to be through teacher's aide or paraprofessional roles in the schools. The program offers a tool which, used appropriately by tutors, should teach nonlearning children to read at the time when their peers are learning and when reading is needed for school tasks. Were it applied on a widespread basis, the consequence should be a drastic reduction in the number of young children failing to achieve basic reading competence on schedule. Since most of these children come from low-income and/or minority group backgrounds, we are talking about an educational gain that will be felt most strongly precisely where the needs are greatest. It is difficult to argue that the gain would not matter. It is difficult as well, after what is presented in this book, to argue that the gain cannot be brought about within the practical constraints of American public education. Perhaps, then, the time has come to put the program to work.

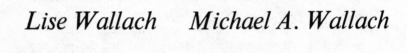

Lise Wallach   Michael A. Wallach

Appendix A
Tutor's Manual

Contents

Introduction   227

Part I   Learning to Recognize Shapes of Letters and the Sounds They Are Usually For

     Materials   229
     Steps   231
     Procedure for Successive Sessions   275
     Summary   276

Part II   Learning to Sound Out Simple Words

     Materials   278
     Steps   278
     Procedure for Successive Sessions   288
     Summary   289

Part III   Reading Simple Stories

     Materials   290
     Steps   291
     Procedure for Successive Sessions   298
     Summary   300

Introduction

This manual contains a set of procedures for helping a child learn to read.

In Part I, he learns to recognize separate sounds at the start of words, like the sound *a* in "ant," and *b* in "book." He also learns to recognize the shapes of letters and to connect these with the sounds.

In Part II, the child gets practice in sounding out some simple words.

In Part III, he learns to read simple material written for children starting to read.

It is important to follow the procedures as they are given. Always make it possible for the child to do what is asked of him by helping him as needed in the ways described. Always give such help soon enough to keep the child confidently going on.

Treat the child at all times with respect and encouragement.

Part I
Learning to Recognize
Shapes of Letters
and the Sounds
They Are Usually For

Materials for Part I

Letter-cards: one card for each letter of the alphabet, printed as a small letter (not a capital).

Letter-tracing sheets: sheets for each letter of the alphabet, which contain the printed small letter, an "alpha-picture" embodying that letter in a picture of something whose name starts with that letter's sound, and dotted lines for tracing that letter.

Letter-drawing sheets: sheets like the letter-tracing sheets except that the dotted lines for tracing are omitted.

Alpha-picture chart: a large card showing, for each letter, its alpha-picture and how it is printed both small and as a capital.

Pencils: preferably thick pencils without erasers (too much time can be wasted if the child tries to erase errors).

Game-pictures: cards with pictures of objects whose names start with the sounds of the different letters. The names are written in script on the backs of the cards. You will need to group the game-pictures for use by letter. Here is a list of the game-pictures for each letter:

a: apple, ambulance, anchor, ax, astronaut, antenna, arrow

b: bed, bus, banana, bat, ball, balloon, book, bell, bike, bridge

c: candle, clock, comb, carrot, cannon, cup, camera

d: dress, doughnut, dice, drum, dam, drops (or drip), drill, domino, dome

e: engine, eggs, elbow, elephant, Eskimo

f: fan, fork, fish, feather, finger, fire, flag

g: ghost, garage, gun, gate, golf club, glasses, gum, garbage can (or garbage), gas pump (or gas), grapes

h: hat, hammer, heart, horseshoe, house, hamburger, helicopter

i: igloo, ink, Indian, inch, inchworm

j: jet, jam, jacket, jeep, jump rope, jacks, jail, jewel, juke box

k: kite, king, kettle, ketchup, kayak, key, kangaroos (or kangaroo)

l: ladder, lemon, lantern (or lamp or light), lollipop, log, lemonade, lighthouse

m: matches, magnet, mitten, map, milk, mailbox, mask, moon, mop, music

n: nail, nut, nest, net, needle, necklace, newspaper, nail file

o: octopus, ostrich, olive

p: pipe, pear, pumpkin, pencil (or paper), pig, pen, pail, present (or package), pie, parachute

q: quotation mark (or quotes), question mark, quarter, quilt

r: radio, rabbit, rocket, record, raft, rake, rainbow, rocking chair

s: scissors, sun, saw, star, spoon, swings (or swing or swing set), slide (or sliding board)

t: table, television (or TV), turtle, telephone, truck, telescope, tank, towel, target

u: umbrella, Uncle Sam, underwear, up

v: vest, volcano, vase, vacuum cleaner, valley, vise, violin

w: window, witch, wagon, watermelon, well, whale, wheel, wheelbarrow

x: X ray, explosion

y: yo-yo, yarn, yolk, yam, yard

z: zebra, zero, zigzag, zoo, zipper

Steps for Part I

Follow these steps, for each letter in the alphabet, in alphabetical order (a b c d e f g h i j k l m n o p q r s t u v w x y z). Go through all the steps with each letter before going on to the next letter.

Step 1. Introduction to the Sound

Tell the child that a lot of words start with the sound _____, and make the sound which the letter you are on is usually for. The sounds for each letter are given below. Some of them are hard to make without adding other sounds too. For example, one can't say *b* without making it sound a little like "buh" or something like that. When you are making the sound for a letter just try to add as little other sound as you can.

This "sound name" is what you should call the letter whenever you talk about it. Don't use the alphabet name unless the child himself does, and even then you should still use the sound name most of the time.

After saying that a lot of words start with the sound _____, read aloud the tongue-twister sentence illustrating that sound, emphasizing the sound whenever it is at the start of a word. After reading the whole sentence, work on each of the words in it that start with the sound you are on. First you say the word and have the child repeat it after you. Then you say it once more, separating the starting sound from the rest of the word, with a pause in between. Then have the child say it that way too. Then go on to the next word.

The sounds and tongue-twister sentences for each letter are:

a: not as in "April" but as in "apple."

Say, "A lot of words start with the sound *a*. Like in this sentence: *A*ndrew *a*nd *A*lice *a*sked if *A*nnie's *a*ctive *a*nimals were *a*ngry."

Then work on each *a* word separately, starting with Andrew.

You:	Andrew
Child:	Andrew
You:	A-ndrew
Child:	A-ndrew
You:	and
Child:	and
You:	a-nd
Child:	a-nd
	. . . etc.

b: not like the word "bee" but as in "banana."

Say, "A lot of words start with the sound *b*. Like in the sentence: *B*ill and *B*etty *b*aked *b*rown *b*read for *B*arbara's *b*aby."

You:	Bill
Child:	Bill
You:	B-ill
Child:	B-ill
You:	Betty
Child:	Betty
You:	B-etty
Child:	B-etty
	. . . etc.

c: not like the word "sea" but as in "corn." (Note: this is the same sound as the letter k is usually for also.)

Sentence: *C*arol and *C*laire *c*an *c*ook *c*arrots, *c*orn, *c*abbage, and *c*andy.

d: not like the first three letters of "deep," but just the first letter.

Sentence: *D*avid's *D*addy's *d*og *d*idn't *d*ig *d*irt in the *d*ark.

e: not as in "equal" but as in "enemy."

Sentence: *E*verybody saw *E*ddie and the *E*skimo *e*nter the *e*levator on the *e*lephant.

f: not like the first three letters of "effort" but as in "find."

Sentence: The *f*unny *f*urry *f*ly *f*lew *f*ar to the *f*lowers.

g: not as in "gee whiz" but as in "gum."

Sentence: *G*ary was *g*lad to play *g*ames in *g*randmother's *g*reen *g*arden.

h: not like "aitch" but as in "house."

Sentence: *H*arry *h*ad a *h*orrible *h*eadache and *h*ated to *h*ear *H*enry *h*owl.

i: not like the word "I" but as in "ink."

Sentence: The *i*mportant *I*ndian was *i*ll with *i*njuries *i*nside the *i*gloo.

j: not like the name "Jay" but as in "job."

Sentence: *J*ohn got *j*uice and *j*elly on his *j*acket when *J*udy *j*umped on him.

k: not like the name "Kay" but as in "king." (Note: Tell the child this is the same sound he already learned for the letter c.)

Sentence: *K*enny wasn't *k*ind in *k*indergarten; he *k*icked *K*ate in the *k*itchen.

l: not like the first two letters of "elevator" but as in "lemon."

Sentence: *L*isa *l*ost the *l*arge *l*emon for the *l*izard Lenny *l*oved.

m: not like the first two letters of "Emily" but as in "mother."

Sentence: On *M*ondays *M*ichael's *m*other *M*ary *m*ostly *m*opped.

n: not like the first two letters of "end" but as in "no."

Sentence: *N*obody was *n*ice to *N*ancy's *n*eighbor *N*ick, but he was *n*ever *n*asty.

o: not like the word "Oh!" but as in "octopus."

Sentence: *O*liver had an *o*peration in *O*ctober, and *O*scar gave him an *o*ctopus.

p: not like the word "pea" but as in "pencil."

Sentence: *P*eter *P*iper *p*icked a *p*eck of *p*ickled *p*eppers.

q: not like the word "queue" but as in "quotes." (Note: The sound the letter q is usually for is really a combination of two sounds—*k w.*)

Sentence: "Be *q*uiet," said the *q*ueen *q*uickly, "or I'll *q*uarrel with your *q*uestion!"

r: not like the word "are" but as in "rose."

Sentence: *R*uth and *R*achel *r*an after *R*ichard's *r*abbit in the *r*ain.

s: not like the first two letters of "Esther" but as in "save."

Sentence: *S*am *s*aid he was *s*orry he put *s*alt in *S*ally's *s*andwich.

t: not like the word "tea" but as in "table."

Sentence: *T*ommy *t*ricked *T*im and *t*ook his *t*rain off the *t*rack.

u: not like the word "you" but as in "ugly."

Sentence: *U*ncle was *u*pset because he was *u*nable to put his *u*mbrella *u*p.

v: not like "vee" but as in "valley."

Sentence: *V*irginia *v*isited *V*icky and gave her *v*iolets and *v*egetables with *v*itamins.

w: not like "double you" but as in "welcome."

Sentence: *W*hen the *w*eather is *w*arm *w*e *w*ill *w*alk *w*ith *W*illiam in the *w*ild *w*oods.

x: not as in "xylophone" but like the first two letters of "extra." (Note: This is the one time the sound name is the same

as the alphabet name. It is really a combination of three sounds
—e k s. And it is mostly written "ex" instead of "x.")

Sentence: The *ex*cited *ex*perts *ex*plained that the *ex*tra *X*
rays were *ex*cellent.

y: not like the word "why" but as in "young."

Sentence: *Y*esterday *y*ou *y*elled in the *y*ard for a *y*ellow *y*o-
yo.

z: not like "zee" but as in "zipper."

Sentence: The *z*ebra *z*oomed *z*ig-*z*ag in the *z*oo.

Step 2. The Two-Picture Game

Take out all the game-pictures with names that start with the
letter you are working on. They are listed at the beginning of
the manual. Take out an equal number of other game-pictures
with names that all start with letters that are different from
each other. For most letters you can use any of the game-
pictures, but some sounds are too similar, so some exceptions
are given at the end of Step 2. The number of game-pictures
for each letter is also given at the end of Step 2.

Mix up the two kinds of pictures, so the child won't be able
to tell which pictures start with the letter you are working on
just because they are in a separate pile.

Show the child two of the pictures at a time, one that has a
name starting with the letter you are on, and one that doesn't.
Put the pictures for the letter you are working on to the left
sometimes and to the right sometimes, so the child won't be
able to tell which they are just because they are always in the
same place.

Have the child say what the two pictures show and make
sure he understands what each picture is supposed to be a
picture of. Also make sure the pictures get called by the names
that are on their backs. If the child says a different name, don't
say he is wrong, but ask him if he can think of anything else
it could be called besides. Tell him what it is supposed to be
called if he doesn't get it by himself.

Have the child say which picture starts with the sound
_____ (the sound you are working on). Sometimes a child
will try to point between the pictures, or at both of them, not
really committing himself to one or the other. Get him to make
a definite choice before you continue.

If he chooses the right picture, tell him it is right.

Whenever the child chooses the wrong picture as the one
which starts with the sound you are on, say, "No. It's _____
(the name of the picture he chose), not _____ (the name
as it would be if it started with the sound you are on in place
of the sound it does start with)." Then point to the right picture and say "_____ (its name) starts with _____ (the
sound you are on). Say __-_____ (the name with a pause
after the starting sound)." Have him repeat the name with a
pause after the starting sound.

After each pair of pictures, show the child another pair,
again one whose name starts with the sound you are on and
one that doesn't, and so on, until he has picked the correct
picture seven times in a row. When you have shown him all
the pictures you took out, shuffle them and keep going as long
as necessary, until the child picks the correct pictures seven
times in a row.

If the child has a hard time with this game, do the following
for awhile after he has named each of the two pictures. Point
to the picture on the left and say its name with a pause after
the starting sound, and have the child say it after you. Then
do the same for the picture on the right. Only then ask which
one starts with _____ (the sound you are on). Then proceed
as before, depending on what he says.

*For each letter you work on, here are the num-
ber of game-pictures for that letter, the other letters whose
game-pictures you can use, and examples of possible pairs of
pictures and what to say if the child chooses the wrong one:*

a: 7 game-pictures.

Other letters whose game-pictures you can use—all letters
except *e, i,* and *x.*

Example: *anchor* and *bat*. If the child chooses *bat*, you say, "No. It's bat, not at." Point to the anchor and say, "Anchor starts with *a*. Say 'a-nchor.' " Have the child repeat "a-nchor."

Another example: *apple* and *rocket*. If the child chooses *rocket*, you say, "No. It's rocket, not a-ocket." Point to the apple and say, "Apple starts with *a*. Say 'a-pple.' " Have the child repeat "a-pple."

Another example: *ax* and *octopus*. If the child chooses *octopus*, you say, "No. It's octopus, not actopus." Point to the ax and say, "Ax starts with *a*. Say 'a-xe.' " Have the child repeat "a-xe."

b: 10 game-pictures.

Other letters whose game-pictures you can use—all letters.

Example: *bell* and *flag*. If the child chooses *flag*, you say, "No. It's flag, not blag." Point to the bell and say, "Bell starts with *b*. Say 'b-ell.' " Have the child repeat.

Another example: *bus* and *eggs*. If the child chooses *eggs*, you say, "No. It's eggs, not beggs." Point to the bus and say, "Bus starts with *b*. Say 'b-us.' " Have the child repeat.

c: 7 game-pictures.

Other letters whose game-pictures you can use—all letters except *k, q,* and *x*.

Example: *carrot* and *drum*, child chooses *drum*. Say: "No. It's drum, not crumb." (Point.) "Carrot starts with *c*. Say 'c-arrot.' "

Another example: *clock* and *igloo*, child chooses *igloo*. Say: "No. It's igloo, not kigloo." (Point.) "Clock starts with *c*. Say 'c-lock.' "

d: 9 game-pictures.

Other letters whose game-pictures you can use—all letters.

Example: *dress* and *lantern*, child chooses *lantern*. Say: "No. it's lantern, not dantern." (Point.) "Dress starts with *d*. Say 'd-ress.' "

Another example: *dice* and *Indian*, child chooses *Indian*. Say: "No. It's Indian, not Dindian." (Point.) "Dice starts with *d*. Say 'd-ice.' "

e: 5 game-pictures.

Other letters whose game-pictures you can use—all letters except *a, i,* and *x.*

Example: *elbow* and *record,* child chooses *record.* Say: "No. It's record, not eckerd." (Point.) "Elbow starts with *e.* Say 'e-lbow.' "

Another example: *eggs* and *whale,* child chooses *whale.* Say: "No. It's whale, not eh-ale." (Point.) "Eggs starts with *e.* Say 'e-ggs.' "

Another example: *elephant* and *octopus,* child chooses *octopus.* Say: "No. It's octopus, not ectopus." (Point.) "Elephant starts with *e.* Say 'e-lephant.' "

f: 7 game-pictures.

Other letters whose game-pictures you can use—all letters.

Example: *flag* and *lollipop,* child chooses *lollipop.* Say: "No. It's lollipop, not follipop." (Point.) "Flag starts with *f.* Say 'f-lag.' "

Another example: *fire* and *ostrich,* child chooses *ostrich.* Say: "No. It's ostrich, not fostrich." (Point.) "Fire starts with *f.* Say 'f-ire.' "

g: 10 game-pictures.

Other letters whose game-pictures you can use—all letters.

Examples: *gum* and *lemonade,* child chooses *lemonade.* Say: "No. It's lemonade, not gemonade." (Point.) "Gum starts with *g.* Say 'g-um.' "

Another example: *grapes* and *antenna,* child chooses *antenna.* Say: "No. It's antenna, not gantenna." (Point.) "Grapes starts with *g.* Say 'g-rapes.' "

h: 7 game-pictures.

Other letters whose game-pictures you can use—all letters.

Example: *heart* and *pie,* child chooses *pie.* Say: "No. It's pie, not high." (Point.) "Heart starts with *h.* Say 'h-eart.' "

Another example: *hamburger* and *Uncle Sam,* child chooses *Uncle Sam.* Say: "No. It's Uncle Sam, not Huncle Sam." (Point.) "Hamburger starts with *h.* Say 'h-amburger.' "

i: 5 game-pictures.

Other letters whose game-pictures you can use—all letters except *a, e,* and *x.*

Example: *igloo* and *king,* child chooses *king.* Say: "No. It's king, not ing." (Point.) "Igloo starts with *i.* Say 'i-gloo.' "

Another example: *inch* and *ostrich,* child chooses *ostrich.* Say: "No. It's ostrich, not istrich." (Point.) "Inch starts with *i.* Say 'i-nch.' "

Another example: *Indian* and *rainbow,* child chooses *rainbow.* Say: "No. It's rainbow, not i-ainbow." (Point.) "Indian starts with *i.* Say 'I-ndian.' "

j: 9 game-pictures.

Other letters whose game-pictures you can use—all letters.

Example: *jewel* and *telephone,* child chooses *telephone.* Say: "No. It's telephone, not jelephone." (Point.) "Jewel starts with *j.* Say 'j-ewel.' "

Another example: *jump rope* and *inch,* child chooses *inch.* Say: "No. It's inch, not jinch." (Point.) "Jump rope starts with *j.* Say 'j-ump rope.' "

k: 7 game-pictures.

Other letters whose game-pictures you can use—all letters except *c, q,* and *x.*

Example: *king* and *lemon,* child chooses *lemon.* Say: "No. It's lemon, not kemon." (Point.) "King starts with *k.* Say 'k-ing.' "

Another example: *kangaroo* and *apple,* child chooses *apple.* Say: "No. It's apple, not kapple." (Point.) "Kangaroo starts with *k.* Say 'k-angaroo.' "

l: 7 game-pictures.

Other letters whose game-pictures you can use—all letters.

Example: *ladder* and *raft,* child chooses *raft.* Say: "No. It's raft, not laughed." (Point.) "Ladder starts with *l.* Say 'l-adder.' "

Another example: *lighthouse* and *anchor,* child chooses *anchor.* Say: "No. It's anchor, not lanchor." (Point.) "Lighthouse starts with *l.* Say 'l-ighthouse.' "

m: 10 game-pictures.

Other letters whose game-pictures you can use—all letters.
Example: *music* and *record*, child chooses *record*. Say:
"No. It's record, not meckord." (Point.) "Music starts with *m*.
Say 'm-usic.' "
Another example: *mailbox* and *olive*, child chooses *olive*.
Say: "No. It's olive, not molive." (Point.) "Mailbox starts with
m. Say 'm-ailbox.' "

n: 8 game-pictures.

Other letters whose game-pictures you can use—all letters.
Example: *nail* and *cup*, child chooses *cup*. Say: "No. It's
cup, not nup." (Point.) "Nail starts with *n*. Say 'n-ail.' "
Another example: *necklace* and *inchworm*, child chooses
inchworm. Say: "No. It's inchworm, not ninchworm." (Point.)
"Necklace starts with *n*. Say 'n-ecklace.' "

o: 3 game-pictures.

Other letters whose game-pictures you can use—all letters
except *u*.
Example: *ostrich* and *needle*, child chooses *needle*. Say:
"No. It's needle, not o-eedle." (Point.) "Ostrich starts with *o*.
Say 'o-strich.' "
Another example: *olive* and *ink*, child chooses *ink*. Say:
"No. It's ink, not onk." (Point.) "Olive starts with *o*. Say
'o-live.' "
Another example: *octopus* and *mop*, child chooses *mop*.
Say: "No. It's mop, not op." (Point.) "Octopus starts with *o*.
Say 'o-ctopus.' "

p: 10 game-pictures.

Other letters whose game-pictures you can use—all letters.
Example: *pig* and *dome*, child chooses *dome*. Say: "No. It's
dome, not pome." (Point.) "Pig starts with *p*. Say 'p-ig.' "
Another example: *pipe* and *astronaut*, child chooses *astronaut*. Say: "No. It's astronaut, not pastronaut." (Point.) "Pipe
starts with *p*. Say 'p-ipe.' "

q: 4 game-pictures.

Other letters whose game-pictures you can use—all letters except *c, k,* and *x.*

Example: *question mark* and *fork,* child chooses *fork.* Say: "No. It's fork, not quork." (Point.) "Question mark starts with *q.* Say 'qu-estion mark.' "

Another example: *quilt* and *Indian,* child chooses *Indian.* Say: "No. It's Indian, not Quindian." (Point.) "Quilt starts with *q.* Say 'qu-ilt.' "

r: 8 game-pictures.

Other letters whose game-pictures you can use—all letters.

Example: *radio* and *bed,* child chooses *bed.* Say: "No. It's bed, not red." (Point.) "Radio starts with *r.* Say 'r-adio.' "

Another example: *rake* and *umbrella,* child chooses *umbrella.* Say: "No. It's umbrella, not rumbrella." (Point.) "Rake starts with *r.* Say 'r-ake.' "

s: 7 game-pictures.

Other letters whose game-pictures you can use—all letters except *x* and *z.*

Example: *swings* and *table,* child chooses *table.* Say: "No. It's table, not sable." (Point.) "Swings starts with *s.* Say 's-wings.' "

Another example: *saw* and *elephant,* child chooses *elephant.* Say: "No. It's elephant, not sellephant." (Point.) "Saw starts with *s.* Say 's-aw.' "

t: 9 game-pictures.

Other letters whose game-pictures you can use—all letters.

Example: *telescope* and *inchworm,* child chooses *inchworm.* Say: "No. It's inchworm, not tinchworm." (Point.) "Telescope starts with *t.* Say 't-elescope.' "

Another example: *truck* and *pumpkin,* child chooses *pumpkin.* Say: "No. It's pumpkin, not tumpkin." (Point.) "Truck starts with *t.* Say 't-ruck.' "

u: 4 game-pictures.

Other letters whose game-pictures you can use—all letters except *o.*

Example: *Uncle Sam* and *zigzag,* child chooses *zigzag.* Say: "No. It's zigzag, not uh-igzag." (Point.) "Uncle Sam starts with *u.* Say 'U-ncle Sam.' "

Another example: *up* and *sun,* child chooses *sun.* Say: "No. It's sun, not un." (Point.) "Up starts with *u.* Say 'u-p.' "

Another example: *underwear* and *anchor,* child chooses *anchor.* Say: "No. It's anchor, not unchor." (Point.) "Underwear starts with *u.* Say 'u-nderwear.' "

v: 7 game-pictures.

Other letters whose game-pictures you can use—all letters.

Example: *vise* and *octopus,* child chooses *octopus.* Say: "No. It's octopus, not voctopus." (Point.) "Vise starts with *v.* Say 'v-ise.' "

Another example: *valley* and *raft,* child chooses *raft.* Say: "No. It's raft, not vaft." (Point.) "Valley starts with *v.* Say 'v-alley.' "

w: 8 game-pictures.

Other letters whose game-pictures you can use—all letters.

Example: *whale* and *volcano,* child chooses *volcano.* Say: "No. It's volcano, not wolcano." (Point.) "Whale starts with *w.* Say 'wh-ale.' "

Another example: *witch* and *igloo,* child chooses *igloo.* Say: "No. It's igloo, not wigloo." (Point.) "Witch starts with *w.* Say 'w-itch.' "

x: 2 game-pictures.

Other letters whose game-pictures you can use—all letters except *a, c, e, i, k, q, s,* and *z.*

Example: *X ray* and *octopus,* child chooses *octopus.* Say: "No. It's octopus, not eksoctopus." (Point.) "X ray starts with *x.* Say 'X ray.' "

Another example: *X ray* and *telephone*, child chooses *telephone*. Say: "No. It's telephone, not eckselephone." (Point.) "X ray starts with *x*. Say 'X ray.' "

Another example: *explosion* and *ladder*, child chooses *ladder*. Say: "No. It's ladder, not eksadder." (Point.) "Explosion starts with *x*. Say 'ex-plosion.' "

y: 5 game-pictures.

Other letters whose game-pictures you can use—all letters.

Example: *yo-yo* and *lantern*, child chooses *lantern*. Say: "No. It's lantern, not yantern." (Point.) "Yo-yo starts with *y*. Say 'y-o-yo.' "

Another example: *yam* and *ambulance*, child chooses *ambulance*. Say: "No. It's ambulance, not yambulance." (Point.) "Yam starts with *y*. Say 'y-am.' "

z: 5 game-pictures.

Other letters whose game-pictures you can use—all letters except *s* and *x*.

Example: *zero* and *explosion*, child chooses *explosion*. Say: "No. It's explosion, not z-plosion." (Point.) "Zero starts with *z*. Say 'z-ero.' "

Another example: *zoo* and *record*, child chooses *record*. Say: "No. It's record, not zecord." (Point.) "Zoo starts with *z*. Say 'z-oo.' "

Step 3. The Yes-No Game

Again use all the game-pictures with names that start with the letter you are working on, the same ones as in Step 2. Take out a different set—again the same number—of other game-pictures with names that all start with letters that are different from each other. Again only pick game-pictures whose names start quite differently from those for the letter you are on. See the end of Step 2 for the other game-pictures that can be used for each letter you work on, and for the number of game-pictures. Try to use mostly game-pictures for different letters than you used in Step 2. You can use letters early in the alphabet for Step 2, and later in the alphabet for Step 3.

Mix up together all the game-pictures you are using, the ones for the letter you are working on and the different ones. Show them to the child one at a time. Have him say what the picture shows. Make sure he understands what it is supposed to be a picture of. Also make sure it gets called by the name on the back. If the child says a different name, don't say he is wrong, but ask him if he can think of anything else it could be called besides. Tell him what it is supposed to be called if he doesn't get it by himself.

Then have the child say whether the name starts with the sound _____ (the sound you are working on). If he gives the right answer, tell him it is right.

Whenever the child says a picture's name starts with the sound you are on and it doesn't, say "No. It's _____ (the name of the picture), not _____ (the name as it would be if it started with the sound you are on in place of the sound it does start with). _____ (the name of the picture) doesn't start with _____ (the sound you are on)."

For example, if the child says "hat" starts with _a_, you say, "No. It's hat, not at. Hat doesn't start with _a_."

Or if the child says "lemon" starts with _k_, you say, "No. It's lemon, not kemon. Lemon doesn't start with _k_."

Whenever the child says a picture's name doesn't start with the sound you are working on and it does, you say the name once more, now with a pause after the starting sound. Tell the child that it does start with the sound you are on. For example, if you are working on _a_ and he says that "ambulance" doesn't start with that sound, you say something like: "A-mbulance. That does start with _a_."

When you have finished with one picture, put it aside, and have the child do the same things with the next picture in the pile, and so on. When you have used up all the pictures in one pile, shuffle them and continue. Keep going until the child has said correctly seven times in a row whether the name starts with the sound you are on or not.

If the child has a hard time with this game, do the following for a while after he names each picture. You say the name again with a short pause after the starting sound, and have the child say the name that way too. Only then ask him whether the name starts with _____ (the sound you are working on). Then proceed as before, depending on what he says.

For example, suppose you are working on *a* and the child has kept making mistakes just about as often as he has been giving correct answers. Suppose the next picture in the pile is apple. Have him tell you what it shows. After he says, "apple," you say "a-pple," and have him say "a-pple" too. Only then, ask, "Does apple start with *a*?" Then proceed as before, depending on what he says.

Or suppose the next picture is nail. After he says "nail," you say "n-ail," and have him say "n-ail" too. Only then, ask, "Does nail start with *a*?"

Step 4. Letter Tracing

Take one of the letter-tracing sheets (these are the sheets with dotted letters) for the letter you are working on. Show the child the alpha-picture at the top left. See that he understands what the picture is supposed to be.

Tell him that the dark lines are the letter for the sound _____ (make the sound) at the start of the name of the alpha-picture. (If the child knows the alphabet name, tell him that it is right, and that the letter is *also* for the sound _____.) Make it clear to the child that the name starts with this sound by saying the name, first, normally, and then with the starting sound separated by a pause from the rest of the name.

Have him say the name of the alpha-picture these ways too, and also have him make the sound the letter is for by itself.

Then have the child trace the dotted letters. Have him do the letters in order from left to right, finishing each row of letters before going to the row underneath it. If he doesn't trace in the right way, show him how. Have him practice until he can do it fairly well, giving him more of the sheets with dotted letters if he needs them.

The alpha-pictures for each letter, and the way each letter should be made, are:

a: ant

> You: This is supposed to be an ant. The dark lines here (point) are the letter for *a* (make the sound), the sound at the start of ant. You repeat after me, ant.
> Child: ant
> You: a-nt
> Child: a-nt
> You: *a*
> Child: *a*

b: bird

> You: This is supposed to be a bird. The dark lines here (point) are the letter for *b* (make the sound), the sound at the start of bird. You repeat after me, bird.
> Child: bird
> You: b-ird
> Child: b-ird
> You: *b*
> Child: *b*

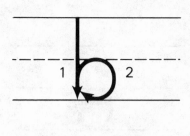

c: cake

d: door

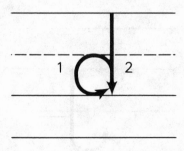

e: elephant

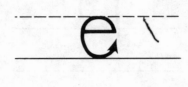

f: foot

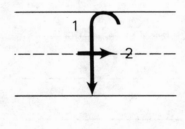

g: glass

h: hair

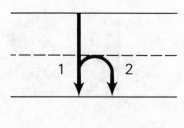

i: inch

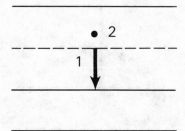

j: juggler

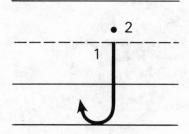

k: key

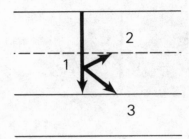

l: leaf

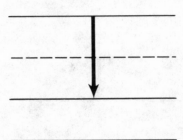

m: marbles

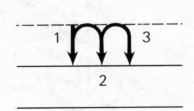

n: nose

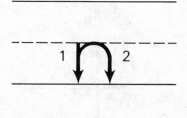

o: olive

p: pot

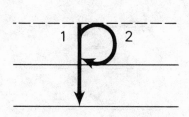

q: quilt

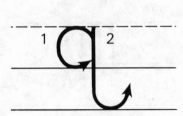

r: rope

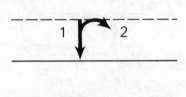

s: snake

t: tree

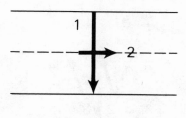

u: underwear

v: violin

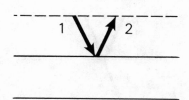

w: waves

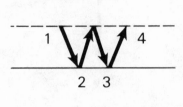

x: explosion

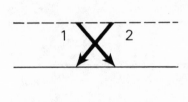

y: yard

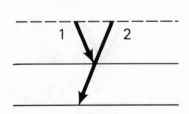

z: zipper

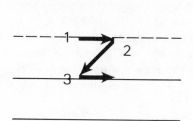

Step 5. Letter Drawing

Take one of the letter-drawing sheets (these are the sheets without dotted letters, with only lines across the page) for the letter you are working on. Have the child look at the alpha-picture on the top left and ask him what the picture shows. Remind him if necessary.

Then ask him what the dark lines are. If he gives the correct sound, tell him he is right.

If the child gives the alphabet name instead of the sound name, also tell him he is right. Then tell him the letter is *also* for a sound, and ask him to tell you the sound too.

If the child can't say the sound, you say it. Again make it clear to him that this is the sound the name of the alpha-picture starts with. Say the name first normally, and then also with the starting sound separated by a pause from the rest of the name. Have the child say the name these ways too, and also have him make the sound the letter is for by itself.

Have the child practice drawing the letter, as shown in Step 4. (This time he doesn't have the dotted outlines to help him.) Again have him do the letters in order from left to right, completing each row before going on to the row underneath. If he seems to have too much trouble, let him do some more tracing as in Step 4, then try Step 5 again, and so on, going back and forth a number of times.

Have him practice, giving him more sheets if he needs them, until he can draw the letter without anything to trace fairly well or until you have spent a half hour on Steps 4 and 5. Do not spend more than a half hour on both these steps together.

If you are working on *a*, this is the last step, and you go on to Step 1 for *b*. Otherwise continue through Steps 6–10.

Step 6. The Picture-Matching Game with the Letter-Drawing Sheets

Take out the letter-drawing sheets and the game-pictures listed with the letter you are working on as shown at the end of Step 6. (Use clean sheets that haven't been written on.)

Put one of the letter-drawing sheets in front of the child. Again have the child look at the alpha-picture on the top left and ask him what the picture shows. Remind him if necessary.

Then ask him what the dark lines are. If he gives the correct sound, tell him he is right.

If the child gives the alphabet name instead of the sound name, also tell him he is right. Then tell him the letter is *also* for a sound, and ask him to tell you the sound too.

If the child can't say the sound, you say it. Again make it clear to him that this is the sound the name of the alpha-picture starts with. First, say the name normally, then with the starting sound separated by a pause from the rest of the name. Have the child say the name these ways too, and also have him make the sound by itself.

Then put another letter-drawing sheet in front of the child. Ask in the same way what the picture shows and what the dark lines are. Then do the same with the last letter-drawing sheet (except when you are on *b*, when there are only two).

Then mix up all the game-pictures you took out and show them to the child one at a time. Have him say what the picture shows, and see that it gets called by the name it is supposed to be. Then have him say the sound that the name starts with.

If he says the wrong sound, you say the name again, first normally, and then once more, with a pause after the starting sound. Then say the right sound by itself. Have him say the name these ways too, and then the right sound by itself also.

For example, if the child says apple starts with *p*, say, "Apple. A-pple. Apple starts with *a*." Have him say apple, a-pple, and *a*.

When the child has said the correct starting sound, ask him to put the picture on the letter-drawing sheet which has the letter for that sound.

If the child puts the picture on the sheet with the right letter, tell him that is right. Then take the picture off and put it aside.

If he puts the picture on a sheet with a wrong letter, say, "That's _____ (the sound the letter he put the game-picture with is for), the sound at the start of _____ (the name of the alpha-picture for that letter). _____ (the name of the game-picture) starts with _____ (the starting sound). Can you find the letter for _____ (that sound)?"

If necessary, show him the right letter and tell him, "Here's _____ (the sound the game-picture starts with). _____ (the name of the alpha-picture) starts with _____ (the sound it starts with) like _____ (the name of the game-picture) does."

Have the child put the picture in the right place. Then you take it off and put it aside.

For example, if the child puts the apple on the letter-drawing sheet for *b*, say, "That's *b*, the sound at the start of bird. Apple starts with *a*. Can you find the letter for *a*?" If necessary, show him and say, "Here's *a*. Ant starts with *a* like apple does." Have the child put the apple on the letter-drawing sheet for *a*. Then take it off and put it aside.

Then have the child do the same thing with the next game-picture, and so on. Continue until the child puts seven pictures in a row on the right sheets, *whether or not* he says their starting sounds correctly right away. If you have shown him all the game-pictures you took out before he gets seven in a row right, reshuffle the game-pictures and rearrange the letter-drawing sheets so they are in a different order too, and go on. Repeat as often as necessary.

If the child has a hard time *giving the right starting sounds* for the names of the game-pictures, do the following for awhile after the child names each game-picture: Repeat the name and have the child repeat it after you. Then say the name with a pause after the starting sound and have the child repeat that. Only then ask, "What's the starting sound?" If necessary, say the starting sound yourself and have the child repeat it after you.

For example, after the child names the candle game-picture:

> You: candle
> Child: candle
> You: c-andle
> Child: c-andle
> You: What's the starting sound?

And if the child doesn't say *c*, you say it and have him repeat it after you.

Remember that the child has to put seven pictures in a row on the right sheets before going on, but he does *not* have to give the starting sounds correctly by himself.

If the child has a hard time *putting the pictures on the right letters* after the starting sound has been given, do the following for awhile just before he is to choose which letter is for that sound: Say, "_____ (the name of the game-picture) starts with _____ (its starting sound)." Pointing to each letter in turn from left to right, say, "This is for _____ (the sound it is for), this is for _____ (the sound it is for)," and so on. Then, if necessary, say, "Put the _____ (the name of the game-picture) on the letter for _____ (the starting sound)."

For example, for the candle game-picture with the sheets for *a, b,* and *c,* after the child has said the starting sound *c*, say "Candle starts with *c*." Point to each of the sheets in turn from left to right and say, "This is for *b*, this is for *c*, this is for *a*" (fitting what you say to the order of the sheets). Then, if necessary, say, "Put the candle on the letter for *c*."

          For each letter you work on in Step 6, here are the letter-drawing sheets to use, and the game-pictures to use:

(*a:* not worked on in this step.)

b: Letter-drawing sheets and game-pictures for *a* and *b*.

c: Letter-drawing sheets and game-pictures for *a, b,* and *c*.

d: Letter-drawing sheets and game-pictures for *a, b,* and *d*.

e: Letter-drawing sheets and game-pictures for *c, d,* and *e*.

f: Letter-drawing sheets and game-pictures for *c, e,* and *f*.

g: Letter-drawing sheets and game-pictures for *b, d,* and *g*.

h: Letter-drawing sheets and game-pictures for *b, g,* and *h*.

i: Letter-drawing sheets and game-pictures for *d, g,* and *i*.

j: Letter-drawing sheets and game-pictures for *h, i,* and *j*.

k: Letter-drawing sheets and game-pictures for *i, j,* and *k*.

l: Letter-drawing sheets and game-pictures for *e, k,* and *l*.

m: Letter-drawing sheets and game-pictures for *a, f,* and *m*.

n: Letter-drawing sheets and game-pictures for *c, e,* and *n*.

o: Letter-drawing sheets and game-pictures for *b, j,* and *o*.

p: Letter-drawing sheets and game-pictures for *a, k,* and *p*.

q: Letter-drawing sheets and game-pictures for *d, i,* and *q*.

r: Letter-drawing sheets and game-pictures for *f, n,* and *r*.

s: Letter-drawing sheets and game-pictures for *n, p,* and *s*.

t: Letter-drawing sheets and game-pictures for *j, k,* and *t*.

u: Letter-drawing sheets and game-pictures for *c, i,* and *u*.

v: Letter-drawing sheets and game-pictures for *s, u,* and *v*.

w: Letter-drawing sheets and game-pictures for *o, v,* and *w*.

x: Letter-drawing sheets and game-pictures for *b, o,* and *x.*

y: Letter-drawing sheets and game-pictures for *u, v,* and *y.*

z: Letter-drawing sheets and game-pictures for *d, w,* and *z.*

Step 7. The Word-Matching Game with the Letter-Drawing Sheets

This step is just like Step 6 except that now you tell the child words instead of showing him game-pictures.

Take out a letter-drawing sheet for each letter listed with the letter you are working on as shown at the end of Step 7. (Again, use clean sheets.)

Put one of the letter-drawing sheets in front of the child. Again have him look at the alpha-picture and ask him what the picture shows. Remind him if necessary.

Then ask him what the dark lines are. If he gives the correct sound, tell him he is right.

If the child gives the alphabet name instead of the sound name, also tell him he is right. Then tell him the letter is *also* for a sound and ask him to tell you the sound too.

If the child can't say the sound, you say it. Again make it clear to him that this is the sound the name of the alpha-picture starts with. First say the name normally, and then with the starting sound separated by a pause from the rest of the name. Have the child say the names these ways too, and also have him make the sound by itself.

Then put another letter-drawing sheet in front of the child. Ask in the same way what the picture shows and what the dark lines are. Then do the same with the last letter-drawing sheet (except when you are on *b,* where there are only two).

Then say the first word listed at the end of Step 7 for the letter you are on, and use it in a phrase or sentence to help the child recognize it. Tell him what it means if he doesn't know it.

Have the child repeat the word, and then have him say the sound that it starts with. If he says the wrong sound, you say the word again normally, and then once more with a pause after the starting sound. Then say the right sound by itself. Have him say the word these ways too and then the right sound by itself also.

When the child has said the correct starting sound, ask him to point to the letter for that sound.

If the child points to the right letter, tell him that is right.

If he points to a wrong letter, say "That's _____ (the sound the letter he pointed to is for), the sound at the start of _____ (the name of the alpha-picture for that letter). _____ (the word you gave him) starts with _____ (the starting sound). Can you find the letter for _____ (that sound)?"

If necessary, show him the right letter and tell him, "Here's _____ (the sound the word you gave him starts with). _____ (the name of the alpha-picture) starts with _____ (the sound it starts with) like _____ (the word you gave him) does."

Then go on to the next word in the list at the end of Step 7, and do the same things again, and so on. Play this game until the child has pointed to the right letter for seven words in a row, *whether or not* he says their starting sounds correctly right away. If you get through the whole list of words before he gets seven in a row right, rearrange the letter-drawing sheets so they are in a different order and start from the beginning of the list again. Repeat as often as necessary.

If the child has a hard time *giving the right starting sounds* for the words you tell him, do the following for awhile after he says each word. Repeat the word and have the child repeat it again after you. Then say the word with a pause after the starting sound and have the child repeat that. Only then ask, "What's the starting sound?" If necessary, say the starting sound yourself and have the child repeat it after you.

Remember that the child has to point to the right letter for seven words in a row before going on, but he does *not* have to give the starting sounds correctly by himself.

If the child has a hard time *pointing to the right letters* after the starting sound has been given, do the following for awhile just before he is to choose which letter is for that sound: Say, "_____ (the word you gave him) starts with _____ (its starting sound)." Pointing to each letter in turn from left to right, say, "This is for _____ (the sound it is for), this is for _____ (the sound it is for)," and so on. Then, if necessary, say, "Point to the letter for _____ (the starting sound)."

For each letter you work on in Step 7, here are the letter-drawing sheets to use, and the list of words to use:

(*a:* not worked on in this step.)

b: Letter-drawing sheets for *a* and *b.*

Words: arrow, animal, bear, ask, box, accident, button, busy, alphabet, bake, apple, build, bone, angry, bike, ax, anchor, brown

c: Letter-drawing sheets for *a, b,* and *c.*

Words: angry, curtain, comb, bad, animal, apple, boat, carrot, basket, answer, cookies, ax, building, crayons, borrow, accident, clock, bread, alphabet, cry, banana, arrow, call, best

d: Letter-drawing sheets for *a, c,* and *d.*

Words: dry, cook, arrow, do, dig, animal, dinner, candy, ask, come, draw, accident, dark, clean, ax, anchor, color, cabbage, door, cat, apple, doughnut, cream, duck, acrobat

e: Letter-drawing sheets for *b, c,* and *e.*

Words: bear, clock, can, egg, biscuit, elephant, everybody, box, cup, empty, cover, bowl, blue, elbow, cap, clown, break, Eskimo, Band-Aid, cold, crown, end, candle, bug

f: Letter-drawing sheets for *a, d,* and *f.*

Words: finger, fire, duck, arrow, flower, animal, dark, doughnut, foot, ask, fix, apple, dirt, fold, drop, flat, funny, ax, free, angry, drawer, fuss, answer, dog *g:* Letter-drawing sheets for *c, e,* and *g.*

Words: game, clock, elevator, enemy, garage, cute, cookies, glad, egg, cool, everything, green, cage, empty, gum, grand-mother, end, gold, elbow, cut, give

h: Letter-drawing sheets for *a, c,* and *h.*

Words: hard, hope, cap, answer, heavy, anchor, curtain, hand-kerchief, accident, head, clock, apple, hungry, crown, happy, crack, acrobat, hiccup, anger, cook, hello, clap, animal, candy

i: Letter-drawing sheets for *c, f,* and *i.*

Words: itch, cabbage, inside, fat, call, ill, flower, important, come, igloo, find, cookies, imagine, coat, fox, famous, ink, clothes, injury, finger, funny, instrument, fly, cold, free

j: Letter-drawing sheets for *a, b,* and *j.*

Words: jail, afternoon, baby, jam, bug, astronaut, ball, jacket, job, bend, joke, ask, jump, advertisement, bite, jar, brick, judge, animal, bottom, ax, best, jelly

k: Letter-drawing sheets for *b, f,* and *k.*

Words: boy, kitchen, finish, kettle, frog, button, fly, kind, box, keep, key, bag, fan, kick, family, Band-Aid, kill, brown, blue, father, kindergarten, find, bed, king, four

l: Letter-drawing sheets for *h, j,* and *l.*

Words: jelly, lamp, heavy, judge, leg, jacket, hand, little, hole, hot, joke, leave, hit, happy, lamb, jump, large, jail, lost, help, jar, lady, jam, hill

m: Letter-drawing sheets for *c, h,* and *m.*

Words: hard, mother, cat, mouse, candy, hold, mop, handle, ham, man, cook, mask, clock, horse, money, house, crayon, coming, maybe, hope, mitten, climb, high

n: Letter-drawing sheets for *f, h,* and *n.*

Words: number, family, hello, nap, handkerchief, head, nail, funny, never, hiccup, fix, neighbor, nobody, friend, horn, not, home, fold, flat, now, hope, feel, heavy, nine, fox *o:* Letter-drawing sheets for *a, c,* and *o.*

Words: crown, ostrich, apple, cap, octopus, cookies, ask, operation, acrobat, carrot, cool, olive, ant, cloud, ax, opposite, camera, anchor, opportunity, corner, ox, anger

p: Letter-drawing sheets for *b, e,* and *p.*

Words: pan, big, everywhere, blind, pill, elephant, powder, break, egg, pail, empty, bicycle, play, butter, bake, entrance, pole, pet, elbow, bear, pretty, bring, pear, enemy

q: Letter-drawing sheets for *a, b,* and *q.*

Words: angry, question, box, answer, button, quiet, quilt, busy, after, quick, animal, quarter, build, apple, bone, queen, brown, acrobat, quarrel, ask, quart, basket, bite

r: Letter-drawing sheets for *e, k,* and *r.*

Words: run, edge, kind, rabbit, keep, enter, key, rock, roll, elephant, kick, rat, kill, roar, elbow, elevator, rag, king, ribbon, kindergarten, envelope, kitchen, rain, empty, kettle, egg

s: Letter-drawing sheets for *c, r,* and *s.*

Words: road, sorry, candle, ring, sandwich, rake, cabbage, car, salt, run, sing, cold, say, rip, cage, soap, robber, spider, coin, cap, rocket, seesaw, cloudy, sailboat, roller skates, crown

t: Letter-drawing sheets for *d, p,* and *t.*

Words: dark, take, park, duck, table, draw, trick, pretty, pile, tool, doughnut, truck, tired, poor, desk, terrible, dream, package, play, toast, door, pot, tank, pet, dig

u: Letter-drawing sheets for *h, r,* and *u.*

Words: honey, rainbow, underneath, hand, rocking chair, ugly, umbrella, raisins, help, up, rope, hill, hold, uncle, rake, undressing, run, until, happy, rat, heavy, upstairs, read, horn

v: Letter-drawing sheets for *r, q,* and *v.*

Words: run, ribbon, vegetable, question, roll, violin, quickly, quarter, vinegar, ride, quiet, violet, queen, ring, quarrel, visit, rope, vitamin, quilt, rock, valley, quart, vote *w:* Letter-drawing sheets for *f, m,* and *w.*

Words: wall, fly, mother, witch, mend, fox, why, fun, weather, mix, music, fry, wake, flame, wild, minute, fix, window, fire, mud, make, wing, favorite, maybe

x: Letter-drawing sheets for *j, t,* and *x.*

Words: extra, job, tiger, X ray, excellent, tongue, jam, trouble, excited, jump, exercise, telephone, jail, expect, jacket, train, joke, explain, jar, tent, jelly, explode, tub

y: Letter-drawing sheets for *p, q,* and *y.*

Words: yarn, yes, prune, quilt, play, young, quiet, yellow, question, party, yard, quick, poke, you, pants, year, quarter, queen, yesterday, pills, quarrel, yolk, pen, pot, quart

z: Letter-drawing sheets for *u, v,* and *z.*

Words: zebra, upstairs, vinegar, zoom, zipper, valley, umbrella, vegetable, zero, undress, uncle, zigzag, visit, ugly, vitamin, zoo, unkind, vote

Step 8. The Picture-Matching Game with the Letter-Cards

This step is just like Step 6 except that now the child has to match the pictures to letters instead of to alpha-pictures.

Take out the letter-cards and the game-pictures listed with the letter you are working on as shown at the end of Step 8.

Put one of the letter-cards in front of the child and ask him to tell you what sound that letter is for. Tell him that it is right if he gives the correct one.

If the child gives the alphabet name instead of the sound, tell him that is the right alphabet name, and ask him to tell you the sound too.

If the child can't say the sound, take out the alpha-picture chart and show him the alpha-picture for that letter. Point out how the dark lines are the same as the letter on the card. If he still can't say the sound, you say it, and again make it clear to him that this is the sound the name of the alpha-picture starts with.

Then do the same with the other letter-cards you took out.

After the child has said the correct sound for each of the letter-cards, mix up all the game-pictures you took out and show them to the child one at a time. Have him say what the picture shows and see that it gets called by the name it is supposed to be. Then have him say the sound that the name starts with.

If he says the wrong sound you say the name again, first normally, and then once more, with a pause after the starting sound. Then say the right sound by itself. Have him say the name these ways too, and then the right sound by itself also.

When the child has said the correct starting sound, ask him to put the picture on the letter-card which has the letter for that sound.

If the child puts the picture on the card with the right letter, tell him it is right. Then take the picture off and put it aside.

If he puts the picture on a card with a wrong letter, say, "That's _____ (say the sound it is for). _____ (the name of the game-picture) starts with _____ (the starting sound). Can you find the letter for _____ (that sound)?"

If necessary, show him the right letter.

Have the child put the picture on the right letter-card. Then tell him that's right and put the picture aside.

Then have the child do the same thing with the next game-picture, and so on. Continue until the child puts seven pictures in a row on the right letter-cards, *whether or not* he says their starting sounds correctly right away. If you have shown him all the game-pictures you took out before he gets seven in a row right, reshuffle the game-pictures and rearrange the letter-cards so they are in different places, and go on. Repeat as often as necessary.

If the child has a hard time *giving the right starting sounds* for the names of the game-pictures, do the following for awhile after the child names each game-picture: Repeat the name and have the child repeat it after you. Then say the name with a pause after the starting sound and have the child repeat that. Only then ask, "What's the starting sound?" If necessary, say the starting sound yourself and have the child repeat it after you.

If the child has a hard time *pointing to the right letters* after the starting sound has been given, do the following for awhile just before he is to choose which letter is for that sound: Say, "_____ (the name of the game-picture) starts with _____ (its starting sound)." Pointing to each letter in turn from left to right, say, "This is for _____ (the sound it is for), this is for _____ (the sound it is for)," and so on. Then, if necessary, say, "Put the _____ (the name of the game-picture) on the letter for _____ (the starting sound)."

For each letter you work on in Step 8, here are the letter-cards to use, and the game-pictures to use:

(*a:* not worked on in this step.)

b: Letter-cards and game-pictures for *a* and *b*.

c: Letter-cards and game-pictures for *a, b,* and *c*.

d: Letter-cards and game-pictures for *b, c,* and *d*.

e: Letter-cards and game-pictures for *b, d,* and *e*.

f: Letter-cards and game-pictures for *c, d,* and *f*.

g: Letter-cards and game-pictures for *a, f,* and *g*.

h: Letter-cards and game-pictures for *d, f,* and *h*.

i: Letter-cards and game-pictures for *b, h,* and *i*.

j: Letter-cards and game-pictures for *e, g,* and *j*.

k: Letter-cards and game-pictures for *a, h,* and *k*.

l: Letter-cards and game-pictures for *b, f,* and *l*.

m: Letter-cards and game-pictures for *e, j,* and *m*.

n: Letter-cards and game-pictures for *a, m,* and *n*.

o: Letter-cards and game-pictures for *d, e,* and *o.*

p: Letter-cards and game-pictures for *d, o,* and *p.*

q: Letter-cards and game-pictures for *g, o,* and *q.*

r: Letter-cards and game-pictures for *j, m,* and *r.*

s: Letter-cards and game-pictures for *i, o,* and *s.*

t: Letter-cards and game-pictures for *f, l,* and *t.*

u: Letter-cards and game-pictures for *e, n,* and *u.*

v: Letter-cards and game-pictures for *h, n,* and *v.*

w: Letter-cards and game-pictures for *n, u,* and *w.*

x: Letter-cards and game-pictures for *f, h,* and *x.*

y: Letter-cards and game-pictures for *g, x,* and *y.*

z: Letter-cards and game-pictures for *e, r,* and *z.*

Step 9. The Word-Matching Game with the Letter-Cards

This step is just like Step 7 except that again the child has to match to letters rather than alpha-pictures.

Take out the letter-cards listed with the letter you are working on as shown at the end of Step 9.

Put one of the letter-cards in front of the child, and ask him to tell you what sound that letter is for. Tell him that it is right if he gives the correct one.

If the child gives the alphabet name instead of the sound, tell him that is the right alphabet name and ask him to tell you the sound too.

If the child can't say the sound, take out the alpha-picture chart and show him the alpha-picture for that letter. Point out how the dark lines are the same as the letter on the card. If he still can't say the sound, you say it, and again make it clear to him that this is the sound the name of the alpha-picture starts with.

Then do the same with the other letter-cards you took out.

After the child has said the correct sound for each of the letter-cards, say the first word listed at the end of Step 9 for the letter you are on, and use it in a phrase or sentence to help the child recognize it. Tell him what it means if he doesn't know it.

Have the child repeat the word and then have him say the sound that it starts with. If he says the wrong sound, you say the word again normally and then once more with a pause after the starting sound. Then say the right sound by itself. Have him say the word these ways too and then the right sound by itself also.

When the child has said the correct starting sound, ask him to point to the letter for that sound.

If the child points to the right letter, tell him it is right.

If he points to a wrong letter, say, "That's _____ (the sound it is for). _____ (the word you gave him) starts with _____ (the starting sound). Can you find the letter for _____ (that sound)?"

If necessary, show him the right letter.

Then go on to the next word on the list at the end of Step 9, and do the same things again, and so on. Play this game until the child has pointed to the right letter for seven words in a row, *whether or not* he says their starting sounds correctly right away. If you get through the whole list of words before he gets seven in a row right, rearrange the letter-cards and start from the beginning of the list again. Repeat as often as necessary.

If the child has a hard time *giving the right starting sounds* for the words you tell him, do the following for awhile after he says each word: Repeat the word and have the child repeat it again after you. Then say the word with a pause after the starting sound and have the child repeat that. Only then ask, "What's the starting sound?" If necessary, say the starting sound yourself and have the child repeat it after you.

If the child has a hard time *pointing to the right letters* after the starting sound has been given, do the following for awhile

just before he is to choose which letter is for that sound: Say,
"_____ (the word you gave him) starts with _____ (its
starting sound)." Pointing to each letter in turn from left to
right, say, "This is for _____ (the sound it is for), this is for
_____ (the sound it is for)," and so on. Then, if necessary,
say, "Point to the letter for _____ (the starting sound)."

*For each letter you work on in Step 9, here are
the letter-cards to use, and the list of words to use:*

(*a:* not worked on in this step.)

b: Letter-cards for *a* and *b*.

Words: angry, box, answer, button, busy, after, animal, bell,
apple, bone, brown, at, ball, acrobat, ask, build, basket, ax

c: Letter-cards for *a*, *b*, and *c*.

Words: crown, cap, apple, big, cookies, blind, ask, actor,
carrot, crooked, bicycle, acrobat, break, cool, butter, ant, cloud,
bake, bear, ax, camera, anchor, bring, corner, after

d: Letter-cards for *b*, *c*, and *d*.

Words: boy, cat, dark, candy, button, cook, duck, draw, box,
bag, carriage, doughnut, crayon, Band-Aid, desk, brown, coming, dream, blue, door, bed, climb, dive, catch, corn, dig, bit

e: Letter-cards for *c*, *d*, and *e*.

Words: cabbage, edge, dot, call, donkey, enter, elephant, come,
doorbell, elbow, dusty, elevator, cookies, drink, calf, envelope,
clip, draw, empty, dinner, coat, egg, clothes, dirty, cranberries

f: Letter-cards for *b*, *e*, and *f*.

Words: fly, fox, box, everywhere, fun, button, feel, egg, busy,
empty, fry, build, bone, flame, enter, brown, fix, forward, end,
ball, basket, fire, bite, elbow, favorite, enemy

g: Letter-cards for *e*, *f*, and *g*.

Words: guess, fog, ever, good, family, give, funny, end, fix, grow, get, friend, egg, game, elephant, fold, empty, gas, flat, elbow, enter, girl, gone, feel, garbage, edge, fox

h: Letter-cards for *e*, *g*, and *h*.

Words: everybody, hand, ghost, egg, gone, help, end, grandfather, hill, gum, elephant, give, hold, enter, elbow, hanger, happy, glad, grass, heavy, escalator, horn, goose, honey, envelope, goat, hair, gate, empty

i: Letter-cards for *g*, *h*, and *i*.

Words: ill, grapes, horse, gold, inside, him, inchworm, guard, happy, instrument, injure, hill, gift, hand, ink, got, hiccup, horn, igloo, glad, gate, important, help, garden, itch, garage, hold

j: Letter-cards for *d*, *f*, and *j*.

Words: danger, Jell-O, furniture, dinosaur, daisy, jewel, farmer, fast, job, day, fish, join, jungle, feather, decide, dish, jump, finish, dry, jacket, joke, doctor, fireman, forget, jar, doll, full, judge, fun, down

k: Letter-cards for *d*, *g*, and *k*.

Words: kind, dream, door, keep, game, garage, key, desk, garden, kick, kill, green, doughnut, glad, king, draw, dig, kindergarten, gum, dot, gold, kitchen, get, dark, kettle

l: Letter-cards for *a*, *d*, and *l*.

Words: day, actor, lion, lemon, animals, duck, listen, dark, apple, doughnut, and, after, lift, did, advertise, lamb, dirt, lick, avenue, drop, ask, loud, drawer, drive, lucky, angry

m: Letter-cards for *g*, *i*, and *m*.

Words: igloo, moon, go, gang, milk, inch, gardener, mountain, in, gum, meat, golden, ill, gave, melon, injury, important, green, morning, movie, got, itch, mirror, game, if, mud, glad, mask, instrument

n: Letter-cards for *b*, *d*, and *n*.

Words: bacon, dandelions, noisy, needle, berries, dime, bath, napkin, dollar, newspaper, bird, dig, neck, nails, dance, bottom, birthday, notice, dust, brown, nurse, bump, drive, believe, nearly, different, burn, nest, drag

o: Letter-cards for *f*, *i*, and *o*.

Words: front, ill, ox, inside, octopus, fly, inchworm, fix, olive, friend, instrument, object, injury, forget, operate, opposite, floor, ink, igloo, ostrich, find, itch

p: Letter-cards for *g*, *n*, and *p*.

Words: peanuts, grow, girl, pot, now, glad, pancakes, garden, nap, paper, nickel, park, parade, grandfather, note, green, pig, nothing, gold, policeman, give, next, pony, need, potatoes, garbage, net

q: Letter-cards for *l*, *p*, and *q*.

Words: pajamas, quart, lettuce, ladder, quick, party, learn, quiet, quack, late, pillow, long, quilt, pin, question, laugh, poor, quite, pipe, lie, quotes, pocket, queen, lick, library, quarrel, pick, purple

r: Letter-cards for *o*, *q*, and *r*.

Words: ox, rattle, read, quart, octopus, quiet, remember, quack, olive, raisins, object, reach, quilt, operation, razor, ring, question, quarter, opposite, round, rub, queen, ostrich, rust

s: Letter-cards for *b*, *q*, and *s*.

Words: summer, sun, quarrel, queen, butter, banana, sidewalk, box, quarter, sand, quite, soap, bottle, question, boil, salt, sink, quilt, quack, basket, salad, bus, quiet, quick, better, sing, boy, quart, sell, bump *t:* Letter-cards for *h*, *n*, and *t*.

Words: help, telephone, hurry, night, not, teacher, nice, hungry, tell, naughty, try, necklace, hat, hear, tooth, hope, new, tired, toast, number, hospital, nut, tongue, hammer, take, neighbor

u: Letter-cards for *m*, *s*, and *u*.

Words: under, matches, sand, umbrella, silly, move, sleep, upstairs, ugly, mail, milk, spinach, uncle, sink, middle, mother, spot, undress, mister, unable, smooth, music, until, upset, maybe, sad, magazine, up, soft

v: Letter-cards for *b*, *t*, and *v*.

Words: towel, bad, vanilla, boat, tomato, train, vinegar, trumpet, basket, voice, vote, building, borrow, tickle, vacation, tent, bread, vaccination, best, very, trouble, violet, torn, banana

w: Letter-cards for *g*, *p*, and *w*.

Words: puppy, walk, grow, good, will, pillow, guess, want, weather, give, pail, pumpkin, get, wife, pudding, wonderful, ghost, popcorn, paste, work, game, pull, wish, pour, garden, great, wide

x: Letter-cards for *v*, *w*, and *x*.

Words: extra, wallet, expert, vegetable, vitamins, wool, X ray, excellent, warm, violin, witch, excited, vase, village, exercise, world, vest, experience, way, expect, very, explain, why, vacation, explode, winter, violet

y: Letter-cards for *k*, *l*, and *y*.

Words: yell, kitten, lead, yawn, learn, kite, look, years, key, yesterday, lift, lollipop, kindergarten, you, keep, lunch, kayak, yard, young, leg, laugh, yet, kick, kiss, yellow, lipstick, yarn, kind

z: Letter-cards for *l*, *y*, and *z*.

Words: yell, zero, lamb, lick, yawn, zebra, years, label, zoom, laugh, zipper, yesterday, line, you, zigzag, yard, young, lemon, zoo, yet, listen

Step 10. Giving the Sounds for the Letters

Take out a letter-card for each letter in the alphabet up to and including the letter you are working on.

a b c d e f g h i j k l m n o p q r s
t u v w x y z

For example, if you are working on letter f, take out a letter-card for a, b, c, d, e, and f.

Mix up these letter-cards and show one to the child. Ask him to tell you the sound that letter is for.

If the child gives the alphabet name instead of the sound, tell him that is the right alphabet name, and ask him to tell you the sound too.

If the child gives the wrong sound, or if he can't give a sound at all, take out the alpha-picture chart and show him the alpha-picture for that letter. If he still can't say the sound, you say it and have him say it after you.

It may happen that the child gives a sound which the letter is sometimes for but that this is not the sound you taught him. For example, he may give *j* for the letter g, which is the sound g has in George. Then you should tell him that's right, that the letter does have that sound sometimes, and ask him also to tell you the sound he learned with you. If he can't, use the alpha-picture chart as above.

When the child has said the right sound, tell him it is right, and have him tell you a word that starts with that sound. Count his word as right so long as it starts with a sound like the sound you taught him for that letter. Note that the word doesn't have to be *written* with that letter, for example, "kitchen" is fine for c, "giant" is fine for j, and so on.

If the child can't say a word that starts with the right sound, you tell him the name of the alpha-picture for that letter and have him repeat that.

If the child was able to give you both an acceptable sound for the letter and a word starting with that sound, without your having to tell him, then put that letter-card away. If he needed help either on the sound or on the word, keep the letter-card in a separate pile to use again.

Then go on to the next letter-card and do the same again, and so on. When you have gone through all the letter-cards, then take the ones which you kept in a separate pile because the child needed help on them. Go through those letter-cards the same way again one more time.

Then go on with Step 1 for the next letter of the alphabet, until you have gone through all the letters. Then go on to Part II.

Procedure for Successive Sessions on Part I

Start the first session with Step 1 for a, and continue with Step 2 for a, Step 3 for a, and so on, as far as you get. At the end of the session write down the letter and the step at which to begin next time. If you had to stop in the middle of a step put down that step and start it from the beginning again next time.

Proceed in the same way in successive sessions, going through the steps for each letter of the alphabet in order (a b c d e f g h i j k l m n o p q r s t u v w x y z). Always go through all the steps with each letter before going on to Step 1 with the next letter.

The games will be very difficult for some of the children in the beginning. When this is the case, follow the procedures indicated with each game for use when the game is too hard. When you use these procedures, try the child without them again every once in a while, and stop using them when the child no longer needs them. But keep them so long as the child has trouble without them.

As described with the games, the child is always supposed to get seven right in a row before you go on to the next game. When you use the special procedures that make the game easier, count the right answers he gives then too for getting seven right in a row.

It is important to stick to the procedures as described except when the child himself speeds them up and shows he is able to go faster. Thus, once the child gets familiar with these procedures, he may tell you some of the things you are to ask him before you ask and even before you get through what else you are to do, such as giving phrases or sentences in Steps 7 and 9. This is fine so long as he is able to do everything correctly. But stop him if he says something wrong (for example, if he names a picture wrong or says that a word starts with the wrong sound) before he goes on with what comes next.

Summary of Part I

Start with the letter a and go through Steps 1–5. Then go through Steps 1–10 for b, then for c, d, e, f, g, h, i, j, k, l, m, n, o, p, q, r, s, t, u, v, w, x, y, and z.

Steps

1. Read the tongue-twister sentence. Then say each word that starts with the sound you are on, first normally and then with a pause after the starting sound. Have the child repeat these ways of saying each word.
2. Show the child two game-pictures, one that has a name starting with the sound you are on and one that doesn't. Have the child name the pictures and pick the one that starts with the sound you are on. Continue until he has picked the correct one seven times in a row.
3. Showing the child one game-picture at a time, have him name it and say whether or not it starts with the sound you are on. Continue until he has said this correctly seven times in a row.
4. Explain the alpha-picture and have the child trace the letter, practicing until he can do it fairly well.
5. Go over the alpha-picture again and have the child draw the letter without the dotted outlines. If necessary, go back and forth between tracing and drawing, but don't spend more than a half hour on Steps 4 and 5 together.
6. Put the letter-drawing sheets in front of the child and have him say the sounds. Then, giving the child one game-picture at a time, have him say the sound its name starts with and place it on the alpha-picture for that sound. Continue until he has

placed seven game-pictures in a row on the right alpha-pictures. (Note that he does *not* have to say the sounds correctly without help.)

7. Like 6, but now you say words instead of giving the child game-pictures.

8. Like 6, but now use letters instead of letter-drawing sheets with alpha-pictures.

9. Like 7, but again using letters instead of letter-drawing sheets with alpha-pictures.

10. Have the child say the sound and give a word starting with that sound for each letter of the alphabet up to and including the one you are on. Do the same thing once more with all the letters for which he needed help on either the sound or the word.

Part II
Learning to Sound Out
Simple Words

Materials for Part II

There are no special materials for Part II. The game-pictures, letter-cards, and alpha-picture chart used in Part I are all that is needed for Part II.

Steps for Part II

Step 1. The Which-Picture Game

Follow the instructions below, with each set of game-pictures listed at the end of Step 1. Start with Set 1. When you have finished with Set 1, then do the same things with Set 2, then with Set 3, and so on, until you have gone through all seven sets. Then go on to Step 2.

Take out the set of game-pictures you are on. Spread them out. Tell the child you are going to say the name of one of the pictures, but you won't say it the regular way. Tell him you are going to say the separate sounds that make up its name, and he should guess which picture you mean. He should say the name the regular way and point to the picture.

Then say the separate sounds that make up the name of one of the pictures, as shown at the end of Step 1. Say the sounds, not the names of the letters. Pronounce each sound separately, and after each sound pause a moment before going on to the next sound. For example, for the ball say "*b-aw-l*," and for the bus say "*b-u-s*."

If the child can't tell which picture you mean or guesses a wrong one, have him repeat the sounds after you. If he still can't tell, you say the name the regular way, except leave a pause after the starting sound. For example, for the ball you would now say "*b-awl*," and for the bus you would now say "*b-us*." If he still doesn't recognize the word, say it the same way again but this time make the pause after the starting sound very short. Then if he still doesn't know, say the word the regular way without any pauses.

When he points to the right picture, tell him he is right.

Then tell the child you will say the separate sounds that make up the name of another one of the pictures, and he should again guess which it is. Go through the same procedure with another picture. Again first pronounce each sound separately, and if the child can't pick the right picture, have him repeat the sounds. If he still can't pick the right picture, decrease the pauses as above. Keep doing this with the three different pictures, changing the order around, until the child has identified each picture from the separate sounds alone, without your having to decrease the pauses. (It's all right if he had to repeat the sounds.)

Then put those three game-pictures away and do the same things with the next set of game-pictures listed at the end of Step 1, until you have gone through all seven sets. Then go on to Step 2.

The sets of game-pictures for Step 1 and the separate sounds in their names:

Set 1

ball:	*b-aw-l*
bus:	*b-u-s*
bed:	*b-e-d*

Set 2

jet:	*j-e-t*
jam:	*j-a-m*
jail:	*j-ae-l*

Set 3

pig:	*p-i-g*
pen:	*p-e-n*
pail:	*p-ae-l*

Set 4

fan:	*f-a-n*
fish:	*f-i-sh*
fire:	*f-eye-r*

Set 5

dam:	*d-a-m*
dice:	*d-eye-s*
dome:	*d-oh-m*

Set 6

bat:	*b-a-t*
bell:	*b-e-l*
bike:	*b-eye-k*

Set 7

nut:	*n-u-t*
nail:	*n-ae-l*
net:	*n-e-t*

Step 2. Building and Reading the Names of Some Game-Pictures

Follow the instructions below with each set of game-pictures and letter-cards listed at the end of Step 2. Start with Set 1 and do (a), (b), and (c). When you have finished with Set 1, then do (a), (b), and (c) with Set 2, then with Set 3, and so on, until you have gone through all five sets. Then go on to Step 3.

(a) You build the names with the child
Take out the set of game-pictures you are on and the letter-cards for each letter that occurs in their names. Mix up the letter-cards and spread them out with the letters the right way around.

Tell the child you and he will build the names of the pictures with the letter-cards. Put one picture in front of the child and have him say its name. Then you say its name too, first the regular way and then pronouncing each sound separately with a pause between the sounds. Have the child find the letter-card for each sound, starting with the first, then the second, and then the last. Let him look at the alpha-picture chart if he needs to and help him if necessary. Have him place the letter-cards underneath the picture as they are found, building the word from left to right.

Then point to each letter in turn, from left to right, and have the child say the sound it is for. Help him if necessary. Then move your finger a little faster across the letters and say their sounds more blended together. Finally, move your finger quite fast and say the word the regular way. Have the child say the word the regular way too. (We want the child to understand that together the letters make the word _____, the name of the picture.)

Then, in the same way, build the names of the other two game-pictures with the child.

(b) You build the names for the child to read
Then tell the child that you are now going to build one of the names again but that you won't tell him which. Build any of the three names, this time without saying anything out loud, and then have him try to read it.

Give him help if he needs it in sounding out the letters from left to right and in blending the sounds together into the word.

After the word has been read, mix up the letter-cards again and tell the child that you will again build one of the names and that he should again try to read it. Go through the same procedure again with another name. Keep doing this with the names of the three pictures, in different orders, until the child has managed to read each one correctly without your having to help him.

(c) The child builds the names
Now ask the *child* to pick one of the pictures and try to build its name.

If the child is able to, let him build a name by himself and you "see if you can read it," so that he is doing what you did in (b) and you are doing what he did.

If this is too difficult, you help the child to build one of the names; when it has been correctly built, have him read it to you.

When you are finished with one of the names, have the child pick another picture and build its name, and so on. Continue to help him as necessary. See that the name of each picture gets built at least once. Whether or not the child needed help in building a name, it doesn't have to be built more than once.

When you have gone through (a), (b), and (c) for one set of three game-pictures, then put those game-pictures and their letter-cards away. Do the same things with the next set of game-pictures listed at the end of Step 2, until you have gone through all five sets. Then go on to Step 3.

The sets of game-pictures and letter-cards for Step 2:

Set 1: a, h, m, p, t, y

> hat
> map
> yam

Set 2: a, b, f, j, m, n, t

> bat
> jam
> fan

Set 3: b, g, m, n, s, u

> bus
> gum
> sun

Set 4: b, d, e, j, n, p, t

> bed
> pen
> jet

Set 5: c, g, n, p, t, u

        gun
        nut
        cup

Step 3. Building and Reading Some More Simple Words

Follow the instructions below with each set of words listed at the end of Step 3. Start with Set 1 and do (a), (b), and (c). When you have finished with Set 1, then do (a), (b), and (c) with Set 2, then with Set 3 and so on, until you have gone through all twenty-two sets. Then go to Part III.

(a) You build words with the child
Take out all the letter-cards you will need to build the words in the set you are on. Mix up the letter-cards and spread them out with the letters the right way around.

Tell the child that you and he will build some more words. Tell him the first word is _____ (say the word that is first in the set), like in _____ (say something using the word. You can use the phrases listed with the words at the end of Step 3, or you can make up your own if you want to). For example, when you are on Set 1, say something like: "The first word is pan, like in a pan on the stove."

Then say the word again, first the regular way and then pronouncing each sound separately, with a pause between the sounds. As in the first part of Step 2, have the child find the letter-card for each sound, starting with the first, then the second, and then the last. Have him put the letter-cards in place as they are found, building the word from left to right.

Then point to each letter in turn, from left to right, and have the child say the sound it is for. Help him if necessary. Then move your finger a little faster across the letters and say their sounds more blended together. Finally, move your finger quite fast and say the word the regular way. Have the child say the word the regular way too.

Then tell the child that now you and he will build another word. Tell him the word is _____ (say the word that is second in the set), like in _____ (say something using the word).

Then say the word again, first the regular way and then pronouncing each sound separately, with a pause between the sounds. Have the child find the letter-cards needed. Have him leave the letters that are the same as for the previous word in place and change only what is needed. For example, in Set 1, "man" is to be built after "pan." Have the child put *m* in place of the *p* and leave the *a* and the *n* as they are.

Then, as before, make it clear to the child that, together, the letters make the word. Point to each letter in turn, from left to right, and have the child say the sound it is for. Then move your fingers faster across the letters and say their sounds more blended together. Finally, move your finger quite fast and say the word the regular way. Have the child say the word the regular way too.

After that, tell the child that you and he will build another word, and do the same things with the third word as with the second. Again have him leave the letters that are the same in place and just make what changes are needed.

(b) You build words for the child to read

After the third word in the set has been built and you have made it clear that, together, the letters make the word, then tell the child now you will change it back to one of the words you had before. He should see if he can tell which word it is.

Again leave the letters that are the same in place and change only those letters you need to in order to make a different word in the set. Ask him if he can tell which one you have built. If necessary, ask him "Is it _____ or _____?" saying the two words in the set besides the one you just had. (Make sure you don't always say the right word first.)

Give the child whatever help he needs in sounding out the letters from left to right and in blending the sounds together into the word.

When the word has been correctly read, tell the child that you will again change the word and that he should again try to read it. Build another of the words in the set, again leaving the letters that are the same in place and changing only those letters that you need to. Again ask the child if he can tell which word you have built. Again, if necessary, ask him "Is it _____ or _____?" Also again help him with sounding out and blending if he needs help.

Keep doing this with the three different words in the set, in different orders, until the child has managed to read each one correctly without your having to help him, other than asking "Is it _____ or _____?"

(c) The child builds words
After the child has read the last word in the set correctly without help, tell him that now he should change it to another one of those three words.

If the child is able to, let him choose the word by himself and you "see if you can read it," so that he is doing what you did in (b) and you are doing what he did.

If he doesn't remember the words, tell him what word to make.

If it is too difficult for him to make the word by himself, then you help him to make it. Then have him read it to you.

When you are finished with one of the words, have the child proceed in the same way with another. See that each of the three words in the set gets built at least once. Whether or not the child needed help in building a word, it doesn't have to be built more than once.

When you have gone through (a), (b), and (c) for one set of three words, then put away the letter-cards for those words and do the same things with the next set of words listed at the end of Step 3, until you have gone through all twenty-two sets. Then go on to Part III.

> *The sets of words, letter-cards, and phrases for Step 3:*

Set 1: a, f, m, n, p

> pan: a *pan* on the stove
> man: a boy grows into a *man*
> fan: a *fan* to cool yourself with

Set 2: a, f, p, s, t

        pat: to *pat* a dog
        fat: Santa Claus is always *fat*
        sat: the little girl *sat* on Santa Claus' lap

Set 3: a, g, n, r, t

        rat: a *rat* can bite you
        ran: he *ran* away as fast as he could
        rag: a *rag* to clean with

Set 4: a, c, n, p, t

        cat: a *cat* says "miaow"
        can: a *can* of soup
        cap: a *cap* on your head

Set 5: a, d, m, n, p

        mad: mother was *mad*
        man: the *man* driving the bus
        map: a *map* can help you find some place

Set 6: a, b, d, g, t

        bat: you hit the baseball with a *bat*
        bag: a *bag* of candy
        bad: the food was *bad*

Set 7: a, b, d, s, t

        sat: the boy *sat* in the big chair
        sad: sometimes you feel *sad*
        bad: a *bad* movie

Set 8: a, g, p, t

        tap: *tap* your foot with the music
        pat: *pat* the baby
        tag: to play *tag*

Set 9: f, h, i, s, t

        hit: *hit* the ball
        sit: *sit* on a chair
        fit: the clothes don't *fit*

Set 10: g, i, n, p, t

pig: a *pig* goes "oink, oink"
pit: a *pit* is a hole in the ground
pin: to *pin* a baby's diapers

Set 11: d, h, i, m, t

hid: the child *hid* from the others
him: if the baby cries pick *him* up
hit: you shouldn't *hit* your little sister

Set 12: i, p, s, t

tip: you write with the *tip* of your pencil
pit: to fall in a *pit*
sit: a dog can *sit*

Set 13: e, h, m, n, p

hen: the *hen* laid an egg
pen: you can write with a *pen*
men: the *men* working on the street

Set 14: e, p, t, w, y

pet: a dog is a good *pet*
wet: you get *wet* in the rain
yet: supper is not ready *yet*

Set 15: g, h, o, p, t

pot: you make soup in a *pot*
hot: the stove is *hot*
got: you've *got* many teeth

Set 16: h, m, o, p, t

hop: children and rabbits *hop*
top: the *top* of a big building
mop: to clean the floor with a *mop*

Set 17: g, o, p, t

pot: put potatoes in a *pot*
top: the *top* of a tree
got: he *got* the candy at the store

Set 18: f, g, n, s, u

> sun: it's nice out when the *sun* shines
> gun: the cowboy has a *gun*
> fun: it's *fun* to go down a slide

Set 19: b, n, s, t, u

> bus: to ride in a *bus*
> bun: a hamburger *bun*
> but: I want to go *but* I can't

Set 20: b, g, n, r, u

> run: the boy can *run* fast
> rug: the *rug* on the floor
> rub: you can erase something if you *rub* with an eraser

Set 21: b, g, n, u

> gun: he lost his *gun*
> bun: you eat a *bun*
> bug: you don't want to eat a *bug*

Set 22: b, g, t, u

> tub: a bath in the *tub*
> but: you don't want to *but* you have to
> bug: a very little *bug*

Procedure for Successive Sessions on Part II

In Part II you stay on each step until you have gone through all the sets for that step. Start by doing Step 1 with each of the sets for Step 1. Then do Step 2 (a), (b), and (c) with each of the sets for Step 2. Finally do Step 3 (a), (b), and (c) with each of the sets for Step 3.

If you have to stop a session before finishing (a), (b), and (c)—everything that is to be done with a set—next time start at the beginning again, with (a) for that set. Otherwise go on to the next set. At the end of each session write down the step and set at which you are to begin next time.

Summary of Part II

Go through all the sets of pictures for Step 1, working with each set until the child has identified all three pictures in the set from the separate sounds alone.

Then go to Step 2 and do (a), (b), and (c) with each set in succession. Finally, go to Step 3 and do (a), (b), and (c) with each set in succession. In Step 2 game-pictures are used and in Step 3 only words, but (a), (b), and (c) are essentially the same:

(a) You build words with the child. Each of the three words in a set is to get built once.

(b) You build words for the child to read. Keep doing this with the three names in the set until the child has read each one correctly without help.

(c) The child builds words. Each word should get built once.

Part III
Reading Simple Stories

Materials for Part III

Part III makes use of the reading materials (books of mostly stories and poems) that are worked with in the child's regular classroom. The first stories use a very few words and then gradually more and more are included. The words that are used, and the pages on which they are first introduced, are usually listed at the end of the books.

Sometimes there are special exercise sections, or special stories or poems with lots of new words, that aren't listed at the end. These are intended for the classroom teacher to use in special ways, and you can just skip them, unless you feel it would be particularly useful to go over them. If you do go over them, don't let them take up much time.

For each regular story or poem (or for each part of a story that is especially long) you will need a set of word-cards for the new words that are introduced in it. Use the list at the end of the book to make the word-cards. Break a story into smaller parts if it is unusually long or if more than about twelve different new words occur for the first time in it.

Index cards make good cards to print the words on. They can then all be kept in standard file boxes, in the order of the pages, with dividers between the stories (or the parts of the long stories). On the dividers, simply print the name of each story or poem (with "Part I" or "Part II" where appropriate) and the page on which it begins.

For the word-cards, if a word can begin with a small letter as well as a capital (as most words can), print the word all in small letters, and directly underneath print it again with a capital letter at the start and small letters afterwards. For words that are always written with a capital letter (like a name), just print the word once with a capital letter at the start and small letters afterwards.

On the back of each word-card write the name of the story or poem to which the word belongs. Also write the page on which the word first occurs in the book in normal print, not in some special print or all in capitals, as story titles are sometimes printed. (Note that the page on which a word first occurs printed normally may be later than the page given in the list at the end of the book for when the word is introduced.)

For Part III, then, besides the materials you need for the earlier parts you will need

> the books; and
>
> the file boxes with the word-cards, divided into stories.

You will also need

> strips of heavy paper so that the child can put one underneath the line he is reading as a marker;
>
> lots of small slips of paper, on which you can print words the child misses (little memo pads are good for this); and
>
> an envelope for each child, with his name on it, in which to keep slips for words he has missed.

Steps for Part III

Follow these steps for succeeding stories (or poems) from the reading materials.

Since these reading materials are used in the child's classroom, he may not need to start with the first story. Find out with which story to start the steps by showing him word-cards and having him tell you what they say.

Make sure it is clear to him that the two words written on the top and bottom of most of the word-cards are the same. Tell him the first letter on the bottom is always a capital letter, that it is the same letter as the first letter on the top, and that it is for the same sound.

When the child doesn't know a word or reads it incorrectly, use the *Procedure for teaching words* described below under Step 1.

Start with the set of word-cards for the first story, then go to the second, then the third, and so on. Stop when he has missed three words altogether. Start the steps with him on the first page of the story in which he missed his third word.

Thus, if he already misses three words on the word-cards for the first story, start the steps on the first page of the first story. If he misses one word on the first story and two words on the second, start on the first page of the second story, and so on.

Step 1. Word-Cards for the Page

Take out all the word-cards for the page you are on and follow the *Procedure for going over sets of words* below. If there are no word-cards for this page, go on to Step 2.

Procedure for going over sets of words
Show the child the words one at a time. If he can read a word correctly, tell him that's right and go on to the next word. If he cannot read the word correctly, follow the steps below under *Procedure for teaching words*, stopping and telling him he is right if the child says the word correctly at any point before the end.

Make the procedure a pretty rapid one, always providing the next bit of prescribed help quickly enough that you don't lose the child's attention.

Make sure the child always looks at the word starting with a capital letter as well as the word starting with a small letter when the word is written both ways. You should always go through the steps on the word starting with a small letter first.

When the word has been correctly identified, you can ask "And what is this word?" pointing to the one starting with a capital, as long as it seems necessary.

Procedure for teaching words

(a) If the word is built up from simpler words, show him the simpler words in it. Sometimes a word just has "s" or "es" or "d" or "ed" or "ing" added on at the end, for example "girls," "glasses," "baked," "fixed," and "singing." Sometimes the simple word is changed slightly before such an addition is made. An "e" at the end of the word may be taken off, for example "baking," or a final letter may be repeated, as in "slammed." And sometimes two words can be put together, as in "anybody" or "something."

Whenever there is a simpler word or words in the bigger word, point them out to the child and follow steps (b), (c), and (d) with the simpler word or words first, starting with the one on the left. Sometimes you can just cover up some of the letters in the bigger word. Other times you may want to write the simpler word on a separate piece of paper, especially when it gets changed a little in the bigger word by having, for example, an "e" taken off.

(b) Tell the child the sound of any letter or set of letters where the sound is different from what you taught him. Be sure to try to do this *before* having the child sound the word out (c). The vowels, "a," "e," "i," "o," and "u" will very often have different sounds than the ones you taught. Frequently they have the sounds of their names. They also often have still different sounds, particularly in combinations, for example the two kinds of *oo* sounds in "look" and "soon." There are also frequent other combinations of letters which don't have the sounds you taught, like "th," "ch," and "sh." Sometimes a letter doesn't have a sound at all, like "e" in "have." And usually two of the same letters in a row just have the sound once, like the l's in "tell." (There is no way for the child to know these things at first unless he is told.)

For example, if the word is "home," you would point to the "o" saying, "Instead of *o*, that's *oh*," and to the "e" saying,

"Instead of *e*, this is silent." If the word is "talk," you would point to the "al" and say, "Instead of *a*, *l*, these two together are *aw*." If the word is "moon," you would point to the "oo" and say, "Instead of *o*, *o*, these two together are *oo*."

(c) Then going from left to right, point to the letters in turn. When you get to letters that have sounds different from what you taught the child, you just say those sounds again and have him say them after you. Otherwise have him give the sounds by himself. Let him look at the alpha-picture chart if he needs to.

If the child already blends some of the letters together in sounding out the word, that is excellent. For example, if the word is "Tom," instead of saying *t-o-m*, he may say *to-m*. That is very good. But it should not be required.

(d) When the child has said all the sounds, wait a moment to see if he can recognize the word. If not, again pointing, you say the sounds again.

If he still doesn't recognize the word, again pointing, say the first sounds blended together (for example, *to* . . . for "Tom," *gir* . . . for "girl," and so on) and see if he can finish the word. If he can't, and the word is long enough, give him more and more of the blended sounds (for "father," after *fa* . . . , now say *fath* . . . ; or for "birthday," after *bir* . . . , now say *birth* . . . , and then *birthd* . . .). Finally, say the whole word. Have the child say the word too. Make sure he knows what the word is.

When the child has correctly said the word, go on to the next word, unless there is only one word, in which case you go on to the next step. Go through all the words the same way, following the *Procedure for teaching words* for each word the child does not recognize.

When you have gone through the entire set of words in this way, change the order of the words and show them to him again. Go through them exactly the same way as before, again following the *Procedure for teaching words* for each word the child does not recognize.

Keep going through all the words in this way until the child gets all of them right without making any mistakes and without needing help twice in a row.

If there is a sizable number of words and this task seems difficult for the child, make it easier by first working on only two or three of the words. Then when he has gotten these right without help several times in a row, add one or two more. Keep working in this way until the child is able to get all the words right without help twice in a row.

Step 2. Reading the Page

When the child has gotten all the word-cards for the page right without help twice in a row, turn to the page in the book.

If the page is in the middle of a story or poem which you began in a previous session, help the child remember the part he has already read. If you come to any words that are in some special print or are all in capital letters, like the title of a story, then you read them to the child. Otherwise let the child read.

If the child has trouble keeping his place, let him point to the words or use a strip of paper as a marker underneath the line he is reading. If he needs more help, you point to the words.

If the child doesn't understand something like a question mark or a period, tell him what it is for, and show him how to read the part where it is.

If he comes to a word he can't read or reads it wrong without correcting himself, follow the *Procedure for teaching words* described in Step 1.

Then print the word carefully on a small separate slip of paper, to practice with afterwards. (Be sure to print it the way it is in the book: all in small letters if that is how it is there, or with a capital letter at the start if it has one.)

Most children at this point will not read smoothly or fluently; they will say the words as if they were separate one from another instead of being parts of sentences. That doesn't matter. What is important is that the child make sense of what he is reading. Discuss what is happening in the story (or poem) a little as you go along. Try to ask him questions which will tell you whether he understands what he is reading. (You can use the pictures in your questions, but try not to ask questions which he can answer on the basis of the pictures alone without having to think about what he read.) Sometimes it is hard for the child to really pay attention to the meaning of what he is reading the first time he reads the words. If he didn't seem to understand something, have him read it again.

Step 3. Missed Words for the Page

When the child has read through the page and you have discussed it with him, take the slips you made for the words he missed on this page. Follow the *Procedure for going over sets of words* described in Step 1 with these slips, continuing until he gets them all right without help twice in a row.

(If the child missed no words on this page, omit this step.)

Step 4. Word-Cards for the Page

When the child has correctly recognized all the slips with missed words for the page twice in a row, then again take all the word-cards for the page. Follow the *Procedure for going over sets of words* described in Step 1 with these word-cards again, continuing until he gets them all right without help twice in a row. (Step 4 is thus a repetition of Step 1.)

(If there are no word-cards for the page, omit this step.)

Step 5. Repeating Steps 2, 3, and 4

If the child missed no more than two different words in reading the page, and the reading seemed fairly smooth and easy, go on to Step 6.

If the child did miss more than two different words, or if the reading did not seem fairly smooth and easy, repeat Step 2, having him read the page again. If he misses any words he didn't miss before, write these words on separate slips too and add them to the slips for the words he missed before.

Then repeat Step 3, now using all the slips for words he missed on that page, whether in the last or previous readings.

Then repeat Step 4, going over the word-cards.

Continue on this way repeating Steps 2, 3, and 4 until on Step 2, reading the page, the child misses no more than two different words and reads well. Then repeat Step 3, going over the slips, and Step 4, going over the word-cards, one more time and then go on to Step 6.

Step 6. Succeeding Pages of the Story

Follow Steps 1–5 for succeeding pages until you are finished with the last page of the story.

Now, however, if the child misses some of the same words he missed on a previous page, you don't have to write these down all over again. You can use the slips you made before.

Further, if there are just one or two slips for missed words to go over in Step 3 after the child reads a page, include a few of the slips from earlier pages so you have about four slips altogether. Try to give him more practice this way on words he had particular trouble with.

In the same way, include a few of the cards from earlier pages if there are just one or two cards for a page in Step 4.

Step 7. Missed Words for the Story

After you have gone through Steps 1–5 for the last page of the story, take all the slips for all the words the child missed in this session on all the pages of the story. For these slips follow the *Procedure for going over sets of words* described in Step 1, continuing until he gets them all right without help twice in a row.

(If he missed no words in the story in this session, then omit this step.)

Step 8. Word-Cards for the Story

After the child has gotten all the slips for the story right without help twice in a row, take all the word-cards for all the pages of the story. For these word-cards, follow the *Procedure for going over sets of words* described in Step 1, continuing until he gets them all right without help twice in a row.

(Sometimes there may be no word-cards for an entire story; then omit this step.)

Step 9. Repeating the Story

If the reading was easy for the child, and he didn't miss too many words in the story (no more than about seven different words altogether), go on to Step 1 for the first page of the next story.

If the reading wasn't easy, or the child missed eight or more different words, repeat the preceding steps. Proceed to go over the whole story page by page again exactly as before.

Keep going over the whole story this way until the reading is easy and the child misses no more than about seven different words altogether. Then after finishing the steps through Step 8, go on to Step 1 for the first page of the next story.

Procedure for Successive Sessions on Part III

You start Part III by finding the story on which to begin with the child (see page 291 above). Then you start him on Step 1 for the first page of that story and continue with succeeding steps as far as you get.

At the end of the session, take all the slips you made for words missed in the session and put them in that child's envelope for him to go over at the start of the next session.

Also write down:

1. The page on which you started with the child. (Note also if you are already in a book beyond the first one.)

2. The page on which you are to start the child next time. This page will be the one you are on, if he has not finished the page; otherwise it will be the next page you would go to.

(Thus, if you have begun work on a page but have not completed Step 5 for it, that is the page you write down. If you have completed Step 5 for one page but there are more pages in the story, write down the next page. If you have completed Step 5 for all the pages of the story, write down the first page of the next story if the child is to go on to the next story, or write down the first page of the story you are on if the child is to repeat that story.)

On the second session, start by going over the slips for words missed that you put into the child's envelope at the end of the last session, following the *Procedure for going over sets of words* described under Step 1. Discard the slips when the child has gotten them all right without help twice in a row.

Then, unless you began with the first story last time, take out the word-cards for the last story before the one you began with. Follow the *Procedure for going over sets of words* with these word-cards, continuing until the child has gotten them all right without help twice in a row. Then take out the word-cards for the story you began with, up to the page you got to if you didn't finish the story, and do the same with these word-cards. If you finished that story and went on, continue taking out and going over the word-cards as far as you got, always using one story's set of word-cards at a time.

Then proceed to Step 1 for the page you are to start on, and follow the steps in order. (Thus, you always start with Step 1 again, no matter what step you were on when you stopped.)

At the end of the session again put all the slips for words missed in this session into the child's envelope. (If you didn't finish going over the slips for words missed in the last session, put those slips into the envelope.)

Again write down the page on which to start next time. (You don't need to write down the page on which you started any more, since you will be able to see that from what you wrote down the session before.)

In all succeeding sessions proceed the same way, except to add the following:

If you feel that (due to a long absence, maybe, or just having gone too fast), the child has gotten too far ahead and should be further back, let him start further back again, otherwise following the same procedure.

If Part III is particularly hard for a child, it will help to start the steps on each session back a page or two from the page on which you ended last time.

Also, if a child seems to have forgotten many of the sounds for the letters, take out all the letter-cards again and review the sounds with him in part of each session until he can call them out readily. Shuffle the letter-cards and have him try to give each sound, looking at the alpha-picture chart if necessary. Help him if he needs help.

If you notice that the child keeps needing slips for some of the same words over again, you don't have to discard the slips for these words after they have been gone through at the start of a session. You can keep them aside if you want to, to pull out when needed instead of having to print the word all over again. But discard the ones you don't pull out by the end of the session. The total number of slips you keep for a child shouldn't get too big.

At the end of every week, go over the word-cards for each of the last five stories with the child, story by story, following the *Procedure for going over sets of words* described under Step 1.

Note that you will most likely be starting the child on material he has already gone over in class. This will probably be much easier for him than working on material he has not yet gone over. But in later sessions you may get ahead of where he is in class, so don't be surprised if he suddenly seems to do much more poorly and you need to slow down.

Also, note that you probably won't be able to finish all of the stories. This is all right.

Summary of Part III

On the first session, begin with the first page of the story in which the child misses his third word. Write down that page number. Start with Step 1 and continue as far as you get. Keep the slips for words the child missed for the next session.

On all succeeding sessions, start by going over the missed words you kept the session before. Put them aside after the child gets them all right twice in a row, to be discarded if you don't need them again before the end of that session.

Then go over the set of word-cards for the story before the one on which you started the steps in the last session, until the child gets them all right twice in a row. Then go over the set of word-cards for the next story, and the next, if there is one, continuing up to the page on which you are to start the steps this time. Then start with Step 1 for that page.

Steps

1. Go over the word-cards for the page, until all are right twice in a row.

Procedure for going over sets of words

Show the child the words one at a time. If he can't read a word:

(a) If the word is built up from simpler words, show him the simpler words in it.

(b) Tell the child the sound of any letters where this is different from what you taught him.

(c) Point to the letters from left to right. For the letters that have different sounds than the ones you taught him, you say the sounds again and have him repeat them; for the regular letters have him give the sounds by himself.

(d) Again pointing, you say the sounds again. If he still doesn't recognize the word, again pointing, say the first sounds blended together. Then say more and more of the sounds blended together, until the child recognizes the word. Have him say it.

Go through all the words in this way and then change their order and do it again. Keep doing this until the child gets all the words right without errors and without needing any help twice in a row.

If this is too hard for the child, start by working on only two or three of the words; only after the child has gotten them right several times in a row, add one or two more. Then after the child has gotten all these right several times in a row, add one or two more again, and so on.

2. Have the child read the page, writing down words he misses.

3. Go over the missed words for the page, until all are right twice in a row.

4. Go over the word-cards for the page again, until all are right twice in a row.

5. Repeat Step 2 (reading), Step 3 (going over missed words), and Step 4 (going over word-cards), as necessary, until the reading is fairly smooth and easy, and no more than two different words are missed in Step 2. Then do Step 3 and Step 4 once more.

6. Follow Steps 1–5 for the rest of the pages of the story, including some of the slips and cards from earlier pages where appropriate.

7. Go over all the words missed in this session in the entire story, until all are right twice in a row.

8. Go over all the word-cards for the entire story, until all are right twice in a row.

9. Repeat Steps 2–8 as necessary, until the reading is easy and the child misses no more than about seven different words in the story. Then after finishing the steps through Step 8, go on to Step 1 for the first page of the next story.

At the end of each session, put the slips for all the words missed in this session into the child's envelope, and write down the page on which to start next time.

At the end of each week, go over the word-cards for each of the last five stories again. Go over each story's set until all are right twice in a row.

Appendix B
Alpha-Picture
Chart

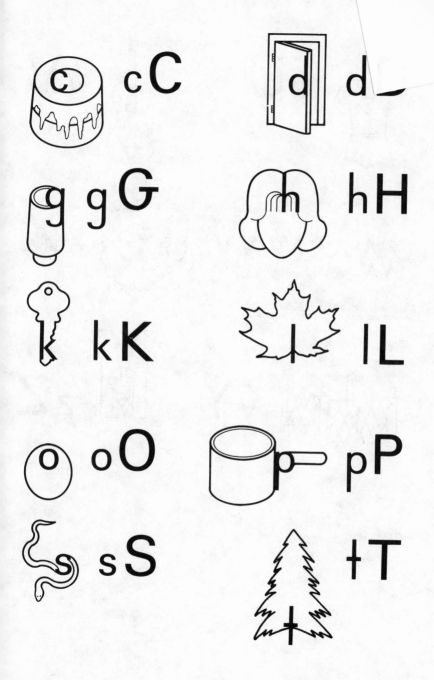

cC

dD

gG

hH

kK

lL

oO

pP

sS

tT

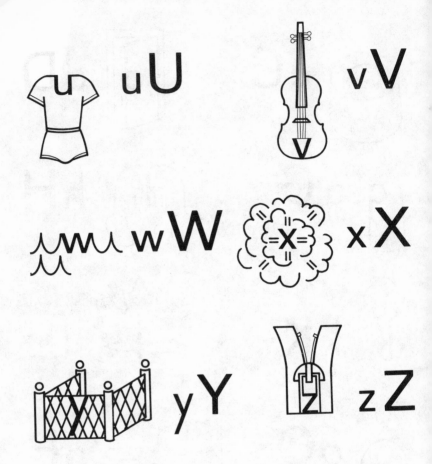

uU vV

wW xX

yY zZ

Appendix C
Key Data by Child

Child	Sex	Teacher	Tutor	Metropolitan percentile	Word Recognition, Classroom Vocabulary	Sentence Reading, Classroom Vocabulary	Spache Words, No. Correct	Spache Passages, Grade Level
1	m	A	—	23	12	10	12	< 1.6
2	m	A	I	40	20	21	37	1.6
3	m	A	—	16	4	0	3	< 1.6
4	f	A	I	27	19	23	36	1.6
5	m	A	—	22	8	4	9	< 1.6
6	f	A	—	19	17	21	34	1.6
7	m	A	—	40	10	10	10	< 1.6
8	m	A	—	4	0	0	0	< 1.6
9	f	A	I	38	24	25	45	2.3
10	m	A	—	35	23	24	53	2.8
11	f	A	—	31	19	15	13	< 1.6
12	m	A	I	13	9	11	4	< 1.6
13	f	B	II	38	17	22	34	1.8
14	m	B	—	16	1	4	4	< 1.6
15	f	B	—	9	7	7	5	< 1.6
16	m	B	II	40	10	7	8	< 1.6
17	m	B	—	17	1	6	3	< 1.6
18	m	B	II	38	22	24	39	2.3
19	m	B	—	38	8	14	15	< 1.6
20	m	B	II	17	17	23	31	< 1.6
21	m	B	—	40	16	20	34	< 1.6
22	f	B	II	31	13	17	15	< 1.6

Child	Sex	Teacher	Tutor	Metropolitan percentile	Word Recognition, Classroom Vocabulary	Sentence Reading, Classroom Vocabulary	Spache Words, No. Correct	Spache Passages, Grade Level
23	f	B	—	15	14	13	17	< 1.6
24	m	C	II	19	13	21	38	1.8
25	m	C	—	13	0	0	2	< 1.6
26	m	C	II	22	18	20	31	< 1.6
27	f	C	—	19	7	10	9	< 1.6
28	m	C	—	26	7	5	8	< 1.6
29	f	C	II	40	8	15	10	< 1.6
30	m	C	—	4	4	5	7	< 1.6
31	f	C	II	26	0	0	1	< 1.6
32	f	C	—	36	18	22	32	1.6
33	f	C	I	29	4	8	9	< 1.6
34	f	D	—	38	17	23	25	< 1.6
35	m	D	—	7	0	0	1	< 1.6
36	m	D	—	31	11	7	5	< 1.6
37	f	D	—	35	16	19	20	1.6
38	f	D	I	38	5	10	8	< 1.6
39	m	D	—	14	6	10	8	< 1.6
40	m	D	—	38	7	14	14	< 1.6
41	m	D	I	27	14	12	5	< 1.6
42	m	D	I	33	24	25	67	2.3
43	f	D	I	9	1	2	3	< 1.6
44	f	E	—	5	0	0	0	< 1.6

Child	Sex	Teacher	Tutor	Metropolitan percentile	Word Recognition, Classroom Vocabulary	Sentence Reading, Classroom Vocabulary	Spache Words, No. Correct	Spache Passages, Grade Level
45	m	E	III	10	5	5	1	<1.6
46	m	E	—	25	5	11	7	<1.6
47	m	E	—	36	6	13	9	<1.6
48	m	E	III	25	16	20	28	1.6
49	m	E	—	25	7	13	8	<1.6
50	m	E	—	19	8	10	18	<1.6
51	m	E	III	40	13	21	25	<1.6
52	f	E	III	25	17	21	27	<1.6
53	f	E	III	27	22	25	49	2.3
54	f	E	III	4	0	0	1	<1.6
55	f	E	—	25	7	17	22	<1.6
56	f	E	—	27	19	23	45	2.3
57	m	E	—	40	15	20	31	<1.6
58	f	F	IV	2	0	0	0	<1.6
59	f	F	—	5	6	6	4	<1.6
60	m	F	IV	29	0	0	0	<1.6
61	m	F	—	36	17	20	25	1.6
62	m	F	—	31	21	24	49	2.3
63	f	F	—	10	8	8	7	<1.6
64	m	F	—	11	0	3	6	<1.6
65	f	F	—	35	24	25	50	2.8
66	m	F	—	7	0	0	0	<1.6

Child	Sex	Teacher	Tutor	Metropolitan percentile	Word Recognition, Classroom Vocabulary	Sentence Reading, Classroom Vocabulary	Spache Words, No. Correct	Spache Passages, Grade Level
67	m	F	IV	1 —	0	0	0	<1.6
68	m	F	—	17	0	0	1	<1.6
69	m	F	IV	16	12	15	18	1.6
70	f	F	IV	27	16	19	29	1.6
71	m	F	—	25	6	6	10	<1.6
72	m	F	IV	25	9	7	7	<1.6
73	f	G	IV	17	21	24	43	2.3
74	m	G	IV	19	12	15	25	<1.6
75	m	G	—	11	0	0	1	<1.6
76	f	G	—	25	14	6	12	<1.6
77	m	G	—	20	0	0	1	<1.6
78	m	H	III	40	19	15	31	1.8
79	m	H	III	12	14	18	29	1.6
80	f	H	—	31	20	21	33	1.8
81	m	H	—	25	8	12	15	1.6
82	m	H	—	36	1	3	5	<1.6
83	f	H	IV	40	18	23	30	1.8
84	m	H	—	16	2	5	6	<1.6
85	f	H	—	14	0	0	0	<1.6
86	f	H	III	17	16	22	30	1.6
87	m	H	—	40	0	5	1	<1.6
88	m	H	—	3	0	0	0	<1.6

References

Anderson, I. H., and Dearborn, W. F. *The psychology of teaching reading.* New York: Ronald, 1952.

Armor, D. J. School and family effects on black and white achievement: a reexamination of the USOE data. In F. Mosteller and D. P. Moynihan, eds., *On equality of educational opportunity.* New York: Vintage Books, 1972.

Arnhoff, F. N., Rubenstein, E. A., and Speisman, J. C. *Manpower for mental health.* Chicago: Aldine, 1969.

Atkinson, R. C. Computerized instruction and the learning process. *American Psychologist,* 1968, *23,* 225–39.

———. Ingredients for a theory of instruction. *American Psychologist,* 1972, 27, 921–31.

———. Teaching children to read using a computer. *American Psychologist,* 1974, *29,* 169–78.

———, and Paulson, J. A. An approach to the psychology of instruction. *Psychological Bulletin,* 1972, *78,* 49–61.

Ausubel, D. P. A teaching strategy for culturally deprived pupils: cognitive and motivational considerations. In J. L. Frost and G. R. Hawkes, eds., *The disadvantaged child.* Boston: Houghton Mifflin, 1966.

Baratz, J. C., and Shuy, R. W., eds., *Teaching black children to read.* Washington, D.C.: Center for Applied Linguistics, 1969.

Bausell, R. B., Moody, W. B., and Walzl, F. N. A factorial study of tutoring versus classroom instruction. *American Educational Research Journal,* 1972, *9,* 591–97.

Bereiter, C. Schools without education. *Harvard Educational Review,* 1972, *42,* 390–413.

———. *Must we educate?* Englewood Cliffs, N.J.: Prentice-Hall, 1973.

———, and Engelmann, S. *Teaching disadvantaged children in the preschool.* Englewood Cliffs, N.J.: Prentice-Hall, 1966.

Berlin, C. I., and Dill, A. C. The effects of feedback and positive reinforcement on the Wepman Auditory Discrimination Test scores of lower-class Negro and white children. *Journal of Speech and Hearing Research*, 1967, *10*, 384–89.

Beshers, J. M. Models of the educational process: a sociologist's perspective. In F. Mosteller and D. P. Moynihan, eds., *On equality of educational opportunity*. New York: Vintage Books, 1972.

Blank, M. Cognitive processes in auditory discrimination in normal and retarded readers. *Child Development*, 1968, *39*, 1091–1101.

———. The treatment of personality variables in a preschool cognitive program. In J. C. Stanley, ed., *Preschool programs for the disadvantaged*. Baltimore: Johns Hopkins University Press, 1972.

Bloom, B. S., Hastings, J. T., and Madaus, G. F. *Handbook on formative and summative evaluation of student learning.* New York: McGraw-Hill, 1971.

Bowles, S., and Levin, H. M. The determinants of scholastic achievement—an appraisal of some recent evidence. *Journal of Human Resources*, 1968, *3*, 3–24.

Bronfenbrenner, U. Developmental research, public policy, and the ecology of childhood. *Child Development*, 1974, *45*, 1–5.

Brown, R. *A first language: the early stages*. Cambridge, Mass.: Harvard University Press, 1973.

Burling, R. *English in black and white*. New York: Holt, Rinehart and Winston, 1973.

Camp, B. W., and van Doorninck, W. J. Assessment of "motivated" reading therapy with elementary school children. *Behavior Therapy*, 1971, *2*, 214–22.

Campbell, D. T. Reforms as experiments. *American Psychologist*, 1969, *24*, 409–29.

———, and Erlebacher, A. How regression artifacts in quasi-experimental evaluations can mistakenly make compensatory education look harmful. In J. Hellmuth, ed., *Disadvantaged child*. Vol. 3, *Compensatory education: a national debate*. New York: Brunner/Mazel, 1970*a*.

———, and Erlebacher, A. Reply to the replies. In J. Hellmuth, ed., *Disadvantaged child*. Vol. 3, *Compensatory education: a national debate*. New York: Brunner/Mazel, 1970*b*.

Cattell, J. McK. Über die Zeit der Erkennung und Benennung von Schriftzeichen, Bildern, und Farben. *Philosophische Studien*, 1885, *2*, 635–50. English translation by R. S.

Woodworth in A. T. Poffenberger, ed., *James McKeen Cattell, man of science.* Vol. 1. Lancaster, Pa.: Science Press, 1947.

Central Advisory Council for Education. *Children and their primary schools.* 2 vols. London: Her Majesty's Stationery Office, 1967.

Chall, J. S. *Learning to read: the great debate.* New York: McGraw-Hill, 1967.

————, Roswell, F. G., and Blumenthal, S. H. Auditory blending ability: a factor in success in beginning reading. *The Reading Teacher*, 1963, *17*, 113–18.

Chicago Daily News. How Chicago grade-school pupils compare. November 1, 1972.

Chicago Today. How your child's school rates. November 1, 1972.

Cicirelli, V. G. The relevance of the regression artifact problem to the Westinghouse-Ohio evaluation of Head Start: a reply to Campbell and Erlebacher. In J. Hellmuth, ed., *Disadvantaged child.* Vol. 3, *Compensatory education: a national debate.* New York: Brunner/Mazel, 1970.

Claiborn, W. L. Expectancy effects in the classroom: a failure to replicate. *Journal of Educational Psychology*, 1969, *60*, 377–83.

Clark, K. B. Social policy, power, and social science research. *Harvard Educational Review*, 1973, *43*, 113–21.

Cloward, R. D. Studies in tutoring. *Journal of Experimental Education*, 1967, *36*, 14–25.

Clymer, T. *A duck is a duck. Level 3 in Reading 360.* Boston: Ginn, 1969*a*.

————. *Helicopters and gingerbread. Level 4 in Reading 360.* Boston: Ginn, 1969*b*.

————, and Gates, D. *May I come in? Level 5 in Reading 360.* Boston: Ginn, 1969.

————, and Jones, V. W. *Seven is magic. Level 6 in Reading 360.* Boston: Ginn, 1969.

Cohen, S. A. *Teach them all to read.* New York: Random House, 1969.

Cole, M., Gay, J., Glick, J. A., and Sharp, D. W. *The cultural context of learning and thinking.* New York: Basic Books, 1971.

Coleman, J. S., et al. *Equality of educational opportunity.* 2 vols. Washington, D.C.: U.S. Government Printing Office, 1966.

Coleman, J. S. The evaluation of *Equality of Educational Opportunity.* In F. Mosteller and D. P. Moynihan, eds., *On Equality of educational opportunity.* New York: Vintage Books, 1972.

Cowen, E. L., Dorr, D., Izzo, L. D., Madonia, A., and Trost, M. A. The Primary Mental Health Project: a new way to conceptualize and deliver school mental health service. *Psychology in the Schools*, 1971, *8*, 216–25.

———, Dorr, D., Trost, M. A., and Izzo, L. D. Follow-up study of maladapting school children seen by nonprofessionals. *Journal of Consulting and Clinical Psychology*, 1972, *39*, 235–38.

———, Gardner, E. A., and Zax, M., eds., *Emergent approaches to mental health problems*. New York: Appleton-Century-Crofts, 1967.

Cramer, W. My mom can teach reading too! *Elementary School Journal*, 1971, *72*, 72–75.

Crano, W. D., Kenny, D. A., and Campbell, D. T. Does intelligence cause achievement? A cross-lagged panel analysis. *Journal of Educational Psychology*, 1972, *63*, 258–75.

Cronbach, L. J. Heredity, environment, and educational policy. In *Environment, heredity, and intelligence*. Harvard Educational Review Reprint Series, no. 2. Cambridge, Mass.: Harvard Educational Review, 1969.

Daniels, L. G. Variables that may be useful when evaluating day care programs for preschool children. In J. C. Stanley, ed., *Preschool programs for the disadvantaged*. Baltimore: Johns Hopkins University Press, 1972.

Dedinsky, M. Schools far behind in U.S. reading tests. *Chicago Today*, November 1, 1972.

Deutsch, C. P. Auditory discrimination and learning: social factors. *Merrill-Palmer Quarterly*, 1964, *10*, 277–96.

Dorr, D., Cowen, E. L., Sandler, I., and Pratt, D. M. Dimensionality of a test battery for nonprofessional mental health workers. *Journal of Consulting and Clinical Psychology*, 1973, *41*, 181–85.

Durrell, D. D., and Murphy, H. A. *Speech-to-print phonics*. New York: Harcourt, Brace and World, 1964.

Dusek, J. B., and O'Connell, E. J. Teacher expectancy effects on the achievement test performance of elementary school children. *Journal of Educational Psychology*, 1973, *65*, 371–77.

Dyer, H. S. Some thoughts about future studies. In F. Mosteller and D. P. Moynihan, eds., *On equality of educational opportunity*. New York: Vintage Books, 1972.

Edmonds, R., et al. A Black response to Christopher Jencks's *Inequality* and certain other issues. *Harvard Educational Review*, 1973, *43*, 76–91.

Elashoff, J. D., and Snow, R. E., eds., *Pygmalion reconsidered.* Worthington, Ohio: Charles A. Jones Publishing Company, 1971.

Elkind, D. "Good me" or "bad me"—the Sullivan approach to personality. *New York Times Magazine,* September 24, 1972.

Elkonin, D. B. Development of speech. In A. V. Zaporozhets and D. B. Elkonin, eds., *The psychology of preschool children.* Cambridge, Mass.: MIT Press, 1971.

Ellson, D. G., Barber, L., Engle, T. L., and Kampwerth, L. Programed tutoring: a teaching aid and a research tool. *Reading Research Quarterly,* 1965, *1,* 77–127.

———, Harris, P., and Barber, L. A field test of programed and directed tutoring. *Reading Research Quarterly,* 1968, *3,* 307–67.

Estes, W. K. *Learning theory and mental development.* New York: Academic Press, 1970.

Evans, J. W., and Schiller, J. How preoccupation with possible regression artifacts can lead to a faulty strategy for the evaluation of social action programs: a reply to Campbell and Erlebacher. In J. Hellmuth, ed., *Disadvantaged child.* Vol. 3, *Compensatory education: a national debate.* New York: Brunner/Mazel, 1970.

Fellows, B. J. *The discrimination process and development.* Oxford, England: Pergamon, 1968.

Feshbach, S., and Adelman, H. Remediation of learning problems among the disadvantaged. *Journal of Educational Psychology,* 1974, *66,* 16–28.

Fitzsimmons, S. J., Cheever, J., Leonard, E., and Macunovich, D. School failures: now and tomorrow. *Developmental Psychology,* 1969, *1,* 134–46.

Flanagan, J. C., and Cooley, W. W. *Project talent: one year follow-up studies.* Pittsburgh: University of Pittsburgh, Project Talent, 1966.

Fleming, E. S., and Anttonen, R. G. Teacher expectancy or My Fair Lady. *American Educational Research Journal,* 1971, *8,* 241–52.

Fletcher, J. D., and Atkinson, R. C. Evaluation of the Stanford CAI program in initial reading. *Journal of Educational Psychology,* 1972, *63,* 597–602.

Furth, H. G., and Wachs, H. *Thinking goes to school: Piaget's theory in practice.* New York: Oxford University Press, 1974.

Gagné, R. M., and Briggs, L. J. *Principles of instructional design.* New York: Holt, Rinehart and Winston, 1974.

Garnica, O. K. The development of phonemic speech perception. In T. E. Moore, ed., *Cognitive development and the acquisition of language.* New York: Academic Press, 1973.

Gartner, A. *Paraprofessionals and their performance: a survey of education, health, and social service programs.* New York: Praeger, 1971.

————, Kohler, M. C., and Riessman, F. *Children teach children: learning by teaching.* New York: Harper and Row, 1971.

Gibson, E. J. *Principles of perceptual learning and development.* New York: Appleton-Century-Crofts, 1969.

Gilbert, J. P., and Mosteller, F. The urgent need for experimentation. In F. Mosteller and D. P. Moynihan, eds., *On Equality of educational opportunity.* New York: Vintage Books, 1972.

Ginsburg, H. *The myth of the deprived child: poor children's intellect and education.* Englewood Cliffs, N.J.: Prentice-Hall, 1972.

Gleitman, L. R., and Rozin, P. Teaching reading by use of a syllabary. *Reading Research Quarterly*, 1973, *8*, 447–83.

Goodman, K. S. The psycholinguistic nature of the reading process. In K. S. Goodman, ed., *The psycholinguistic nature of the reading process.* Detroit: Wayne State University Press, 1968.

————. The 13th easy way to make learning to read difficult: a reaction to Gleitman and Rozin. *Reading Research Quarterly*, 1973, *8*, 484–93.

Greer, C. *The great school legend: a revisionist interpretation of American public education.* New York: Basic Books, 1972.

Grosser, G., Henry, W. E., and Kelly, J., eds., *Nonprofessionals in the human services.* San Francisco: Jossey-Bass, 1968.

Guerney, B. G., ed., *Psychotherapeutic agents: new roles for non-professionals, parents and teachers.* New York: Holt, Rinehart and Winston, 1969.

Hanushek, E. A., and Kain, J. F. On the value of *Equality of Educational Opportunity* as a guide to public policy. In F. Mosteller and D. P. Moynihan, eds., *On equality of educational opportunity.* New York: Vintage Books, 1972.

Harvard Educational Review. *Equal educational opportunity.* Cambridge, Mass.: Harvard University Press, 1969.

Hawkridge, D., Chalupsky, A., and Roberts, A. *A study of selected exemplary programs for the education of disadvantaged children.* Palo Alto, Calif.: American Institutes for Research in the Behavioral Sciences, 1968.

Herrnstein, R. J. IQ. *The Atlantic Monthly*, September, 1971, 43–64.

———. *I. Q. in the meritocracy*. Boston: Little, Brown, 1973.

Hildreth, G. H., Griffiths, N. L., and McGauvran, M. E. *Metropolitan Readiness Tests, form B*. New York: Harcourt, Brace and World, 1966.

———. *Manual of directions, Metropolitan Readiness Tests, forms A and B*. New York: Harcourt, Brace and World, 1969.

Hunt, J. McV. *Intelligence and experience*. New York: Ronald Press, 1961.

———. Environment, development, and scholastic achievement. In M. Deutsch, I. Katz, and A. R. Jensen, eds., *Social class, race, and psychological development*. New York: Holt, Rinehart and Winston, 1968.

———. *The challenge of incompetence and poverty*. Urbana, Ill.: University of Illinois Press, 1969.

———. Heredity, environment, and class or ethnic differences. In Educational Testing Service, *Assessment in a pluralistic society: Proceedings of the 1972 Invitational Conference on Testing Problems*. Princeton, N.J.: Educational Testing Service, 1973.

Jencks, C., et al. *Inequality: a reassessment of the effect of family and schooling in America*. New York: Basic Books, 1972*a*.

Jencks, C. The Coleman Report and the conventional wisdom. In F. Mosteller and D. P. Moynihan, eds., *On equality of educational opportunity*. New York: Vintage Books, 1972*b*.

———. *Inequality* in retrospect. *Harvard Educational Review*, 1973, *43*, 138–64.

Jensen, A. R. How much can we boost IQ and scholastic achievement? In *Environment, heredity, and intelligence*. Harvard Educational Review Reprint Series, no. 2. Cambridge, Mass.: Harvard Educational Review, 1969.

———. *Educability and group differences*. New York: Harper and Row, 1973.

———. Interaction of level I and level II abilities with race and socioeconomic status. *Journal of Educational Psychology*, 1974, *66*, 99–111.

Johnson, D. J., and Myklebust, H. R. *Learning disabilities: educational principles and practices*. New York: Grune and Stratton, 1967.

José, J., and Cody, J. J. Teacher-pupil interaction as it relates to attempted changes in teacher expectancy of academic ability and achievement. *American Educational Research Journal*, 1971, *8*, 39–49.

Katz, M. B. *Class, bureaucracy and schools: the illusion of educational change in America.* New York: Praeger, 1971.

Kavanagh, J. F., and Mattingly, I. G., eds., *Language by ear and by eye: the relationships between speech and reading.* Cambridge, Mass.: MIT Press, 1972.

Kelley, T. L., Madden, R., Gardner, E. F., and Rudman, H. C. *Stanford Achievement Test, primary I battery.* New York: Harcourt, Brace and World, 1964.

Kohl, H. *36 children.* New York: Signet Books, 1968.

———. *Reading, how to.* New York: Dutton, 1973.

Köhler, W. *Gestalt psychology.* New York: Liveright, 1947.

Labov, W., Cohen, P., Robins, C., and Lewis, J. *A study of the non-standard English of Negro and Puerto Rican speakers in New York City.* 2 vóls. Final Report, U.S. Office of Education Cooperative Research Project No. 3288. New York: Columbia University, 1968. Mimeographed.

Lambie, D. Z., and Weikart, D. P. Ypsilanti Carnegie infant education project. In J. Hellmuth, ed., *Disadvantaged child.* Vol. 3, *Compensatory education: A national debate.* New York: Brunner/Mazel, 1970.

Landes, R. *Public education in New York City.* New York: First National City Bank Public Affairs Committee, 1969.

Lazerson, M. Revisionism and American educational history. *Harvard Educational Review,* 1973, *43,* 269–83.

Leontiev, A. N. The nature and formation of human psychic properties. In B. Simon, ed., *Psychology in the Soviet Union.* London: Routledge and Kegan Paul, 1957.

Levin, H. Reading and the learning of variable grapheme-to-phoneme correspondences. Paper presented at the Conference on Perceptual and Linguistic Aspects of Reading, Center for Advanced Study in the Behavioral Sciences, Stanford, Calif., October 31–November 2, 1963.

Liberman, A. M., Cooper, F. S., Shankweiler, D. P., and Studdert-Kennedy, M. Perception of the speech code. *Psychological Review,* 1967, *74,* 431–61.

Maeroff, G. I. A solution to falling reading scores continues to elude big-city schools. *New York Times,* May 27, 1973.

Mathews, M. M. *Teaching to read, historically considered.* Chicago: University of Chicago Press, 1966.

Mattingly, I. G. Reading, the linguistic process, and linguistic awareness. In J. F. Kavanagh and I. G. Mattingly, eds., *Language by ear and by eye: the relationships between speech and reading.* Cambridge, Mass.: MIT Press, 1972.

McCleary, E. K. Report of results of tutorial reading project. *The Reading Teacher,* 1971, *24,* 556–60.

McNeill, D. The development of language. In P. H. Mussen, ed., *Carmichael's manual of child psychology*. Vol. 1. 3d ed. New York: Wiley, 1970.

Meier, J. H., Segner, L. L., and Grueter, B. B. An education system for high-risk infants: a preventive approach to developmental and learning disabilities. In J. Hellmuth, ed., *Disadvantaged child*. Vol. 3, *Compensatory education: A national debate*. New York: Brunner/Mazel, 1970.

Mendels, G. E., and Flanders, J. P. Teachers' expectations and pupil performance. *American Educational Research Journal*, 1973, *10*, 203–12.

Mercer, J. R. A policy statement on assessment procedures and the rights of children. *Harvard Educational Review*, 1974, *44*, 125–41.

Milner, E. A study of the relationship between reading readiness in grade one school children and patterns of parent-child interaction. *Child Development*, 1951, *22*, 95–112.

Mosteller, F., and Moynihan, D. P., eds. *On equality of educational opportunity*. New York: Vintage Books, 1972*a*.

Mosteller, F., and Moynihan, D. P. A pathbreaking report. In F. Mosteller and D. P. Moynihan, eds., *On equality of educational opportunity*. New York: Vintage Books, 1972*b*.

Murphy, H. A., and Durrell, D. D. *Murphy-Durrell Reading Readiness Analysis*. New York: Harcourt, Brace and World, 1965.

National Education Association, Research Division. *Class size*. Washington, D. C.: National Education Association, 1967.

Norman, D. A. *Memory and attention: an introduction to human information processing*. New York: Wiley, 1969.

O'Donnell, M. *Janet and Mark. First preprimer of the Harper and Row Basic Reading Program*. New York: Harper and Row, 1966*a*.

————. *Outdoors and in. Second preprimer of the Harper and Row Basic Reading Program*. New York: Harper and Row, 1966*b*.

————. *City days, city ways. Third preprimer of the Harper and Row Basic Reading Program*. New York: Harper and Row, 1966*c*.

————. *Just for fun. Fourth preprimer of the Harper and Row Basic Reading Program*. New York: Harper and Row, 1966*d*.

————. *Around the corner. Primer of the Harper and Row Basic Reading Program*. New York: Harper and Row, 1966*e*.

————. *Real and make-believe. First reader of the Harper and Row Basic Reading Program*. New York: Harper and Row, 1966*f*.

————. *All through the year. Second reader of the Harper and Row Basic Reading Program.* New York: Harper and Row, 1966g.

Olsen, H. C. Linguistics and materials for beginning reading instruction. In K. S. Goodman, ed., *The psycholinguistic nature of the reading process.* Detroit: Wayne State University Press, 1968.

Ornstein, A. C. Reaching the disadvantaged. In W. W. Brickman and S. Lehrer, eds., *Education and the many faces of the disadvantaged.* New York: Wiley, 1972.

Pearl, A., and Riessman, F. *New careers for the poor.* New York: Free Press, 1965.

Pellegrini, R. J., and Hicks, R. A. Prophecy effects and tutorial instruction for the disadvantaged child. *American Educational Research Journal,* 1972, *9,* 413–19.

Piaget, J. *The construction of reality in the child.* New York: Basic Books, 1954.

Plumer, D. A summary of environmentalist views and some educational implications. In F. Williams, ed., *Language and poverty.* Chicago: Markham, 1970.

Pope, L. *Guidelines to teaching remedial reading to the disadvantaged.* Brooklyn, N.Y.: Faculty Press, 1967.

Rist, R. C. Student social class and teacher expectations: the self-fulfilling prophecy in ghetto education. In *Challenging the myths: the schools, the blacks, and the poor.* Harvard Educational Review Reprint Series, no. 5. Cambridge, Mass.: Harvard Educational Review, 1971.

Rivlin, A. M. Forensic social science. *Harvard Educational Review,* 1973, *43,* 61–75.

Rollins, H. A., McCandless, B. R., Thompson, M., and Brassell, W. R. Project Success Environment: an extended application of contingency management in inner-city schools. *Journal of Educational Psychology,* 1974, *66,* 167–78.

Rosenthal, R., and Jacobson, L. *Pygmalion in the classroom: teacher expectation and pupils' intellectual development.* New York: Holt, Rinehart and Winston, 1968a.

————. Self-fulfilling prophecies in the classroom: teachers' expectations as unintended determinants of pupils' intellectual competence. In M. Deutsch, I. Katz, and A. R. Jensen, eds., *Social class, race, and psychological development.* New York: Holt, Rinehart and Winston, 1968b.

Roswell, F. G., and Chall, J. S. *Roswell-Chall Diagnostic Reading Test of Word Analysis Skills, Grades 2–6.* New York: Essay Press, 1956–59.

Rothbart, M., Dalfen, S., and Barrett, R. Effects of teacher's expectancy on student-teacher interaction. *Journal of Educational Psychology*, 1971, *62*, 49–54.

Rubovits, P. C., and Maehr, M. L. Pygmalion analyzed: toward an explanation of the Rosenthal-Jacobson findings. *Journal of Personality and Social Psychology*, 1971, *19*, 197–203.

———. Pygmalion black and white. *Journal of Personality and Social Psychology*, 1973, *25*, 210–18.

Savin, H. B. What the child knows about speech when he starts to learn to read. In J. F. Kavanagh and I. G. Mattingly, eds., *Language by ear and by eye: the relationships between speech and reading*. Cambridge, Mass.: MIT Press, 1972.

Schoeller, A. W., and Pearson, D. A. Better reading through volunteer reading tutors. *The Reading Teacher*, 1970, *23*, 625–30.

Sellers, T. E. New report: Chicago's pupils still lag. *Chicago Daily News*, November 1, 1972.

Shaver, J. P., and Nuhn, D. Effectiveness of tutoring underachievers in reading and writing. *Journal of Educational Research*, 1971, *65*, 107–12.

Shvachkin, N. K. Razvitiye fonematicheskogo vospriyatiya rechi v rannem detsve. [Development of phonemic perception of speech in early childhood]. *Akademiia Pedagogicheskikh Nauk RSFSR, Izvestiia*, 1948, *13*, 101–32. English translation by E. Dernbach in C. A. Ferguson and D. I. Slobin, eds., *Child language acquisition: readings*. New York: Holt, Rinehart and Winston, in press.

Siegel, S. *Nonparametric statistics for the behavioral sciences*. New York: McGraw-Hill, 1956.

Sigel, I. E., and Olmsted, P. Modification of cognitive skills among lower-class black children. In J. Hellmuth, ed., *Disadvantaged child*. Vol. 3, *Compensatory education: A national debate*. New York: Brunner/Mazel, 1970.

———, Sechrist, A., and Forman, G. Psycho-educational intervention beginning at age 2: reflections and outcomes. In J. C. Stanley, ed., *Compensatory education for children ages two to eight*. Baltimore: Johns Hopkins University Press, 1973.

Slavina, L. S. Specific features of the intellectual work of unsuccessful pupils. In B. Simon, ed., *Psychology in the Soviet Union*. London: Routledge and Kegan Paul, 1957.

Smith, F. *Psycholinguistics and reading*. New York: Holt, Rinehart and Winston, 1973.

Smith, M. S. *Equality of Educational Opportunity:* The basic findings reconsidered. In F. Mosteller and D. P. Moynihan, eds., *On equality of educational opportunity.* New York: Vintage Books, 1972.

————, and Bissell, J. Report analysis: The impact of Head Start. *Harvard Educational Review,* 1970, *40,* 51–104.

Snow, R. E. Unfinished Pygmalion. *Contemporary Psychology,* 1969, *14,* 197–99.

Sobey, F. *The nonprofessional revolution in mental health.* New York: Columbia University Press, 1970.

Spache, G. D. *Diagnostic Reading Scales.* Examiner's Manual. Monterey, Calif.: CTB/McGraw-Hill, 1963*a.*

————. *Diagnostic Reading Scales.* Examiner's Record Booklet. Monterey, Calif.: CTB/McGraw-Hill, 1963*b.*

————. *Diagnostic Reading Scales.* Test Book. Monterey, Calif.: CTB/McGraw-Hill, 1963*c.*

————. *Diagnostic Reading Scales. Rev. ed.,* Examiner's Manual. Monterey, Calif.: CTB/McGraw-Hill, 1972*a.*

————. *Diagnostic Reading Scales. Rev. ed.,* Examiner's Record Booklet. Monterey, Calif.: CTB/McGraw-Hill, 1972*b.*

————. *Diagnostic Reading Scales. Rev. ed.,* Test Book. Monterey, Calif.: CTB/McGraw-Hill, 1972*c.*

Staats, A. W. *Learning, language, and cognition.* New York: Holt, Rinehart and Winston, 1968.

————, and Butterfield, W. H. Treatment of nonreading in a culturally deprived juvenile delinquent: an application of reinforcement principles. *Child Development,* 1965, *36,* 925–42.

————, Minke, K. A., and Butts, P. A token-reinforcement remedial reading program administered by black therapy-technicians to problem black children. *Behavior Therapy,* 1970, *1,* 331–53.

————, Minke, K. A., Goodwin, W., and Landeen, J. Cognitive behavior modification: "motivated learning" reading treatment with subprofessional therapy-clinicians. *Behavior Research and Therapy,* 1967, *5,* 283–99.

Stanley, J. C. Introduction and critique. In J. C. Stanley, ed., *Compensatory education for children ages two to eight.* Baltimore: Johns Hopkins University Press, 1973.

Stein, A. Strategies for failure. In *Challenging the myths: The schools, the blacks, and the poor.* Harvard Educational Review Reprint Series, no. 5. Cambridge, Mass.: Harvard Educational Review, 1971.

Stendler-Lavatelli, C. B. Environmental intervention in infancy and early childhood. In M. Deutsch, I. Katz, and A. R. Jensen, eds., *Social class, race, and psychological development*. New York: Holt, Rinehart and Winston, 1968.

Stephens, J. M. *The process of schooling*. New York: Holt, Rinehart and Winston, 1967.

Stephens, M. W., and Delys, P. External control expectancies among disadvantaged children at preschool age. *Child Development*, 1973, *44*, 670–74.

Stern, C., and Gould, T. S. *Children discover reading*. Syracuse, N.Y.: Random House/Singer, 1963.

———, Gould, T. S., Stern, M. B., and Gartler, M. *Structural Reading Series*. Rev. ed. New York: Random House/Singer, 1968.

Stodolsky, S. S., and Lesser, G. Learning patterns in the disadvantaged. In *Challenging the myths: The schools, the Blacks, and the poor*. Harvard Educational Review Reprint Series, no. 5. Cambridge, Mass.: Harvard Educational Review, 1971.

Thorndike, R. L. Review of R. Rosenthal and L. Jacobson's *Pygmalion in the classroom. American Educational Research Journal*, 1968, *5*, 708–11.

———. But do you have to know how to tell time? *American Educational Research Journal*, 1969, *6*, 692.

———, ed. *International studies in evaluation*. Vol. 3, *Reading comprehension education in 15 countries*. New York: Halsted Press, 1973.

Trowbridge, N. Self concept and socio-economic status in elementary school children. *American Educational Research Journal*, 1972, *9*, 525–37.

Vellutino, F. R., and Connolly, C. The training of paraprofessionals as remedial reading assistants in an inner-city school. *The Reading Teacher*, 1971, *24*, 506–12.

Venezky, R. L. Language and cognition in reading. In B. Spolsky, ed., *Current trends in educational linguistics*. The Hague: Mouton, in press.

Vernon, M. D. *Reading and its difficulties*. Cambridge: Cambridge University Press, 1971.

Wallach, L., and Wallach, M. A. *Tutorial program for cumulative mastery of basic reading*. Chicago: University of Chicago Press, 1976.

Wallach, M. A. Research on children's thinking. In H. W. Stevenson, ed., *Child psychology: The sixty-second yearbook of the National Society for the Study of Education*. Pt. 1. Chicago: University of Chicago Press, 1963.

Weikart, D. P. Relationship of curriculum, teaching, and learning in preschool education. In J. C. Stanley, ed., *Preschool programs for the disadvantaged*. Baltimore: Johns Hopkins University Press, 1972.

———, and Lambie, D. Z. Preschool intervention through a home teaching program. In J. Hellmuth, ed., *Disadvantaged child*. Vol. 2, *Head Start and early intervention*. New York: Brunner/Mazel, 1968.

Wepman, J. M. Auditory discrimination, speech, and reading. *Elementary School Journal*, 1960, *60*, 325–33.

Wertheimer, M. *Productive thinking*. New York: Harper, 1945.

Wessman, A. E. Scholastic and psychological effects of a compensatory education program for disadvantaged high school students: Project ABC. *American Educational Research Journal*, 1972, *9*, 361–72.

Westinghouse Learning Corporation/Ohio University. *The impact of Head Start*. Springfield, Va.: Clearinghouse for Federal Scientific and Technical Information, U.S. Department of Commerce, 1969.

White, S. H. The national impact study of Head Start. In J. Hellmuth, ed., *Disadvantaged child*. Vol. 3, *Compensatory education: a national debate*. New York: Brunner/Mazel, 1970.

Williams, F., ed., *Language and poverty*. Chicago: Markham, 1970.

Wing, C. W., Jr., and Wallach, M. A. *College admissions and the psychology of talent*. New York: Holt, Rinehart and Winston, 1971.

Winschel, J. F. In the dark . . . reflections on compensatory education 1960–1970. In J. Hellmuth, ed., *Disadvantaged child*. Vol. 3, *Compensatory education: a national debate*. New York: Brunner/Mazel, 1970.

Zaporozhets, A. V. Some of the psychological problems of sensory training in early childhood and the preschool period. In M. Cole and I. Maltzman, eds., *A handbook of contemporary Soviet psychology*. New York: Basic Books, 1969.

Zimiles, H. Has evaluation failed compensatory education? In J. Hellmuth, ed., *Disadvantaged child*. Vol. 3, *Compensatory education: a national debate*. New York: Brunner/Mazel, 1970.

Index

Adelman, H., 219
"Alphabetic code" in reading. *See*
   Prerequisite skills: in reading
"Alpha-pictures," 303–5. *See also*
   Tutorial program
Anderson, I. H., 57
Anttonen, R. G., 36, 185
Application of program, practicality of, 215–21
"Applied" and "pure" research,
   artificial barrier between,
   177–78
Armor, D. J., 21, 22, 23, 24, 184
Arnhoff, F. N., 126
Atkinson, R. C., 207
Auditory discrimination tests, 65,
   66, 165, 189
Ausubel, D. P., 56

Baratz, J. C., 52
Barber, L., 37, 54, 187
Barrett, R., 33
Bausell, R. B., 124
Bereiter, C., 43, 126, 215
Berlin, C. I., 66, 189
Beshers, J. M., 39
Beta weight, 22
Bissell, J., 12
Blank, M., 15, 66, 183, 189
Blending and reading. *See*
   Prerequisite skills: in reading

Bloom, B. S., 56
Blumenthal, S. H., 57
Bowles, S., 20
Brassell, W. R., 219
Briggs, L. J., 56
Bronfenbrenner, U., 177
Brown, R., 74
Burling, R., 42, 52
Butterfield, W. H., 54
Butts, P., 54, 187

Camp, B. W., 55
Campbell, D. T., 9, 12, 110
Cattell, J. McK., 58
Central Advisory Council for
   Education, 18
Chall, J. S., 57, 63, 65, 152, 188,
   189
Chalupsky, A., 12
Cheever, J., 43
Chicago Daily News, 111, 112
Chicago Today, 111, 112
Children to be tutored, 123–24,
   194, 210–13, 219. *See also*
   Field research: design of
Cicirelli, V. G., 12
Claiborn, W. L., 36, 185
Clark, K. B., 25
Cloward, R. D., 53
Clymer, T., 130
Cody, J. J., 36

Cognitive and operant ideas in
   tutorial program, 78
Cohen, P., 42
Cohen, S. A., 53
Cole, M., 202, 203
Coleman, J. S., 1, 2, 9, 10, 18, 19,
   20, 21, 23, 24, 25, 29, 31, 38,
   39, 40, 50, 51, 112, 184
Coleman Report. *See* Coleman,
   J. S.
Community adults as tutors. *See*
   Tutors
"Computer assisted instruction,"
   5, 207–10
Confidence. *See* Self-concept
Connolly, C., 53
Constructs versus skills, 6
Cooley, W. W., 18
Cooper, F. S., 66
Cowen, E. L., 126
Cramer, W., 55
Crano, W. D., 9
Cronbach, L. J., 75
Cumulative mastery of skills. *See*
   Prerequisite skills: instruction
   in

Dalfen, S., 33
Daniels, L. G., 12
Data by child, 307–11
Dearborn, W. F., 57
Decoding and reading. *See*
   Prerequisite skills: in reading
Dedinsky, M., 111, 112
Delys, P., 39, 40, 186
Design of field research, 113–25,
   194–96
Deutsch, C. P., 65, 189
Diagnostic Reading Scales,
   137–42, 197–98
Dill, A. C., 66, 189
"Directed tutoring," 125
Dorr, D., 126
Durrell, D. D., 68, 114
Dusek, J. B., 36, 185

Dyer, H. S., 11, 39
"Dyslexia," 210–13

Edmonds, R., 29
Elashoff, J. D., 33, 185
"Electric Company, The," 5, 207
Elkind, D., 39, 186
Elkonin, D. B., 68
Ellson, D. G., 37, 54, 55, 124,
   125, 126, 187
Engelmann, S., 43
Engle, T. L., 37, 54
Erlebacher, A., 12
Estes, W. K., 49
Evaluation in field research,
   130–45, 196–97
Evans, J. W., 108

Fellows, B. J., 65
Fernald School program, 218
Feshbach, S., 219
Field research: design of, 113–25,
   194–96; equivalence of experi-
   mentals and controls in,
   146–49, 197–98; evaluation in,
   130–45, 196–97; results of
   evaluation in, 149–76, 197–
   200; schools in, 110–13;
   setting of, 110–13
Fitzsimmons, S. J., 43
Flanagan, J. C., 18, 34
Flanders, J. P., 36, 185
Fleming, E. S., 36, 185
Fletcher, J. D., 207
Forman, G., 15, 183
Furth, H. G., 204, 205, 206, 207

Gagné, R. M., 56
Game-pictures. *See* Tutorial
   program
Gardner, E. A., 126
Gardner, E. F., 114
Garnica, O. K., 66
Gartler, M., 68
Gartner, A., 54, 126
Gates, D., 130

Gay, J., 202
Gestalt psychology, 58, 59, 68
Gibson, E. J., 65, 66, 82
Gilbert, J. P., 110
Ginsburg, H., 11, 32, 33, 35, 42, 43, 71, 73, 186
Gleitman, L. R., 66, 190, 200, 201, 202
Glick, J. A., 202
Goodman, K. S., 57, 62
Goodwin, W., 54
Gould, T. S., 68
Greer, C., 26
Griffiths, N. L., 113, 194
Grosser, G., 126
Grueter, B. B., 17
Guerney, B. G., 126

Hanushek, E. A., 20
Harris, P., 37, 54, 187
Harvard Educational Review, 50
Hastings, J. T., 56
Hawkridge, D., 12
Head Start, 1, 2, 11, 12, 13, 14, 39, 40
Henry, W. E., 126
Herrnstein, R. J., 1, 179
Hicks, R. A., 36
Hildreth, G. H., 113, 114, 116, 194
"Hothouse" experiments. See Real-world versus "hothouse" experiments
Hunt, J. McV., 2, 16, 19, 179, 183

Illinois Test of Psycholinguistic Ability, 12
Instruction at prerequisite skills. See Prerequisite skills, instruction at
International Association for the Evaluation of Educational Achievement, 25
Izzo, L. D., 126

Jacobson, L., 33, 34, 35, 36
Jencks, C., 1, 2, 8, 10, 18, 29, 38, 51, 179, 184
Jensen, A. R., 1, 2, 72, 73, 74, 179
Johnson, D. J., 212
Jones, V. W., 130
José, J., 36

Kain, J. F., 20
Kampwerth, L., 37, 54
Katz, M. B., 26
Kavanagh, J. F., 47, 65, 189
Kelley, T. L., 114
Kelly, J., 126
Kenny, D. A., 9
Kohl, H., 30, 53
Kohler, M. C., 54
Köhler, W., 58

Labov, W., 42
Lambie, D. Z., 16, 17
Landeen, J., 54
Landes, R., 18
Lazerson, M., 26
"Learning disability," 210–13
Leonard, E., 43
Leontiev, A. N., 45, 46
Lesser, G., 9, 37
"Letter-cards." See Tutorial program
"Letter-drawing sheets." See Tutorial program
"Letter-tracing sheets." See Tutorial program
Levin, H., 82
Levin, H. M., 20
Lewin, K., 177
Lewis, J., 42
Liberman, A. M., 66

McCandless, B. R., 219
McCleary, E. K., 55
McGauvran, M. E., 113, 194
McNeill, D., 42

Macunovich, D., 43
Madaus, G. F., 56
Madden, R., 114
Madonia, A., 126
Maehr, M. L., 32
Maeroff, G. I., 8, 10, 11
Mathews, M. M., 57
Mattingly, I. G., 47, 65, 66, 189
Maturation, waiting for, 70–72
Meier, J. H., 17
Mendels, G. E., 36, 185
Mercer, J. R., 210
Metropolitan Readiness Tests, 12,
    113, 114, 115, 116, 117, 118,
    120, 121, 122, 123, 146, 147,
    148, 149, 160, 161, 194, 198
Milner, E., 47
Minke, K. A., 54, 187
Moody, W. B., 125
Mosteller, F., 1, 18, 19, 26, 40,
    110, 184
Moynihan, D. P., 1, 18, 19, 26,
    40, 184
Munoz, L., 10
Murphy, H. A., 68, 114
*Murphy-Durrell Reading
    Readiness Analysis*, 114
Myklebust, H. R., 212

National Education Association,
    Research Division, 18
New York Times, 8, 10
Nonprofessionals. *See* Tutors
Norman, D. A., 66
Nuhn, D., 53

O'Connell, E. J., 36, 185
O'Donnell, M., 131
Olmsted, P., 14
Olsen, H. C., 214
Open classrooms, 27, 70–72, 179,
    186
Operant and cognitive ideas in
    tutorial program, 78
Ornstein, A.C., 11

Outline of argument, 178–200

Paraprofessionals. *See* Tutors
Paulson, J. A., 207
Pearl, A., 126
Pearson, D. A., 53
Pelligrini, R. J., 36
Phoneme recognition and read-
    ing. *See* Prerequisite skills:
    in reading
Phonics and reading. *See* Pre-
    requisite skills: in reading
Piaget, J., 13, 14, 15, 16, 17, 74,
    182, 183, 204
Plumer, D., 65, 189
Pope, L., 53
Practicality of applying program,
    215–21
Pratt, D. M., 126
Prerequisite skills: alternatives to
    instruction in, 70–76; instruc-
    tion in, 2–5, 41–50, 56–70,
    77–107, 186–94, 200–215; in
    reading, 56–70, 77–107,
    187–94, 200–215
Preschool intervention, 11–18,
    182–83
"Programed tutoring," 55, 125
Psycholinguistic research, 42
"Pure" and "applied" research,
    artificial barrier between,
    177–78

"Radical chic," 29–30
"Reading disability," 210–13
Real-world versus "hothouse"
    experiments, 108–10, 146, 176,
    194, 215
Recruitment of tutors, 127–29,
    195, 217–18. *See also* Tutors
Report card information:
    description of, 144–45;
    results for, 168–75
Revisionist historians of educa-
    tion, 25–26

Riessman, F., 54, 126
Rist, R. C., 30, 31, 32, 33, 35, 185
Rivlin, A. M., 110
Roberts, A., 12
Robins, C., 42
Role-playing. *See* Training of tutors
Rollins, H. A., 219
Rosenthal, R., 33, 34, 35, 36
Roswell, F. G., 57, 65, 189
Rote teaching, 72–75
Rothbart, M., 33
Rozin, P., 66, 190, 200, 201, 202
Rubenstein, E. A., 126
Rubovits, P. C., 32
Rudman, H. C., 114

Sandler, I., 126
Savin, H. B., 47, 57, 66
Schiller, J., 108
Schoeller, A. W., 53
School resources, customary forms of, 18–28, 184
"Schools for thinking," 204
Schools in field research, 110–13
Sechrist, A., 15, 183
Segner, L. L., 17
Self-concept, 38–41, 186
Sellers, T. E., 111, 112
Sentence-reading test: description of: 132–37; results for, 152–55
"Sesame Street," 5, 207
Settings for tutoring, 219–21
Shankweiler, D. P., 66
Sharp, D. W., 202
Shaver, J. P., 53
Shuy, R. W., 52
Shvachkin, N. K., 66
Siegel, S., 148
Sigel, I. E., 14, 15, 183
Skills versus constructs, 6
Slavina, L. S., 48
Smith, F., 57, 61, 62, 188
Smith, M. S., 12, 21, 23, 24, 184

Snow, R. E., 33, 34, 35, 185
Sobey, F., 126
Sound recognition and reading. *See* Prerequisite skills: in reading
Spache, G. D., 132, 136, 137, 138, 139, 140, 141, 142, 154, 156, 157, 158, 159, 160, 161, 162, 164, 167, 197, 198
Spache Consonant Sounds test: description of, 141–42; results for, 161–63
Spache reading-passages and comprehension questions: description of, 138–41; results for, 159–61
Spache Word Recognition lists: descriptions of, 137–38; results for, 154–58
Speisman, J. C., 126
Staats, A. W., 54, 55, 187
Stanford Achievement Test, 114
Stanley, J. C., 43
Starting-sounds test with paired words: description of, 142–43; results for, 163–65
Starting-sounds test with single words: description of, 143–44; results for, 165–68
Stein, A., 31, 32, 33, 35, 185
Stendler-Lavatelli, C. B., 15
Stephens, J. M., 18
Stephens, M. W., 39, 40, 186
Stern, C., 68
Stern, M. B., 68
Stodolsky, S. S., 9, 37
Studdert-Kennedy, M., 66
Supervisors of tutors, 7, 128–30, 195–96, 213, 216–20. *See also* Tutors

Teacher expectancies, 28–38, 185–86
Teachers' aides. *See* Tutors

Thompson, M., 219
Thorndike, R. L., 25, 33, 184, 185
Training of tutors, 91, 128–30,
  216–17. *See also* Tutors
Trost, M. A., 126
Trowbridge, N., 38, 39
Tutorial program: building and
  reading words in, 95–97,
  280–88; general principles
  underlying, 77–81; giving the
  sounds for the letters in, 91,
  274–75; introduction to the
  sound in, 82–84, 231–35; letter
  drawing in, 88, 255–56; letter
  tracing in, 87–88, 245–55;
  observations on operation of,
  91–93, 97–98, 103–7; operant
  and cognitive ideas in, 78;
  overview of, 190–94; procedure
  for teaching words in, 100–101,
  293–94; sound-letter matching
  games in, 88–91, 256–73;
  two-picture game in, 84–85,
  235–43; which-picture game
  in, 93–95, 278–80; yes-no
  game in, 85–86, 243–45
Tutors, 5–7, 37, 50–56, 125–30,
  182, 195–96, 208–10, 215–21

van Doorninck, W. J., 55
Vellutino, F. R., 53
Venezky, R. L., 48, 66, 68, 190
Vernon, M. D., 57

Wachs, H., 204, 205, 206, 207
Wallach, M. A., 71, 74
Walzl, F. N., 125
Weikart, D. P., 15, 16, 17
Wepman, J. M., 65, 189
Wertheimer, M., 58
Wessman, A. E., 25
Westinghouse Learning Cor-
  poration/Ohio University
  evaluation of Head Start, 1,
  2, 12
White, S. H., 12, 13
Whole-word approach and
  reading, 56–70, 187–89
Williams, F., 52
Wing, C. W., Jr., 71
Winschel, J. F., 11
Word recognition test: descrip-
  tion of, 131–32; results for,
  149–52

Zaporozhets, A. V., 68
Zax, M., 126
Zimiles, H., 13, 14